T0292559

Advances in Information Security

Volume 64

Series Editor

Sushil Jajodia, Center for Secure Information Systems, George Mason University, Fairfax, VA 22030-4444, USA

More information about this series at http://www.springer.com/series/5576

Kristin E. Heckman • Frank J. Stech
Roshan K. Thomas • Ben Schmoker
Alexander W. Tsow

Cyber Denial, Deception and Counter Deception

A Framework for Supporting Active Cyber Defense

 Springer

Kristin E. Heckman
The MITRE Corporation
McLean, VA, USA

Frank J. Stech
The MITRE Corporation
McLean, VA, USA

Roshan K. Thomas
The MITRE Corporation
McLean, VA, USA

Ben Schmoker
The MITRE Corporation
McLean, VA, USA

Alexander W. Tsow
The MITRE Corporation
McLean, VA, USA

ISSN 1568-2633
Advances in Information Security
ISBN 978-3-319-25131-8   ISBN 978-3-319-25133-2   (eBook)
DOI 10.1007/978-3-319-25133-2

Library of Congress Control Number: 2015953440

Springer Cham Heidelberg New York Dordrecht London
© Springer International Publishing Switzerland 2015
This work is subject to copyright. All rights are reserved by the Publisher, whether the whole or part of
the material is concerned, specifically the rights of translation, reprinting, reuse of illustrations, recitation,
broadcasting, reproduction on microfilms or in any other physical way, and transmission or information
storage and retrieval, electronic adaptation, computer software, or by similar or dissimilar methodology
now known or hereafter developed.
The use of general descriptive names, registered names, trademarks, service marks, etc. in this publication
does not imply, even in the absence of a specific statement, that such names are exempt from the relevant
protective laws and regulations and therefore free for general use.
The publisher, the authors and the editors are safe to assume that the advice and information in this book
are believed to be true and accurate at the date of publication. Neither the publisher nor the authors or the
editors give a warranty, express or implied, with respect to the material contained herein or for any errors
or omissions that may have been made.

Printed on acid-free paper

Springer International Publishing AG Switzerland is part of Springer Science+Business Media
(www.springer.com)

Preface

The field of cyber security has evolved over the last three decades and today is at a critical juncture. Computer network defense (CND) has reached the limits of what traditional perimeter defenses such as boundary controllers and firewalls, as well as intrusion detection systems, can do to increase an organization's overall security posture. Sophisticated, well-organized attackers collectively known as the advanced persistent threat (APT) continue to bypass these traditional defense mechanisms by exploiting zero-day vulnerabilities. Trying to block access by intruders in many cases is futile: it is more realistic to assume that the defense perimeter is porous and that stealthy adversaries may have established a semi-persistent presence in the defender's network. Both researchers and practitioners acknowledge, at least tacitly, that they need more advanced and active defense security techniques. Such techniques would not merely monitor, detect, and block intrusions, but would actively engage adversaries and study their tactics, techniques, and procedures (TTPs) and craft customized responses and mitigation strategies.

Throughout history, denial, deception, and counterdeception have proven effective force multipliers when used in conflict. As the challenges to U.S. national security increasingly move into the cyber domain, the field of cyber security needs an analogous force multiplier to defend effectively against computer network attacks, intrusions, and pervasive electronic espionage. What role can cyber denial and deception (cyber-D&D) play in such a paradigm? That is the subject of this book.

A significant opportunity exists for advancing CND by adapting and applying classical D&D theory and techniques to CND operations. Such adaptation and application entail connecting classical D&D theory and techniques to cyber defense in order to develop a framework that facilitates greater use of D&D in routine CND operations. As adversaries' attack techniques evolve, defenders' cyber systems must also evolve to provide the best continuous defense. This will usher in a new paradigm, consisting of a highly customized network defense based on understanding the specifics of adversary attacks. By knowing how to engineer cyber systems to better detect and counter the deception aspects of advanced cyber threats, and how to apply D&D against the APT and other threats, cyber defenders will force adversaries to move more slowly, expend more resources, and take greater risks, while themselves possibly avoiding or at least better fighting through cyber degradation.

A review of the cyber security research literature indicates that the use of denial, deception, and counterdeception in the cyber domain is in its infancy when compared to D&D use in the physical world and kinetic warfare.[1] Training in government and academic settings rarely integrates classical deception theory with cyber security. As a result, many computer network defenders have limited familiarity with D&D theory or approaches, let alone how to apply them. This, coupled with disjoint terminology, theory, and lack of a cohesive framework, may have contributed to fewer empirical and operational applications of D&D in cyber security.

Given this, we wished to introduce a wide audience to the role that cyber-D&D can play as part of a larger and more comprehensive active CND scheme. However, this book is not intended as a technical manual for crafting cyber-D&D techniques. Viewing cyber-D&D primarily as a technical initiative or problem would lead to low adoption and failure to counter cyber threats. Instead, concepts for cyber-D&D must be conceived, championed, managed, and matured within the larger organizational, business, and cyber defense context. This book represents our attempt to lay out a blueprint for these broader considerations.

Mc Lean, VA, USA   Kristin E. Heckman
                                                                                           Frank J. Stech
                                                                                        Roshan K. Thomas
                                                                                           Ben Schmoker
                                                                                       Alexander W. Tsow

---

[1] Frank Stech, Kristin E. Heckman, Phil Hilliard, and Janice R. Ballo. "Scientometrics of Deception, Counter-deception, and Deception Detection in Cyber-space," *PsychNology Journal*, v. 9, no. 2, pp. 79–122, 2011.

Acknowledgments

The authors, our significant others, as is their habit, have overestimated their capabilities and underestimated their responsibilities, and the time and resources needed to meet them. Hence we undertook to acknowledge everyone who contributed to the creation of this book, beginning with ourselves. The authors basically ignored family and friends, and, we suspect, other duties and obligations, in order to produce this volume. The authors have expressed their deep gratitude and appreciation for our forbearance, patience, and assistance. We shan't let them forget that. Nevertheless, we believe the end justifies their negligence. We are proud of the product and of the authors.

Having had to listen to the authors' tales of inadequate cyber security and computer systems compromises of all forms, we became aware of the promise of cyber deceptions in active defense of computer systems. But many defenses obviously are still needed, and many horses have left too many barns, so these Acknowledgments will tend to use first names and last initials. The individuals involved are probably already known to foreign intelligence services, but we need not make connecting the dots any easier for them. Those thanked know who they are.

Without question, this book is dedicated to the late Dr. Barton S. Whaley (1928–2013), America's foremost scholar of all matters of deception, and authority on the literature and research on deception and counterdeception. He was a dear friend of Frank and Kristin. His influence permeates this book and will influence deception and counterdeception, in the cyber realm and elsewhere, for years to come.

This volume is very much a product of the MITRE Corporation's dedication to cutting-edge and meaningful research and development. MITRE's support for deception and counterdeception research predates the work reflected in this volume by over a decade. Thanks for such support are due to Richard G., Dave L., Steve H., Anne C., Rod H., and Robert N. (a bit of a deception scholar himself).

Similarly, supporting the connection between deception and counterdeception research and MITRE's long-standing efforts to enhance cyber defenses reflects the vision and foresight of Vipin S., Mark M., Gary G., Marion M., Marnie S., Rich B., Rick S., Kerry B., and MITRE's Engineering Council.

Many at MITRE have partnered with the authors in various deception and counterdeception research projects and other activities. Thanks to Janice B., Phil H., Margaret M., Chris E., Mike T., Mark B., Charles W., Barry C., Lisa C., Frank D., Blake S., Adam P., Mark G., Dave K., Marc B., Irv L., Todd O., Michael W., Stephen D., Audra H., Justin A., and Justin L.

All scholars stand on the shoulders of others. The footnotes and references in this volume reflect the influence and contributions made by the communities of researchers of deception and counterdeception, and the growing cadre of researchers developing cyber denial and deception and counterdeception defenses for computer enterprises. The authors especially want to thank Frank H., Sushil J., V. S., Dorothy D., and Spaf.

Getting anything published is a chore and many have helped publish this book: at MITRE; TThom G, Pam G., Liz F. and at Springer; Susan L-F and Jennifer M.

Finally, we are grateful to Kristin, Frank, Roshan, Ben, and Alex for writing this book, and for not writing more books than they already do.

The spouses and significant others of the authors: *Deja Vú, Egypt Om, Elizabeth Mae, Sharon, Bruce, Alix, Annie, Krista, Sarah, Matthew, Ellen, Amy, Cecelia, and Simone*

Contents

List of Figures

List of Tables

The volume number has been updated. An erratum can be found at
DOI 10.1007/978-3-319-25133-2_11

Chapter 1
Introduction

The openly advertised use of deception creates uncertainty for adversaries because they will not know if a discovered problem is real or a trap. … The principle of deception involves the deliberate introduction of misleading functionality or misinformation into national infrastructure for the purpose of tricking an adversary. … Specifically, deception can be used to protect against certain types of cyber attacks that no other security method will handle. … however, the cyber security community has yet to embrace deception as a mainstream protection measure.

Edward Amoroso (2011) Cyber attacks: Protecting national infrastructure. Burlington MA: Elsevier.

The world has become ever more reliant on computers for critical infrastructure, communications, and commercial operations. The security of computer systems now affects billions of lives, yet architectural and legacy decisions and consequent vulnerabilities allow malicious actors to compromise sensitive information and deny access to legitimate users. In addition, intrusions by dedicated actor groups appear to have become more persistent, threatening, and global (Jajodia et al. 2011).

Many organizations approach computer security strictly as a business requirement, best handled by an internal department or outsourced to third-party service providers. Network defenders attempt to forestall break-ins by using traditional perimeter defense technologies such as firewalls and guards, mandatory and discretionary access controls, and intrusion detection and prevention technologies. Such perimeter defenses are insufficient, and the size and complexity of the attack surfaces in modern computer systems present too many vulnerabilities. Further, perimeter defenses do not allow the computer network defense (CND) community to assess damage on the basis of the information stolen, or to understand the attacker's intent, as defenders have no access to most of the communication between the attacker and the compromised system. Malicious actors take advantage of social engineering and client-side exploits to evade perimeter defenses, while proprietary file formats and perpetually vulnerable code allow compromise of machines on the order of millions.[1] Access controls fail because an adversary can take over an insider's credentials and privileges. Intrusion detection technology generates too many false positives—that is, alarms resulting from the legitimate activities of authorized users—to be deemed effective.

---

[1] Symantec Internet Security Threat Report 2011.

© Springer International Publishing Switzerland 2015
K.E. Heckman et al., *Cyber Denial, Deception and Counter Deception*,
Advances in Information Security 64, DOI 10.1007/978-3-319-25133-2_1

While traditional tools are important components of a defensive posture, they are not sufficient to stop dedicated adversaries such as the advanced persistent threat (APT) and those who launch zero-day attacks (attacks that exploit a previously unknown vulnerability). To combat these extant threats,[2] the CND community should augment detection and response with the capability to carefully monitor and study adversaries. Research in evolutionary biology shows that deceptive creatures have an evolutionary advantage over their competitors (Smith 2004)—which could extend into the virtual world. Physical combatants use denial and deception (D&D) to enhance their ability to exploit their opponent in order to fight and survive—network defenders should do the same. In this book we present ways to shift the balance of power in CND through better understanding of malicious actors and methods for manipulating perceptions[3]:

1. Diversion. Direct an adversary's attention from real assets toward bogus ones.
2. Resource Depletion. Waste an adversary's time and energy on obtaining and analyzing false information.
3. Uncertainty. Cause the adversary to doubt the veracity of a discovered vulnerability or stolen information.
4. Intelligence. Monitor and analyze adversary behavior during intrusion attempts to inform future defense efforts.
5. Proactivity. Use deception techniques to detect previously unknown attacks that other defensive tools may miss.

Cyber-D&D may also help organizations to meet strategic goals such as deterrence by including psychological and technical implementations of deception[4]:

Deception works in a fundamentally different way than conventional security methods. Conventional security tends to work directly on, or against, the hacker's actions, e.g., to detect them or to prevent them. Deception works by manipulating the hacker's thinking, to make him act in a way that is advantageous to the defender. Being fundamentally different, deception can be strong where conventional security is weak (and vice-versa). While deception is not always useful, it can be an important and effective way of compensating

[2] One cyber security company defines an APT as "a group of sophisticated, determined and coordinated attackers that have been systematically compromising ... government and commercial computer networks for years. ... well-funded, organized groups of attackers. ... They are professionals, and their success rate is impressive." Mandiant (2010) *M-Trends: The advance of the persistent threat.* https://www.mandiant.com/resources/mandiant-reports/

[3] Bodmer, S., M. Kilger, G. Carpenter, and J. Jones (2012) *Reverse Deception: Organized Cyber Threat Counter-Exploitation.* McGraw-Hill: New York, pp. 31–32.

[4] Although the concept of D&D is well known and has been used to great effect in the physical world, it has received less attention in the cyber domain. However, there are some notable exceptions of systematic research on cyber deception. For example, Janczewski and Colarik's (2008) *Cyber warfare and cyber terrorism* published several interesting research papers on cyber deception by Neil C. Rowe (and colleagues) at the Naval Postgraduate School. Professor Rowe has published extensively on cyber deception. Research on cyber deception has also been performed at Dartmouth College's Institute for Security, Technology, and Society (ISTS) by (among others) Professors George Cybenko, Eugene Santos, and Paul Thompson; and at Columbia University by Professors Salvatore J. Stolfo and Angelos D. Keromytis.

for conventional security's inherent vulnerabilities, and [...] it may be advantageous to combine the two explicitly.[5]

While classical deception theory in the physical world has been comprehensively researched and documented, little systematic research and analysis has been devoted to the concepts of deception, counterdeception, and deception detection in the cyber domain.[6] Scientometric analyses revealed that the cyber security literature rarely uses classic deception terminology or cites classic deception researchers. When researchers do use classic deception terminology to describe various deceptive cyber tactics, they tend to characterize the tactics from a technological perspective rather than a social, behavioral, or cognitive one. Moreover, the analyses showed that so far no standardized vocabulary has emerged to describe the phenomenon of deception in cyber security, nor have deceptive cyber-tactics been mapped into the classic components of D&D tactics.

1.1 Summary

This book represents an attempt to advance the application of D&D concepts and techniques into the cyber realm by establishing conceptual foundations and suggesting practical applications. It presents terminology, theory, models, and an overall framework for the operational application and management of cyber-denial, cyber-deception, and cyber-counterdeception (cyber-D&D&CD) in the larger context of cyber security. The book first builds understanding of D&D and its applications, exploring approaches to adapting classical D&D&CD tactics and techniques to the cyber realm. To do so, we augment the notion of an attacker's "cyber kill chain" by proposing a "deception chain" for planning, preparing, and executing cyber-D&D operations, and connect both of these models into an intrusion campaign and a defensive deception campaign. We examine the risk, unintended consequences, compromise, failure, and the benefits, challenges, and drawbacks of utilizing cyber-D&D. We then explore two intrusion scenarios—one real, based on Stuxnet, and one fictional, based on defending against an APT in a scenario where both the offense and defense used cyber-D&D.

After establishing the theoretical foundations, we present practical approaches that government organizations and businesses can apply as they integrate cyber-D&D into their security practices. Specifically, we describe methods for exercising cyber-D&D&CD, and introduce a capability maturity model (CMM) for assessing an organization's defensive and offensive cyber-D&D capabilities, as well as a strawman CMM for cyber-CD capabilities. In addition, we present a spiral model

---

[5] James J. Yuill. "Defensive Computer-Security Deception Operations: Processes, Principles and Techniques." Dissertation: North Carolina State University, Raleigh NC, 2006, p. 1.

[6] Frank Stech, Kristin E. Heckman, Phil Hilliard, and Janice R. Ballo. "Scientometrics of Deception, Counter-deception, and Deception Detection in Cyber-space," *PsychNology Journal*, v. 9, no. 2, pp. 79–122, 2011.

for cyber-D&D lifecycle management that can help organizations to iteratively and rapidly increase the overall effectiveness of their cyber-D&D capability through continuous process improvements.

The book concludes with suggestions for future research that could help bring cyber-D&D into the mainstream of cyber security practices.

Chapter 2
Bridging the Classical D&D and Cyber Security Domains

> The reason why deception works is that it helps accomplish any or all of the following four security objectives:
>
> - Attention—The attention of an adversary can be diverted from real assets toward bogus ones.
> - Energy—The valuable time and energy of an adversary can be wasted on bogus targets.
> - Uncertainty—Uncertainty can be created around the veracity of a discovered vulnerability.
> - Analysis—A basis can be provided for real-time security analysis of adversary behavior.
>
> Edward Amoroso (2011) *Cyber attacks: Protecting national infrastructure.* Burlington MA: Elsevier.

This chapter uses a traditional framework called the D&D methods matrix as a foundation for describing the basics of D&D in the physical world, extends the D&D matrix to cyber security, and then outlines a set of techniques for applying D&D in the cyber security context. These descriptions can be combined with the cyber-D&D TTP taxonomy in Appendix A to guide understanding of how D&D is used in the cyber domain. We examine the organizational requirements for planning and executing successful defensive cyber-D&D operations, introducing both physical and virtual D&D tactics relevant to each quadrant of the D&D methods matrix.

2.1 Classical D&D

Deception has proven useful in war, diplomacy, and politics (Bodmer et al. 2012; Rowe and Rothstein 2004; Whaley 2007a) for four general reasons. First, deception can divert an aggressor's attention from actual targets and resources, increasing the deception user's freedom of action. Second, deception may cause an opponent to adopt a course of action that works to the defender's advantage. Third, deception can help the defender gain the element of surprise over an adversary. Finally, deception may protect actual resources from destruction.

Deception is fundamentally psychological. We may think of deceptive behaviors by one actor (the deceiver) as influencing the behaviors of another (the target). Deceptions should have a concrete purpose: namely, the deceiver deceives the target

© Springer International Publishing Switzerland 2015
K.E. Heckman et al., *Cyber Denial, Deception and Counter Deception*,
Advances in Information Security 64, DOI 10.1007/978-3-319-25133-2_2

Table 2.1 D&D methods matrix

| Deception objects | D&D methods | |
	Deception: Mislead (M)-type methods revealing	Denial: Ambiguity (A)-type methods concealing
Facts	*Reveal Facts: NEFI* • Reveal true information to the target • Reveal true physical entities, events, or processes to the target	*Conceal Facts (Dissimulation): EEFI* • Conceal true information from the target • Conceal true physical entities, events, or processes from the target
Fictions	*Reveal Fictions (Simulation): EEDI* • Reveal to the target information known to be untrue • Reveal to the target physical entities, events, or processes known to be untrue	*Conceal Fictions: NDDI* • Conceal from the target information known to be untrue • Conceal from the target physical entities, events, or processes known to be untrue

Source: Adapted from Bennett and Waltz (2007)

to cause the target to behave in a way that accrues advantages to the deceiver. This is the deceiver's deception goal; the target's actions are the deceiver's desired deception effect. Thus, while the constituents of deception concepts and plans are psychological, the consequences of executing those plans are physical actions and reactions by the deceiver and the target.

Two essential deception methods create this causal relationship between psychological state and physical behavior. *Denial* represents deceiver behavior that actively prevents the target from perceiving information and stimuli; in other words, using hiding techniques that generate ambiguity in the target's mind about what is and is not real. *Deception* denotes deceiver behavior that provides misleading information and stimuli to actively create and reinforce the target's perceptions, cognitions, and beliefs. This generates a mistaken certainty in the target's mind about what is and is not real, making the target certain, confident, and ready to act—but wrong.

The objects underlying these D&D methods, as shown in Table 2.1, are facts and fictions that are either revealed via deception methods or concealed via denial methods. These facts and fictions can be information or physical entities. The term *non-essential friendly information* (NEFI) refers to facts that the deceiver reveals to the target. Factual information that the defender cyber-D&D team must protect is termed *essential elements of friendly information* (EEFI), while the key fictions that the defender cyber-D&D team must reveal to the target of the deception are termed *essential elements of deception information* (EEDI). Finally, fictions that the deceiver must conceal from the target are referred to as *non-discloseable deception information* (NDDI).

Classical D&D literature focuses on the shaded quadrants the table—that is, on simulation to reveal fictions and dissimulation to conceal facts. The other two quadrants—revealing facts and concealing fictions—are also important to a successful D&D campaign. As with simulations and dissimulations, an effective D&D campaign results in the target perceiving and accepting the revealed facts, while failing to perceive the deceiver's concealed fictions.

2.1.1   Reveal Facts

The upper left quadrant of the table shows deception (also called Mislead or M-type methods) for revealing selected facts—the NEFI. Given that these facts are verifiable, the deceiver must carefully edit and tailor them so that they can be leveraged to craft and reinforce the deception story presented to the target. The target should believe and accept the factual information, physical entities, events, and processes that the deceiver reveals, but these must be carefully engineered to lead the target away from perceiving and understanding the whole truth. The deceiver can also influence the target to disbelieve or reject the facts by discrediting them: revealing facts about the truth to the target in such a way that the target will discredit those facts and disbelieve the truth.

2.1.2   Reveal Fictions—Simulation

The shaded lower left quadrant shows revealing fictions—the EEDI—also known as simulation. This is an essential basis for creating false perceptions. In order for revealed fictions to deceive the target successfully, the fictions must "rest on a firm foundation of previous truth" (Masterman 2000). That is, the target must believe at least some of the revealed facts shown in the upper left quadrant when those facts are necessary to support the defender's simulation.

In the present context, simulation means the invention, revelation, and leveraging of information, physical entities, events, or processes that the deceiver knows to be untrue. Informational fictions can include disinformation (i.e., the revelation of false or misleading information), paltering (i.e., revealing facts that apparently support the reality of a fiction[1]), and lying (i.e., the deliberate transfer of known untruths). To increase the believability of disinformation, paltering, and lies, the deceiver can disseminate this information via a communication channel that also disseminates facts, such as press releases, white papers, or media outlets containing NEFI. In addition, the deceiver creates physical fictions and reveals them to the target via a variety of methods, such as decoys, diversions (e.g., feints, demonstrations), forgeries, doubles, and dummies of equipment or personnel. Psychological states (e.g., mood, emotion) can be simulated during interpersonal communications via the presentation of false facial expressions, body language, and vocal cues.

---

[1] *Paltering* is "less than lying … the widespread practice of fudging, twisting, shading, bending, stretching, slanting, exaggerating, distorting, whitewashing, and selective reporting. Such deceptive practices are occasionally designated by the uncommon word *paltering*." Frederick Schauer and Richard Zeckhauser. "Paltering" in Brooke Harrington, ed. *Deception: From Ancient Empires to Internet Dating*. Stanford, CA: Stanford University Press, 2009, pp. 38–54.

A previously classified espionage case, recently adapted into the movie *Argo*,[2] provides a good example of how to reveal fictions that rest on a firm foundation of truth. A small team of CIA specialists developed a plan for exfiltrating six U.S. State Department employees who had fled during the 1979 takeover of the U.S. Embassy in Tehran, Iran, and were "houseguests" at the Canadian Embassy in Tehran. The cover story for the exfiltration was that the employees belonged to an advance scouting party for the production of a Hollywood science-fiction movie, *Argo*. To ensure the credibility of the cover story, the team intertwined operational deception elements with genuine Hollywood business processes: the number and role of individuals involved in an advance scouting party, physical offices with functional telephones for the fake production company, studio press coverage in the most popular Hollywood trade papers, the use of a real movie script as a prop, a fake production portfolio, and customary "Hollywood-style" attire for the houseguests and their CIA escorts, to name a few. The operation was a D&D success; the six houseguests were exfiltrated from Iran, while in the United States the fake production company had received 26 new scripts (including one from Steven Spielberg) prior to being dismantled several weeks after the exfiltration.

2.1.3   Conceal Facts—Dissimulation

The shaded upper right quadrant of Table 2.1 presents denial, also called Ambiguity or A-type methods, for concealing the EEFI. Here the deceiver conceals the truth, thereby denying the target. Dissimulation, or hiding the real, involves the concealment of true information, physical entities, events, or processes from the target. Just as revealing facts forms an essential basis for revealing fictions, concealing fictions is an essential basis for concealing facts. For example, a double agent should reveal many facts as well as those few fictions the double agent's controllers want to dupe the adversary into believing. Equally important, the double agent should hint at hidden and concealed fictions as if they were hidden facts. An agent who "knows and reveals all" is too good to be true; thus, to be believable, the double agent must hide both some facts *and* some fictions, so that the adversary must work to obtain them, presumably through the other deception channels managed by the double agent's controlling organization. Luring the adversary to expend effort on piecing together these hidden fictions is one method the deceiver can use to "sell" the deception fiction to the adversary.

---

[2] *Argo* is a 2012 film distributed by Warner Bros. Pictures. This case was also adapted into a television movie in 1981, *Escape from Iran: The Canadian Caper*, directed by Lamont Johnson. Anthony (Tony) Mendez, the CIA officer involved in this case, has written about his experiences: "A Classic Case of Deception," *Studies in Intelligence*, Winter 1999/2000, p. 1–16; and *Argo: How the CIA and Hollywood Pulled off the Most Audacious Rescue in History*, 2012 co-authored with Matt Baglio and published by Viking Adult.

Winston Churchill stated, "In time of war, when truth is so precious, it must be attended by a bodyguard of lies." The truth can also be concealed via secrecy, which denies the target access to the deceiver's most crucial truths, such as genuine intentions, capabilities, time lines, and of course, the D&D plan itself. Information can be kept secret via technological means such as steganography, cryptography, and honeypots, nets, tokens, clients that hide the real cyber environment. Physical entities, events, and processes can be kept secret via methods such as camouflage, concealment, and secure facilities. As with simulation, the presentation of false facial expressions, body language, and vocal cues during interpersonal communications can prevent the target from recognizing true psychological states

As an example of concealment, in 1962 the Soviets had to devise a cover story for their plan to emplace ballistic missiles, medium-range bombers, and a division of mechanized infantry in Cuba. Operations security (OPSEC) minimized the number of top civilian and military officials planning the operation; however, to execute the operation, these planners had to mislead both Soviet and foreign citizens about the destination of the equipment and forces. As a code name for the operation, the Soviet General Staff used ANADYR—the name of a river flowing into the Bering Sea, the name of the capital of the Chukotsky Autonomous District, and the name of a bomber base in that region. To support the code name illusion, the forces deployed to Cuba were told only that they were going to a cold region, and were supplied with winter equipment and 'costumes' including skis, felt boots, and fleece-lined parkas.[3] Personnel who needed climate specifics, such as missile engineers, were told that they were taking intercontinental ballistic missiles to a site on Novaya Zemlya, a large island in the Artic where nuclear weapons had historically been tested.[4] The ANADYR denial was so successful that it fooled even senior Soviet officers sent to Cuba. One general asked General Anatoli Gribkov, a senior member of the Soviet General Staff involved in planning the operation, why winter equipment and clothing had been provided. Gribkov replied, "It's called ANADYR for a reason. We could have given away the game if we had put any tropical clothing in your kits." [5]

2.1.4 Conceal Fictions

The lower right quadrant of Table 2.1 shows concealing fictions, or NDDI: that is, hiding from the target information, physical entities, events, or processes that the deceiver knows to be untrue. This is the least intuitive quadrant in the matrix. To illustrate the concept of concealing fictions, Bennett and Waltz (2007) use the example of statements by "spin doctors," which notoriously bear multiple

---

[3] Gribkov, A. I., Smith, W. Y., & Friendly, A. (1994). *Operation ANADYR: U.S. and Soviet generals recount the Cuban missile crisis.* Chicago: Edition q, p. 15.
[4] Fursenko, A. A., & Naftali, T. J. (1997). *One hell of a gamble: Khrushchev, Castro, and Kennedy, 1958–1964.* New York: Norton, p. 191.
[5] Gribkov and Smith (1994) p. 15.

interpretations. Such statements enable the spin doctors to use strategies to either avoid revealing that they are lying or to avoid revealing that their actions are a hoax. In the former strategy, the spin doctor denies a fiction by suppressing a lie, and in the latter, by curbing information that might expose a sham. The deceiver benefits by concealing from the target particular known fictions that support the deceiver's D&D plan. The concealment should arouse the target's interest and focus attention on piecing together these missing elements of deceiver information. For example, the deceiver may have a double agent sending deception information to the target (e.g., a concocted mixture of real but innocuous facts and deception—facts and fictions supporting the deceiver's deception) while hiding from the target the EEFI that the agent actually works for the deceiver. The agent's communications should hint at but conceal other fictions consistent with the deceiver's deception, motivating the target to collect and fill in those missing pieces. As the target works to assemble the jigsaw puzzles, the deceiver feeds the target's collection though other controlled deception channels. The pieces slowly fall into place, and the target assembles the picture the deception planners intended the target to perceive and believe.

One real-world example of concealing fictions comes from early twentieth century warfare. Colonel G. F. R. Henderson served as the British chief of intelligence for an assignment during the South African War (Holt 2007). During this assignment, Field Marshal Lord Roberts was to lift the siege of Kimberly using a traditional feint. Henderson's assignment was to deceive the Boers by keeping their attention on the location of Roberts's feint, and denying them the location of Roberts's planned attack. To mystify and mislead the enemy, Henderson sent out fictitious orders in the open (i.e., simulation), but then canceled them in cipher (i.e., concealing a fiction). Henderson's D&D succeeded: the Boers' attention stayed focused on the feint, they missed Roberts's movements, and the siege was lifted.

Likewise, during the Second World War, the British understood camouflage to mean not just hiding the real but showing the fake in such a way that its "fakeness" was concealed.[6] The American 23rd Headquarters Special Troops[7] followed suit and created faulty camouflage – that is, camouflage designed to draw attention to fake objects. They hid the fake by making it seem real enough that it was worth hiding. By doing so they sought to persuade the enemy to make decisions by altering the adversary's perception: things were not as they appeared.

For example, in the summer of 1944 the 23rd were assigned their first large-scale operation, ELEPHANT, in a town called St. Lô while the Allies massed their forces for the Battle of Normandy. Although Operation ELEPHANT was a disaster for the 23rd, the unit learned many valuable lessons.[8] If they camouflaged equipment such

---

[6] Gerard, P. (2002) *Secret Soldiers: The Story of World War II's Heroic Army of Deception.* New York: Penguin Group.

[7] The 23rd Headquarters Special Troops was a group of U.S. Army artists and designers engaged in a variety of D&D activities against the Germans in World War II.

[8] One month after the operation, headquarters staff concluded that "The results of this operation are uncertain...However, no movement of forces to counter the move of the Armored division was made by the enemy and captured documents indicated that the unit which was simulated was still

as tanks too well, the enemy would never know it was there. If the camouflage was too conspicuous, the enemy would suspect it was a sham. The 23rd discovered a compromise: they mimicked the mistakes real tankers made when pulling into a "harbor" for the night. Such mistakes included leaving a length of the barrel sticking out of the net, leaving a gas can exposed to catch the morning light and flash a telltale glint to an enemy spotter, draping the net too loosely so that the shape of the tank stood out, and leaving a gap in the foliage surrounding the "tank."

2.1.5   Deception Dynamics

As this chapter has shown so far, denial and deception go hand in hand. The deceiver uses denial to prevent the detection of EEFI by *hiding the real*, and deception to induce misperception by using EEDI to *show the false*.[9] The deceiver assembles an illusion by creating a ruse to hide *and* to show. As shown in the D&D methods matrix, the deceiver also has to *hide the false*, that is, the NDDI, to protect the D&D plan, and *show the real*, that is, the NEFI, to enhance the D&D cover story. Deception is a very dynamic process and planners will benefit from the interplay of techniques from more than one quadrant in a deception operation. Table 2.2 builds on the D&D methods matrix in Table 2.1 to present some D&D techniques at a high level.

Several historical examples illustrate these dynamics of deception. For example, during Operation ELSENBORN, the 23rd was to convince the enemy that the 4th Infantry Division was at Elsenborn Barracks, a Belgian army rest camp just behind the front lines between Eupen and Malmedy.[10] The 23rd handled all of the 4th's actual radio traffic for one week prior to the operation while the 4th was still holding a sector of the front. When the 4th Infantry moved out to the Hürtgen Forest as reinforcements, radiomen from the 23rd continued radio communications using fake messages indicating that the 4th was slated for rest and recreation (R&R) at Elsenborn. The 23rd had coordinated with the signal operators of the 9th Infantry, which had been at Elsenborn the week before this operation, to stage a 3-day radio exercise. When the 23rd arrived at Elsenborn, they continued broadcasting as part of the supposed "exercise." This provided them an excuse to stay on the air and

---

considered to be the actual Armored division in its original location several days after the conclusion of the operation." Despite doing just about everything wrong, the 23rd had gotten lucky. One week after the operation, Lt. Fox wrote a memo to Col. Reeder, the commanding officer of the 23rd, and his colonels about the lessons to be learned: "…The successful practice of military deception by the 23rd Hqs requires the proper amount of SHOWMANSHIP and ARMY PROCEDURE. [emphasis in original]" To Fox, the 23rd had a "…lack of appreciation of the Fine Art of the theatre." Gerard, P. (2002) *Secret Soldiers: The Story of World War II's Heroic Army of Deception.* New York: Penguin Group, pp. 153–155.

[9] As shown in the D&D methods matrix, the deceiver also has to *hide the false*, that is, the NDDI, to protect the D&D plan, and *show the real*, that is, the NEFI, to enhance the D&D cover story.

[10] Gerard, P. (2002) *Secret Soldiers: The Story of World War II's Heroic Army of Deception.* New York: Penguin Group.

Table 2.2 D&D methods matrix with examples

	D&D Methods	
Deception objects	Deception: Misleading-type methods revealing	Denial: Ambiguity-type methods concealing

Facts	*Reveal Facts: NEFI*
	  Information:
	  • Release true information that benefits the deceiver by being disbelieved or rejected by the target (double bluff ruse)
	  • Discredit true information so the target disbelieves it, e.g., make the information too obvious (double play ruse)
	  • Coat-trail trivial facts to divert the target from larger truths
	  • Create negative spin (take the blame for a lesser crime; exhibit contrition to conceal lack of true remorse)
	  • Engage in paltering
		Conceal Facts (Dissimulation): EEFI
		  Information:
		  • Implement secrecy and security programs (INFOSEC, SIGSEC, OPSEC)
		  • Withhold information to create a false or misleading impression

	Physical:
	  • Display real facilities or equipment (to condition the target, or to build a source's credibility with target)
	  • Display duplicates
	  • Display distractors, misleading clues, coat-trailing evidence
	  • Engage in feints, demonstrations (real)
	  • Disseminate positive evidence to distract or mislead the target
		Physical:
		  • Deploy camouflage, concealment, signal and signature reduction; stealth designs; disguises; secure facilities
		  • Dazzle to hinder perception (fine print)
		  • Engage in nonverbal deceit
		  • Engage in "Red Flagging" by hiding in plain sight (blending)
		  • Hide negative evidence (dissimulated) by offering alternative or simulated evidence

Fictions	*Reveal Fictions (Simulation): EEDI*
	  Information:
	  • Disseminate disinformation; lie; provide information known to be untrue
	  • Dazzle (to overwhelm understanding)
		Conceal Fictions: NDDI
		  Information:
		  • Suppress a lie
		  • Apply positive spin

	Physical:
	  • Deploy decoys; mimics; mock-ups; dummies; forgeries, doubles; disguises
	  • Engage in diversions; feints; demonstrations
	  • Nonverbal deceit
	  • Positive evidence (simulated) to mislead from real negative evidence (faking a crime scene)
		Physical:
		  • Hide a sham
		  • Cover up falsehoods to avoid arousing target's suspicion
		  • Disseminate negative evidence (simulated) to conceal positive evidence (cleansing a crime scene)

Source: Adapted from Bennett and Waltz (2007)

communicate misinformation when they would have normally been silent given the 4th's R&R. The 23rd thus executed a fake within a fake.

On many occasions the 23rd used the magician's "pull:" the trick of getting the audience to look at the flourishing right hand (i.e., showing the false) while the canny left hand performed the trick (i.e., hiding the real). They would demonstrate Allied buildup and strength where in fact none existed. Instead, the 23rd was masquerading as forces that had moved under cover and silence to another critical attack location. While the Germans were busy watching and sometimes engaging the 23rd's flourishing right hand, they were lulled into complacency where the uncanny left revealed an Allied attack with forces that were believed to be located elsewhere.

Juan Pujol, a World War II double agent codenamed GARBO by the British, has been called the "most successful double agent ever."[11] GARBO not only simulated and dissimulated, he also revealed facts and concealed fictions. When the Second World War broke out, Pujol decided he wanted to spy for the British. 'I must do something,' he told himself. 'Something practical; I must make my contribution towards the good of humanity.' Hitler was 'a psychopath,' Pujol concluded, and so he must support the Allies. 'I wanted to work for them, to supply them with confidential information which would be of interest to the Allied cause, politically or militarily.' In January 1941, the 29-year-old Catalan approached the British Embassy in Madrid, with an offer to spy against the Germans. The embassy firmly turned Pujol away.

Pujol next tried the Germans, pretending to be a keen fascist willing to spy against the British—in the hope that, once recruited by the Nazis, he could then betray them. The Germans told him they were 'extremely busy'; then, mostly to get rid of him, the Germans said that they might use him if he could get to Britain via Lisbon. Pujol's German intelligence case officer, Kühlenthal, duly equipped Pujol with secret ink, cash, and the codename 'Agent Arabel.' Once in Lisbon, Pujol again contacted the British, and again was turned away. Pujol was in a dilemma, since he needed to send intelligence to the Germans as soon as possible. On 19 July 1941, he sent a telegram to Kühlenthal announcing his safe arrival in Britain *[Reveal fiction]* although he was still in Portugal *[Conceal fact]*. Denied the opportunity to gather real intelligence for either side, Pujol decided to invent it, with the help of the Lisbon public library, second-hand books, and whatever he could glean from newsreels. He remained in Lisbon for 9 months, inventing what he thought his Nazi spymasters wanted to hear *[Reveal fact; Reveal fiction]*.

In Lisbon Pujol continued to pester the British to recruit him. Despite producing evidence to show he was now in the employ of the Germans, he was repeatedly turned down. Pujol approached the American naval attaché in Lisbon, who contacted his opposite number in the British Embassy, who duly, but very slowly, sent a report to London. Finally, British MI6 realized that the German agent sending the bogus messages to the Germans must be Juan Pujol García, the Spaniard who had repeatedly approached them in Lisbon.

Now working for British MI5, GARBO sent important, real information to his German handlers, carefully timing his messages to arrive too late to be useful to the Germans *[Reveal facts]*. Pujol's British controllers wondered how the Germans

[11] Macintyre, B. (2012) *Double Cross: The true story of the D-Day spies.* Great Britain: Bloomsbury Publishing. Also see: Andrew, C. M. (2009) *Defend the realm: the authorized history of MI5.* Alfred A. Knopf : New York.; Pujol, J. and N. West (1986) *GARBO.* Grafton Books: London.; McCamley, N.J. (2003) *Secret Underground Cities: An account of some of Britain's subterranean defence, factory and storage sites in the Second World War.* Leo Cooper: London.

could fail to see their agents as people 'who seldom or never say anything untrue, but who equally never say anything which is new.' In German eyes, GARBO's failure to supply high-grade information in a timely way was not his fault *[Conceal fact]* but theirs; and the more often he tried *[Reveal fact]* and failed *[Conceal fact]*, the more they loved him.

Another interesting twist in GARBO's career is a classic case of concealing fictions. Roger Hesketh,[12] who during the war served as a member of the deception section of Supreme Headquarters, Allied Expeditionary Force, provided an additional insight into the complexities of intricate story simulations: the value of creating interesting but flexible story elements that might have utility in future, as-yet-undetermined deception episodes. Though special means and other deception operations, the Allies built up various cover story contexts for future use. For GARBO, the deception planners concocted a mystery: strange secret goings-on at the famous caves of Chislehurst, well known to the Germans from as long ago as World War I. The British fed bits of this mystery (but not the full story) to GARBO, who used them to tease and tantalize his German deception target. GARBO and his notional subagents and nets conveyed:

> … a rather mysterious story concerning the caves at Chislehurst … For many months GARBO had been hinting at strange developments in these caves [One of GARBO's sub-agents worked in the Chislehurst caves and another was a guard at the caves] which were in some way connected to the coming invasion *[Conceal fiction]*…The Germans took GARBO's reports about the Chislehurst caves seriously, even if their interest was sometimes tinged with incredulity. When the invasion came, a suitable occasion for exploiting the story did not present itself and … the Germans were ultimately informed that the caves had been used for storing arms for the *Maquis* [French underground]. *[classic blow-off for cooling out the mark]*

GARBO conveyed to the Germans pieces of a mystery for which even he did not have the whole story. Plan *Bodega* was an

> … entirely fictitious development, in preparation for the opening of the second front of a huge underground depot with a network of underground tunnels or the distribution of arms and ammunition to airfields and anti-aircraft defenses in the London area. …the build-up of this project (Plan *Bodega*) might later be exploited for deception purposes in conjunction with Operation *Overlord* but in fact no use was made of it. [13]

2.2 Translating D&D to Cyber Security

Classical D&D techniques can be extended to cyber security. Some "translation" of D&D techniques from the physical to the virtual world may be necessary. Table 2.3, which further builds on the cyber-D&D methods matrix, suggests some analogies by outlining a high-level set of cyber-D&D techniques (combinations of two or

---

[12] Hesketh, R. (2000) *FORTITUDE: The D-Day Deception Campaign*. Overlook: New York.
[13] Howard, M. (1995) *Strategic Deception in the Second World War*. Norton: New York.

Table 2.3 D&D methods matrix with Cyber-D&D techniques

Deception objects	D&D methods	
	Deception: M-type methods: Revealing	Denial: A-type methods: Concealing
Facts	*Reveal Facts: NEFI* • Publish true network information • Allow disclosure of real files • Reveal technical deception capabilities • Reveal misleading compromise details • Selectively remediate intrusion	*Conceal Facts (Dissimulation): EEFI* • Deny access to system resource • Hide software using stealth methods • Reroute network traffic • Silently intercept network traffic
Fictions	*Reveal Fictions (Simulation): EEDI* • Misrepresent intent of software • Modify network traffic • Expose fictional systems • Allow disclosure of fictional information	*Conceal Fictions: NDDI* • Hide simulated information on honeypots • Keep deceptive security operations a secret • Allow partial enumeration of fictional files

Source: Adapted from Bennett and Waltz (2007)

more tactics), organized according to whether they are facts or fictions, and whether they are revealed via deception methods or concealed via denial methods. This "packaging" of tactics can be an indicator of a sophisticated deception capability for CD purposes.

Figures 2.1 and 2.2 are Venn diagrams of the offensive and defensive tactics, techniques, and procedures (TTPs), respectively. The categorization reflects whether a particular TTP generally reveals or conceals facts or fictions, or some combination thereof. These diagrams illustrate that the advantage in using D&D clearly lies on the side of the attacker, given the sheer number of offensive D&D TTPs. Also, as compared to the methods reflected in Table 2.2, the majority of the offensive cyber-D&D TTPs shown in Fig. 2.1 fall along the simulation-dissimulation axis. This suggests potential opportunity space for crafting new TTPs that reveal facts and conceal fictions along the other axis. Appendix A contains further analysis and presents a full cyber-D&D taxonomy: a comprehensive list of all these offensive and defensive cyber-D&D TTPs,[14] categorized according to the D&D methods matrix.

These figures do not show all possible cyber-D&D TTPs, partly because those TTPs do not have naming conventions that make them readily identifiable, possibly due to the immaturity of the cyber-D&D field.[15] Furthermore, given the ever-evolving

---

[14] The offensive TTP entries include examples of how they would be used by a financially motivated actor as well as by an espionage-motivated actor. The defensive TTP entries include examples of how they would be used against a financially motivated actor and a targeted espionage actor.

[15] As shown in Stech et al.'s 2011 paper "Scientometrics of Deception, Counter-deception, and Deception Detection in Cyber-space," the absence of a clear set of conventional terminology suggests the immaturity of that domain.

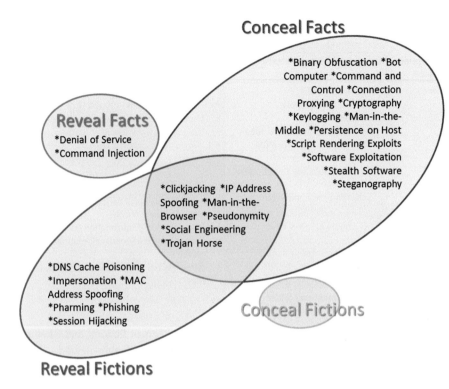

Fig. 2.1 Offensive Cyber-D&D tactics

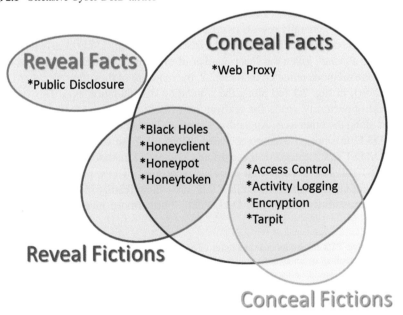

Fig. 2.2 Defensive Cyber-D&D tactics

nature of computer networking, technology, and software, these TTPs necessarily evolve as well, with some becoming obsolete, some being adapted, and new ones being created. As such, these diagrams have a moving window of validity.

2.3   Using D&D in Cyber Security

In *Defensive Computer-Security Deception Operations*, Yuill[16] asserts that cyber-D&D complements other cyber security methods:

> After years of research and development, computer security remains an error-prone task and, in some respects, perhaps a losing battle. Computer security's chronic problems call for wholly new approaches. Deception works in a fundamentally different way than conventional security. Conventional security tends to work directly with the hacker's actions, e.g., to prevent them or to detect them. Deception manipulates the hacker's thinking to make him act in a way that is advantageous to the defender. Being fundamentally different, deception can be strong where conventional security is weak.

This section, organized by the four quadrants of the D&D methods matrix, elaborates on each of the high-level cyber-D&D techniques presented in Table 2.3. Each subsection suggests some potential implementations of D&D for cyber security, particularly incident response in the context of a deception operation.

2.3.1   Reveal Facts

Revealing facts to an opponent can be an effective way of detecting malicious actors. By **publishing a limited amount of true information**[17] about their network, personnel, and missions, defenders can selectively attract attention or reduce attacker sensitivity to defensive network surveillance (Bennett and Waltz 2007). For example, defender deception tactics may include revealing employee attendance at upcoming conferences via their company blog or public mailing list. Malicious actors who employ targeted social engineering may adapt their tactics to the new context; for example, a message to an employee could purport to follow up on a session at the conference. The resulting information would become a marker to distinguish spear phishing attempts from untargeted malicious email.

Defenders may show their hand by **revealing their deception capabilities** in a way that makes their opponent disbelieve information gleaned from past intrusions. The defender could build a virtual honeypot environment nearly identical to the organization's actual environment, with usernames, email accounts, software registration, and server names configured to accurately reflect real configurations. If they

---

[16] James J. Yuill. *Defensive Computer-Security Deception Operations: Processes, Principles and Techniques.* Dissertation North Carolina State University, Raleigh NC, 2006, p. 200.

[17] Phrases shown in boldface are techniques originally presented in Table 2.3.

discover the duplication, malicious actors may doubt the authenticity of the data found in both previous and future intrusions, and become wary when interacting with supposedly compromised systems. Sophisticated planners integrate such deception capability signatures into their production networks to create further doubt in the event of a true compromise.

Malicious actors intrude into networks to gain access to sensitive information. One channel of disclosure is to launch an actor's implant inside a virtual honeypot. By **seeding the deception environment with real documents** that have been publicly released or previously compromised, or that contain non-sensitive information, the environment presents a sense of realism with limited risk to the target organization. If a phishing email launched the intrusion attempt, the original message and its presence in the targeted user account also act as confirming evidence of the adversary's success.

Planners must consider deception along several dimensions of impact. For example, publicity about an intrusion can damage an organization's public image and stature. With the right emphasis, an organization can **reveal this apparent weakness to emphasize a capable security program** in order to discourage further intrusion attempts. Misleading phrasing such as "unverified claims of network compromise are being investigated as a matter of routine by teams of internal security specialists" adds a degree of urgency to intruder operations. A successful disclosure encourages the intruders to reveal operational methods and support, such as implants, tools for subsequent compromise and enumeration, command and control (C2) hop points that the intruders might hold back if they believed they had more time to execute. This tactic is most effective when the deceivers understand the adversary's open source collection abilities.

In a similar vein, but more direct, **overt—but incomplete—remediation actions can accelerate an intruder's pace of operations**. During incident response, network defenders isolate and sanitize infected machines in a coordinated fashion.[18] After initial containment, security personnel could remove a subset of intruder access while leaving some portions intact to allow malicious actors to discover the remediation activities. The tactic encourages adversaries to reveal more TTPs in their efforts to reestablish footholds in the post-"remediation" environment.

2.3.2   Conceal Facts

Either side can conceal facts to gain advantages during a computer network intrusion. Ordinary access control policies—a formalization of **resource denial**—and their implementation form the long-standing first line of cyber defense. Firewalls, service proxies, email filtering, role-based account assignment, and protocol

---

[18] Jim Aldridge, Targeted Intrusion Remediation: Lessons From The Front Lines, Blackhat 2012, https://www.blackhat.com/usa/bh-us-12-briefings.html#Aldridge

encryption all deny resources to legitimate network users in the event their systems become compromised.

Adversaries may create **a denial of service (DoS) condition** through traffic floods or excessive failed access attempts as partial fulfillment of their mission. More insidious intrusions can render physical resources inaccessible through compromise of industrial control systems.

At a lower level, malware can intercept anomaly detection and other warning messages, stopping them from reaching the resources that process them. For example, **stealth methods can conceal the presence of malware** from security software by altering kernel data structures to prevent display in process, service, and device listings. Malicious code commonly obfuscates its control and dataflow dependencies to inhibit analysis once the implants have been discovered. Encryption or steganography may conceal adversarial command traffic to infected machines, preventing defenders from realizing that their information is being stolen.

Defenders also benefit from **software stealth techniques to hide security software services**, such as host activity sensors, antivirus, and data loss prevention clients. Other defensive denial tactics include encrypting documents to prevent exposure of intellectual property, and disallowing commonly abused system commands such as 'dsquery' or 'netcat' to prevent use by malicious actors. While this does not prevent actors from transferring equivalent tools to victims, it forces the attackers to take more risks in the process.

Proxies and anonymization services **reroute traffic to conceal the source address of a machine**. For example, the Tor network routes encrypted data through a series of machines. As a defense, many organizations simply block the public list of last-hop machines. Threat actors often use more *ad hoc* proxy networks for their C2, combining compromised systems with distributed virtual hosting services. Routing traffic through other machines in this manner makes it more difficult for network defenders to effectively filter and investigate malicious activity, particularly when hosts span multiple owners and jurisdictions

Rerouting adversarial traffic forms the foundation of *active defense* technologies. Defenses such as "sinkholing" route known bad Domain Name System (DNS) requests to non-existent Internet Protocol (IP) addresses or perhaps to internal sensors. More aggressive responses would route malicious actors to honeypot systems.[19] Defenders may also choose to deter malicious actors by performing system shutdown or logoff actions for contrived reasons. This straightforward response may be part of a plan to disable malicious access if the attackers appear close to discovering that they are in a ruse environment. As the responses become more active, such tactics more closely align with *revealing fictions* in place of *concealing facts*.

Organizations that gate access to the Internet with proxies have a structure for vetting requests to external resources. Conventional systems deny access to untrusted hosts, but active defenders may permit such connections at an enhanced level of monitoring while denying essential resources to the suspect host. Some enterprises attempt

---

[19] See Chap. 5 for an illustration.

man-in-the-middle intercepts on encrypted connections to web sites by issuing their own trusted certificates. While this practice may raise privacy concerns, its pay-off enables detection of malware that uses the Secure Sockets Layer/Transport Layer Security (SSL/TLS) for communication—especially significant given the recent events involving the Heartbleed bug in supposedly secure systems.

2.3.3   Reveal Fictions

Trend Micro reports that malware most commonly infects machines as a result of users' installing software from the Internet or opening malicious email attachments.[20] This finding underlies the defensive practices of network security operations centers that make large investments in Internet content and email filtering. Most users would not knowingly compromise their organization's network,[21] so malicious actors commonly lie to gain and preserve footholds in protected networks. Attackers can **misrepresent the intent of software and media in order to install malware**, for example by using fake antivirus programs,[22] Trojanized software in third-party application markets,[23] and pornography sites.[24] Phishing offers another instance of overt fiction intended to mislead users into opening documents that install malware. Malicious actors abuse webpage layout engines to simulate user interface elements that can trick victims into interacting with malicious content. In one notable example from 2012, the Flame malware used a control panel interface that resembles an innocuous web administration panel, presumably to evade discovery by suspicious system administrators.[25]

While defenders can reroute local DNS queries to deny access to malicious resources, one powerful adversarial tactic is to **poison DNS responses with attacker-controlled IP addresses**. After corrupting the records, the adversary creates a mock-up of a website or service that users expect to see in an effort to exploit their trust in the destination. Common goals include collecting user login credentials or pushing content that exploits vulnerabilities in visiting systems to establish a malicious implant.

In addition to hijacking domains, malicious operators can passively monitor traffic to compromise poorly implemented authentication systems.[26] This **session hijacking** exploits the stateless nature of the Hypertext Transfer Protocol (HTTP)

---

[20] https://blog.trendmicro.com/trendlabs-security-intelligence/most-abused-infection-vector/

[21] http://www.verizonenterprise.com/resources/reports/rp_data-breach-investigations-report-2012_en_xg.pdf

[22] http://static.usenix.org/events/leet10/tech/full_papers/Rajab.pdf

[23] http://www.f-secure.com/static/doc/labs_global/Research/Threat_Report_H2_2013.pdf

[24] http://www.bluecoat.com/documents/download/2014-mobile-malware-report

[25] https://www.securelist.com/en/blog/750/Full_Analysis_of_Flame_s_Command_Control_servers

[26] http://codebutler.com/firesheep/

by targeting the authentication cookies with which websites create sessions. After obtaining the authentication cookies, the attacker may replay them to impersonate an already-authenticated legitimate user.

Defender missions also benefit from presenting selected fictions. Malware, like other software, comes from a code base that its developers alter over time to suit their ends. Zeus, Poison Ivy and Gh0st RAT are well known public examples of remote access tools (appropriately known as RATs), and threat specialists (e.g., Mandiant 2013) enumerated dozens more. Once the defender organization bins the threats posed by the RATs, it may analyze the C2 protocols that the tools use for the implants of their high-priority campaigns. This analysis informs the development of protocol parsers, modifiers, and defender-controlled compatible implants. Together, these technologies can **intercept and modify network traffic** to give attackers a deceptive view of supposedly compromised systems. Emulated implants provide basic capabilities, such as file listing and remote shell execution, but disallow hard-to-emulate operations such as file uploading or screenshot capture. Unsupported commands can silently fail with a network timeout, require an interminable amount of time to complete, or appear to be blocked by policy.

More generally, because the primary purpose of a honeypot is to be vulnerable to compromise, defenders can use *honeypots* to deceive attempted intruders by presenting a wholly fake system. Honeypots fall into two categories: low-interaction honeypots that passively respond to malicious actors and high-interaction honeypots that require care and feeding for best results. Like emulated implants, low-interaction honeypots are shallow simulations of systems that respond plausibly to attempted compromise. A honeypot can simulate a service on a node; for example, Kippo acts as a Secure Shell (SSH) listener that collects brute force attacks and allows basic interactions with a lightweight file system.[27] Instead of hosting a real SSH server on port 23, a honeypot system would listen with Kippo, giving intruders an apparent opportunity to attack.

Another approach, known as tarpitting, simulates nodes on IP addresses that are not allocated in the production network. LaBrea, named after the famous tar pits in Los Angeles, was one proposed solution to the flash infection of 339,000 machines over 14 h caused by the Code Red worm (Haig 2002). The concept was to slow Code Red's scanning by presenting fictional machines in unallocated IP space that permitted the worm to establish Transmission Control Protocol (TCP) connections on all ports but subsequently timed out. This approach tied up the logic of Code Red as it waited for TCP responses rather than infecting new machines. LaBrea's timeout response had a minimal impact on enterprise operations because production traffic only touched legitimate machines, not the unallocated IP space.

Benefits of low-interaction honeypots include flexible deployment and the ability to gather information on malicious actors without the risk of compromising real machines. These honeypots have proven effective against relatively unsophisticated actors who rely on automated exploitation scripts but do not possess the technical ability to discover the deceptive environment. Integrating low-interaction honeypots

---

[27] https://code.google.com/p/kippo/

into production networks by re-allocating unused IP space gives an organization visibility into attempts to map and exploit hosts on their internal network.

By contrast, high-interaction honeypots offer a deeper level of simulation than the minimally implemented services intended to thwart automated tools. These honeypots seek to deceive a live adversary by presenting a range of services and vulnerable machines. Successful deployment enables network defenders to collect data on how malicious actors behave in the latter phases of an intrusion. For example, *honeyd* generalizes LaBrea's approach by providing deeper responses to traffic destined for unallocated IPs (Provos and Holz 2007). At the node level, *honeyd* simulates responses to network traffic at layer 3 and above by handing off interaction to both local and remote processes—for instance, a real HTTP web server on port 80, or a listener such as Kippo on port 23. Besides responding to local network traffic, *honeyd* simulates traversal of arbitrary network topologies with virtual routers and connections to other, non-local networks.

High-interaction honeypots require regular monitoring by network defenders, who should add artifacts over time to take advantage of changing adversary interests. Typically, defenders create plausible documents, emails, and user activity prior to launching a high-interaction honeypot. These so-called *honeytoken* documents need not be fully backstopped, but should be interesting to the adversary in question. Tracking honeytokens allows an organization to discover leaks or adversary distribution methods. As an example, if a malicious actor steals a fake list of email addresses during a deception operation, those emails may be subject to bulk public disclosure or be re-used to send phishing messages to the fake users. Tools such as pastycake[28] or Google Alerts can monitor popular distribution sites to detect public exposure of the "stolen" documents, and organizations can perform additional monitoring on the "stolen" email accounts.

The creation of fictional information, or honeytokens, such as fake user accounts, requires the defending organization to add them to its phone directory, email system, and employee domain. Organizations must treat any attempt to interact with these accounts as very suspicious, and investigate them immediately. On a production network, these accounts can be added to groups without dangerous privileges and have logon scripts that prevent abuse. As a proactive measure, organizations can use decoy email addresses for high-value targets such as executives or system administrators. Email addresses disclosed to external parties can be monitored for phishing attempts without affecting internal communications.

Finally, exposing a past deception to malicious actors may deter future intrusion attempts, depending on the attacker's perception of the organization's overall defensive posture. It may also cause actors to question the validity of any information taken from the organization's network in the past. The APT develops indicators of deception and uses them to guide subsequent engagements. A defender who integrates such features into production environments can make a real success seem like a honeypot to the adversary, potentially resulting in a loss of interest.

---

[28] https://github.com/9b/pastycake

2.3.4 Conceal Fictions

Most denial technologies can become vulnerable through misconfiguration, failure to patch, or exercise of a capability for which the adversary has demonstrated counter-measures. Defenders should tune the weakening strategy to the adversary's standard operating procedures (SOPs), so that the attacker can discover the "hidden" resource. Possibilities include selecting moderate to weak passwords for accounts or encrypted media, using exploitable webpages to obtain fictional resources (e.g., the page may be subject to SQL [Structured Query Language] injection vulnerabilities), and deploying outdated access control technologies to protect internal resources. As adversaries work through more "clues," these denial methods should collectively guide the hostile actors to focus their efforts on resources of limited value.

Planting fictional but inaccessible documents can entice interaction by malicious actors without the risk of disclosure. For example, a document purporting to be a planned business acquisition may contain a random collection of bytes disguised as an encrypted file. Using such files on an internal network can attract both malicious insiders and external attackers who have compromised perimeter security. Discoverable metadata about files can enhance the perceived value of such files, for instance by indicating that the files were authored by executives or well-known engineers.

Defenders may also craft documents written in highly technical or domain-specific language. Tools used by malicious actors often have no way of reading documents directly due to concerns about detection and file size. Enticing titles and timestamps may be enough to prompt a malicious actor to upload these files to their server, thereby providing valuable information on their collection requirements and infrastructure. By implanting watermarks in these files, a defender can also prove compromise of intellectual property.

Proprietors of secured and protected credit card databases might choose to include a sizable percentage of fictional "fluorescent" identities and account numbers designed not to work, but to report the attempted use as fraud; (for physical transactions) report the use and summon security; or (for cyber transactions) honor the transaction, while reporting the use and installing covert tracking and beaconing software (e.g., via a clickable purchase link) on the user's machine. All of these fictitious accounts would be concealed and protected and would only work against the attacker if obtained illegally.

Defenders usually wish to hide deception to manipulate their opponents. To this end, they often **configure honeypots to return tampered values in response to system commands** such as 'uptime' or 'systeminfo' to enhance plausibility and conceal the deceptive nature of the environment. To create a fake honeypot, defenders construct a real system that appears to have the known characteristics of a honeypot system.[29] To reinforce the façade, systems can appear as poorly concealed pieces of low-interaction emulation software when queried in certain ways.

---

[29] Neil C. Rowe. "Deception in defense of computer systems from cyber-attack," in A. Colarik and L. Janczewski eds. *Cyber War and Cyber Terrorism.* Hershey, PA: The Idea Group, 2007.

At the policy level, an organization may choose to **hide the existence of deception capabilities** with an OPSEC plan (Bennett and Waltz 2007). In contrast to publicly disclosing deception efforts, the OPSEC approach leaves malicious actors confident in their ability to compromise an organization. Security operations are sensitive as a matter of course, but deception operations are also vulnerable to counter-exploitation if disclosed without prior knowledge of deception planners.

2.4   D&D Operations

Planning and executing successful D&D operations requires a wide range of capabilities. They include an understanding of the theoretical and technical elements of cyber-D&D and an organizational capacity to plan, prepare, support, coordinate, control, and execute complex deception plans.[30] This D&D organizational element should be closely tied to the overall IT operations, cyber security and operational security elements, and threat intelligence efforts.

The deception cover story created and executed by the D&D team, as well as the EEDI, may be entirely truthful. For example, the story might represent a realistic course of action (COA) that the deceiver does not intend to execute. The D&D team could use plans for the rejected COA as the basis for the deception cover story. In this case, much of the deceiver's preparation for the selected COA will be identical or similar to actions that would be taken to implement the rejected COA. This ambiguity, together with an effective deception cover story, will cause the deception target to misconstrue preparations for the real COA as being consistent with the COA of the cover story.

For this approach to succeed, the deceiver organization must perform several critical tasks. The deceiver must induce failure in the target's perception or interpretation of environmental information and thus influence subsequent target actions. This means that the deceiver must either hide the "deception core" (EEFI) from the target, or simulate fictitious properties for EEFI (that is, create EEDI) to mislead the target. Then, the deceiver must develop a theory of the target's mind and behavior, including how the target seeks, scans, and accesses information in the environment; how the target categorizes and interprets this information; and how the target takes action, including further information sampling in the environment. Figure 2.3a, b show the tasks supporting the defender D&D team's deception goals through the use of D&D tactics.

The D&D team can use denial tactics to disrupt the target's perceptions of EEFI and NDDI (see Tables 2.4 and 2.5, respectively), while the deceiver's deception tactics disrupt the target's cognitive interpretation and understanding of the deceiver's true activities. The deceiver would convey the EEDI and NEFI so that the target misunderstands the deceiver's actions (see Tables 2.6 and 2.7, respectively). In other words, the deceiver's denial (ambiguity-type) tactics interfere with the target's

---

[30] See Chap. 7 for an analysis of organizational capability for cyber-D&D.

a

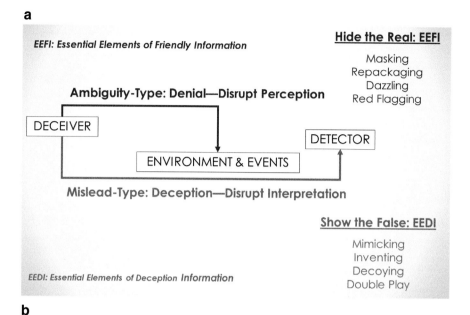

b

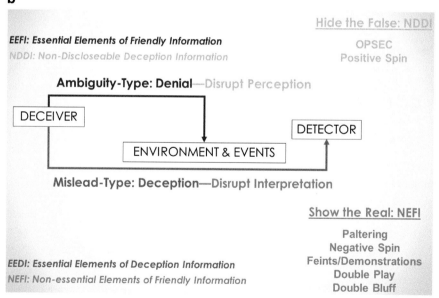

Fig. 2.3 (**a**) D&D types and tactics: EEFI and EEDI (**b**) D&D types and tactics: NDDI and NEFI

perceptions, while the deceiver's deception (mislead-type) tactics distort the target's interpretation of data.

The *deception goal* should always be to induce the target to take actions that will confer advantages on the defender. Those actions constitute the *deception effect*.

Table 2.4 Denial tactics (A-type: hiding the real: EEFI)

Masking	Conceal key characteristics of one entity while matching those of another *Using pseudonyms, Steganography*
Repackaging	Add and change labels or characteristics *Showing different web site content based on geo-IP location, Cryptography, Footprinting*
Dazzling	Obscure characteristics, add overpowering alternative characteristics *Software obfuscation*
Red Flagging	Obvious display of key characteristics, "waving a red flag" *Disposable email addresses*

Table 2.5 Denial tactics (A-type: hiding the false: NDDI)

OPSEC	Employ an operational security program for protecting secrets *Keep deceptive security operations a secret*
Positive Spin	Exaggerate positive elements to suppress negative falsehoods *Allow partial enumeration of fictional files*

Table 2.6 Deception tactics (M-type: showing the false: EEDI)

Mimicking	Copy characteristics; create fictitious entities *Fake Twitter accounts, Clickjacking, DNS Cache Poisoning*
Inventing	Create new characteristics; synthesize realistic indicators *Phishing email*
Decoying	Create alterative characteristics byforming immaterial entities or indicators *Honeypots*
Double Play	Maintain characteristics; show the real in such a suspicious manner as to cast doubt on it *Evercookies*

Table 2.7 Deception tactics (M-Type: Showing the Real: NEFI)

Paltering	Reveal facts that are misleading *Reveal misleading compromise details*
Negative Spin	Reveal minor facts so as to conceal major facts *Allow disclosure of select real files*
Feints/Demonstrations	Attempt to divert adversary attention toward one area in order to weaken attention to another area *Reveal select technical deception capabilities*
Double Play	Discredit true information so target disbelieves it *Selectively remediate intrusion*
Double Bluff	Release true information that benefits the deceiver by being disbelieved or rejected *Publish true network information*

Table 2.8 Deception team information and actions, and intended target reactions

Deception team information & actions (friendly)	Deception target intended reactions (adversary)
Attract adversary's attention to EEDI and cover story information and actions	Take notice of the EEDI and cover story
Hold adversary's interest in EEDI and cover story information and actions	Assess EEDI and cover story as relevant and monitor them
Confirm adversary's expectations and experiences regarding EEDI and cover story	Assess revealed elements of EEDI and cover story as congruent with expectations
Modify adversary's expectations and experiences regarding EEFI	Fail to take notice of EEFI hidden elements

The D&D team must have the knowledge and ability to develop D&D operations that protect the EEFI and the NDDI while contributing to the broader organization's goals and objectives by creating EEDI, NEFI, and cover stories[31] that can be expected to produce the deception effect. Table 2.8 summarizes the D&D team's information and actions and the intended reactions by the target.

The D&D team actions and information shown in the table presuppose that the deceiver has considerable information and intelligence about the target: how the target reacts to information and actions, what appeals to the target's interests, the target's expectations, and the target's blind spots.[32] The more intelligence the deceiver has about the target, the better the defender cyber-D&D team can develop EEDI and cover stories to mislead and deceive the target.

The information elements of the EEDI and the principal and secondary deception cover stories may include simulation (manipulation) or dissimulation (concealment) of several information dimensions:

- Actions:

  - Intention (What is the activity?)
  - Place/target (Where is the activity?)
  - Payoff (Why is the activity happening?)
  - Style/Method (How is the activity carried out?)

- Actors:

  - Players (Who is engaged in the activity?)
  - Strength (How many people are involved?)

---

[31] The deception planner should prepare several cover stories that will be supported throughout a specific deception campaign. By sustaining more than one viable cover story, the deceivers have a fallback story if the principal cover story is compromised, or if the deception target does not seem to react to the principal cover story.

[32] For ideas on identifying and exploiting blind spots in deception planning, see Van Hecke, M. L. (2007) *Blind spots: Why smart people do dumb things.* Prometheus Books: Amherst NY; and Sternberg, R. ed. (2002) *Why Smart People Can Be So Stupid.* Yale University Press: New Haven, CT.

- Stages:

  - Channel (By what means is the activity conducted?)
  - Pattern (In what way/order is the activity conducted?)
  - Time (When is the activity conducted?)

The deception cover stories must present believable information and actions covering all of these elements, just as a screenplay must address as many as possible of the audience's questions about and interests in the action and actors on the screen. Not all of these information elements need be false. In fact, the best deception cover stories make the greatest possible use of true information and activities, and present just enough EEDI and false or misleading information to cause the target to form the wrong picture of events, while making the target actors fully confident they understand the picture accurately.

Whaley (2007c) described a ten-step process for planning, preparing, and executing deception operations. These steps for creating effective deceptions (modified slightly to include the EEFI, EEDI, NEFI, NDDI terminology introduced in Table 2.1) are:

1. Use Blue[33] organizational goals to develop the deception goal, deception effect, and deception success criteria.
2. Collect intelligence on the Red adversary and estimate Red's preconceptions, expectations, and reactions.
3. Use real Blue COAs (that will not be executed) to develop the deception cover story: design the deception effect as Red's natural reaction to the Blue COA cover story.
4. Perform thorough Blue information value analysis (with cyber security and OPSEC partners): identify what must be hidden from Red (EEFI) and what must be revealed to Red (EEDI).
5. Plan denial actions to hide real information that provides Red with unique, unambiguous signatures of Blue plans and actions (EEFI), as well denial actions to hide the fictions that support Blue's D&D plan; detail the necessary steps to mask, repackage, dazzle, or red flag all EEFI and NDDI.
6. Plan to show the false: detail the necessary steps to use real information and actions (NEFI) and to mimic, invent, decoy, or double play the EEDI and actions (virtual and other) for the deception cover stories.
7. Develop the deception plan: organize the necessary D&D means and resources needed to support the cyber-D&D plan.
8. Manage the cyber deception operations: build the matrix of NEFI, EEDI, EEFI, NDDI, and deception cover stories to manage, coordinate, and control deception actions, information, and operations in conjunction with overall cyber operations, cyber security, and OPSEC partners.

---

[33] Whaley uses "Blue" to refer to the friendly, deceiver organization and "Red" to refer to the adversary target.

9. Monitor the deception operations: observe Red behaviors, actions, and reactions (virtual and otherwise); estimate the effectiveness of the deception cover stories; coordinate D&D actions with all ongoing virtual and other operations.
10. Reinforce deception operation successes: redirect unsuccessful deception operations by using concealment, simulations, or other channels to reinforce, sustain, and maintain the deception cover story; ensure the deception operations produce the planned deception effect; and redirect deception operations that are not producing the expected reactions and effects on the Red deception target.

It is important to note that steps 1–6 of the deception process comprise *deception planning*, step 7 is *deception preparation*, and steps 8–10 are *deception execution*. The deceiver achieves the best results by planning deceptions well in advance of the operations they are intended to protect; deception preparations and execution should occur while other operational planning continues. Then, by the time the real operation commences, the deceiver has planted and supported the deception cover story, which manipulates the target to misperceive and misconstrue the ongoing events, erroneously confident that it comprehends the deceiver's operation.

Chapter 3
Intrusions, Deception, and Campaigns

The goal of deploying deception to detect hackers is to change the underlying economics of hacking, making it more difficult, time consuming and cost prohibitive for infiltrators to attack a web application … But the ultimate deception is misinformation. Imagine supplying the hacker with fake successes, responses, files and assets to exploit. This wastes the attackers' time and makes them feel like they have successfully hacked, unknowing that they are instead compromising a virtual world.

> Edward Roberts (2012) Deception and the art of cyber security, *SC Magazine*, February 28, 2012. www.scmagazine.com/deception-and-the-art-of-cyber-security/article/229685/

Cyber intrusion tactics and strategies have advanced considerably over the last two decades. Analysts have drawn on empirical observations to formulate high-level models of cyber intrusions. The four-tiered pyramidal model of intrusions in Fig. 3.1 depicts various granularities of abstractions in such models.

Starting from the bottom, an attack step represents an atomic action which furthers the larger intrusion goal, such as to corrupt a log file or escalate a process privilege.

The second level, a cyber attack, typically consists of a carefully orchestrated set of attack steps. It requires the attacker to sequence the steps and string them together in careful ways, with the outputs of each step used as inputs to subsequent steps. Thus, analysts typically model attacks by a formalism such as an attack tree.

Next in the pyramid is the cyber kill chain, generally recognized as a useful, high-level meta-model of attacks. The kill chain models the distinct phases of cyber intrusions, starting with reconnaissance and ending with execution and maintenance. A kill chain for a particular intrusion may consist of multiple attacks mapped to its various phases.

At the top of the pyramid is the intrusion campaign: a strategic construct used by adversary decision makers in articulating and achieving strategic objectives. The small size of the pyramid's apex conveys that strategic intrusion campaigns are few and far between. A government may organize a single strategic intrusion campaign over a given (extended) time period. That campaign may encompass multiple kill chains, with each kill chain consisting of numerous attacks and each attack in turn consisting of many attack steps.

Our analysis reveals opportunities for cyber-D&D at each phase of this model. In this chapter we examine cyber-D&D options for the various phases, and propose a model for planning, preparing, and executing cyber-D&D operations. These models

© Springer International Publishing Switzerland 2015
K.E. Heckman et al., *Cyber Denial, Deception and Counter Deception*,
Advances in Information Security 64, DOI 10.1007/978-3-319-25133-2_3

Fig. 3.1 High-level model
of cyber intrusions

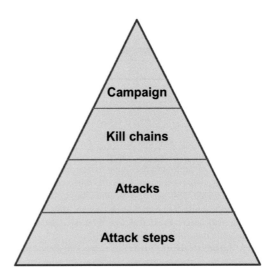

attempt to capture the phases of both individual cyber attacks and their aggregate
behavior. The chapter concludes with an examination of how to advance mission
goals across intrusion campaigns by developing deception campaigns.

3.1   Intrusion Attempts

Amoroso (2011) defines three types of cyber threat actors[1]:

(a) External Adversary—criminal groups, nation-states, and protest organizations
(b) Internal Adversary—disgruntled employees and malicious insiders
(c) Supplier Adversary—commercial vendors and business partners

Amoroso also posits two types of cyber-attack[2]:

1. *Targeted attacks* target organizations and focus on acquiring highly specific
   information for monetary, espionage, or sabotage purposes. Targeted attacks
   might cause DoS or damage to cyber systems (e.g., destroying files). For example,
   a targeted attack may attempt to gain access to a contractor performing military
   research.
2. *Opportunistic attacks* target a wide variety of organizations and indiscriminately
   infect systems. Compromised machines are exploited to obtain personal

---

[1] For detailed examples and descriptions of cyber threat actors, see Sean Bodmer, Max Kilger,
Gregory Carpenter, and Jade Jones. *Reverse deception: Organized cyber threat counter-exploitation.*
McGraw-Hill: New York, 2012.

[2] For detailed examples and descriptions of cyber attacks, see Edward Amoroso. *Cyber-attacks:
Protecting national infrastructure.* Elsevier: Burlington, MA, 2011, p. 5.

Table 3.1 Types of cyber threat actors, attack types, and attack preferences

Types of cyber threat actors	Types of attacks	
	Targeted attacks	Opportunistic attacks
External adversary	Espionage, Sabotage, Ransom, Identity Theft	Financial Gain, Protest, Embarrassment
Internal adversary	Espionage, Financial Gain, Sabotage, Revenge, Embarrassment	Espionage, Financial Gain, Revenge, Embarrassment
Supplier adversary	Espionage, Financial Gain	Financial Gain

information for monetary gain or espionage. For example, a malicious site compromising home computers to steal bank account numbers, credit card account numbers, and passwords.

Table 3.1 identifies the types of attacks preferred by different adversaries.

Attempted intrusions by motivated and well-resourced cyber threat actors have a high chance of success because of their mission-focused persistence. As noted in Chap. 1, most organizations rely on perimeter-based security measures that have limited effectiveness against client-side compromises of internal machines. The persistent adversary escalates capabilities in response to defensive actions, so while software updates and network security devices are necessary preventive measures, they are not sufficient to protect against compromise.

As infrastructure which enables network intrusions becomes globally distributed over virtual hosting services and compromised machines, blacklisting of domain names and Internet addresses quickly becomes unsustainable as a defensive technique. While these approaches are effective against less sophisticated threats, defense against motivated actors requires defending against entire classes of attacks and sharing threat information among targeted organizations.

3.2   Cyber Kill Chain

Malicious actors follow a common model of behavior to successfully compromise valuable information in a target network. In general, cyber threats, such as state-actor APTs[3] and advanced cyber criminals,[4] employ a cyber attack strategy, divided into phases, called the kill chain.[5] Figure 3.2 illustrates the concept of a cyber kill

---

[3] See, for example, Mandiant, *M-Trends: the advanced persistent threat,* 2010; and Mandiant, *APT1: Exposing One of China's Cyber Espionage Units,* 2013.

[4] For detailed examples and descriptions of cyber threat actors, see Sean Bodmer et al. (2012).

[5] See Eric M. Hutchins, Michael J. Cloppert, and Rohan M. Amin, "Intelligence-Driven Computer Network Defense Informed by Analysis of Adversary Campaigns and Cyber Kill Chains," *6th Annual International Conference on Information Warfare and Security,* Washington, DC, 2011. http://www.lockheedmartin.com/content/dam/lockheed/data/corporate/documents/LM-White-Paper-Intel-Driven-Defense.pdf. The labels used here for the phases are slightly modified from those in the Lockheed-Martin paper (which are in parentheses).

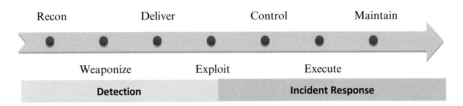

Fig. 3.2 Cyber kill chain for computer network intrusions

chain for computer network intrusions, originally formulated by Lockheed Martin,[6] [7] to inform CND operations.

For a network intrusion to succeed, the attacker completes each step of the kill chain. From the defender's perspective, steps prior to a successful exploit offer opportunities to detect intrusion attempts; during the post-exploit phases defenders can deploy incident response and forensics. These sets of steps are often referred to as "left of exploit" and "right of exploit," respectively.

Hutchins et al. (2011), who applied the "kill chain" concept to cyber attacks, define the kill chain phases as:

1. *Reconnaissance*—Research, identification and selection of targets, often represented as crawling Internet websites such as conference proceedings and mailing lists for email addresses, social relationships, or information on specific technologies.
2. *Weaponization*—Coupling a remote access Trojan with an exploit into a deliverable payload, typically by means of an automated tool (weaponizer). Increasingly, client application data files such as Adobe Portable Document Format (PDF) or Microsoft Office documents serve as the weaponized deliverable. [Note that another, increasingly common weaponized deliverable is drive-by browser exploits. These attacks only require a victim to visit a webpage, rather than open an email attachment or file.]
3. *Delivery*—Transmission of the weapon to the targeted environment. The three most prevalent delivery vectors for weaponized payloads by APT actors, as observed by the Lockheed Martin Computer Incident Response Team (LM-CIRT) for the years 2004–2010, are email attachments, websites, and USB removable media.
4. *Exploitation*—After the weapon is delivered to victim host, exploitation triggers intruders' code. Most often, exploitation targets an application or operating system vulnerability, but it could also more simply exploit the users themselves by convincing them to execute a file they downloaded from the Internet.

---

[6] http://www.lockheedmartin.com/content/dam/lockheed/data/corporate/documents/LM-White-Paper-Intel-Driven-Defense.pdf

[7] Although originally referred to as the "Intrusion Kill Chain" by the authors of the related seminal paper, the concept is now more generally referred to as "Cyber Kill Chain." See http://www.lockheedmartin.com/us/what-we-do/information-technology/cyber-security/cyber-kill-chain.html

5. *Installation*—Installation of a remote access Trojan or backdoor on the victim system allows the adversary to maintain persistence inside the environment. [These additional footholds may have different signatures and hosts than the initial implants in hopes of surviving an incident response that targets only the first method of access. APTs often steal legitimate credentials for subsequent system access, rather than relying on their initial remote access terminals. Ensuring the freshness of this access is part of the maintenance phase.]

6. *Command and Control (C2)*—Typically, [since firewalls deny incoming traffic for initiating connections,] compromised hosts must beacon outbound to an Internet controller server to establish a C2 channel. [Since APTs have diverse missions and targets, their implants usually APT malware especially requires some degree of manual interaction.] Once the C2 channel establishes, intruders have "hands on the keyboard" access inside the target environment. The next step is to enable their mission by uploading the appropriate set of tools.

7. *Actions on Objectives*—Only now can intruders take actions to achieve their original objectives. While data exfiltration is among the most common objective, there are other equally concerning actions including data corruption, denial of service, lateral movement, misattribution, corruption of physical systems, and deception.

The kill chain framework has the flexibility to adapt to specific domains. We illustrate this with three short examples in which we use boldface to identify each kill chain phase.

In cybercrime, the perpetrator might **reconnoiter** and control third-party sites; **weaponize** an exploit kit; **deliver** the exploit via drive-by traffic; **exploit** systems with unpatched applications, such as Internet Explorer or Java; **install** a backdoor; **collect** credentials and/or identify potential victims; **execute** financial transfers via machine access; and **persist** using custom-built software and/or tools.

In technical espionage, an APT can **reconnoiter** companies and/or employees associated with a relevant technology conference; create a malicious PDF via a **weaponization** toolkit that would be of interest to conference attendees; **deliver** messages via a fake email account with the malicious PDF attachment; **exploit** systems with a particular vulnerability; **install** a custom backdoor and/or reverse shell; search and **exfiltrate** technology-related information via the compromised system; **execute** password dumpers and move laterally; and **maintain** access on multiple systems with additional backdoors.

The designer of the Stuxnet worm conducted **reconnaissance** on individuals with physical access; **weaponized** a zero-day exploit for cross domain access and/or disruption; **delivered** the zero-day exploit via infected Universal Serial Bus (USB) drives planted with contractors; **exploited** the synchronous data link control for the process logic controllers on site; relayed **C2** via nodes with Internet connections to collect documentation; **executed** disruption via preprogrammed code; and **maintained** access for 36 days via staged infections.

Because incident response is very costly, cyber defenders must approach security proactively and keep the attacker "left of exploit;" that is, prevent the attacker from reaching the exploit stage. This requires evolution from traditional defensive postures toward active defense strategies driven by cyber threat intelligence. Cyber-D&D is a central component of active defense because it dynamically shapes adversarial actions rather than passively waiting to react at a time and context of the adversary's choosing.

Information operations (IO) doctrine (Department of Defense, 2014) identifies six basic tactics: detect, deny, disrupt, degrade, deceive, and destroy. The last five constitute the so-called "D5 cyber effects." Hutchins et al. (2011) describe all of them as potentially appropriate to use in a "defender's kill chain" to mitigate intrusions by disrupting their sequence of actions leading to success:

> For the defender, *the most important lessons of the kill chain are that it clearly shows that the adversary must progress successfully through every stage before it* [they] *can achieve its* [their] *desired objectives, and any one mitigation disrupts the chain and defeats the adversary.* The more mitigations the defenders can implement across the chain, the more resilient the defense becomes.[8] (italics added)

Deception can and often should be combined with other tactics. Where Hutchins et al. (2011) see deception tactics as applicable (in combination with other IO tactics) at the last two phases of the kill chain, we argue that deception tactics apply to all phases of the cyber kill chain as shown in Fig. 3.3 and outlined below.

3.2.1 Reconnaissance

3.2.1.1 Attack

Malicious actors first perform reconnaissance on the target organization's publicly accessible resources, attempting to find vulnerabilities in web servers, operating systems, and web applications. The attacker harvests employee names, interests, and email accounts from postings on social media sites to enable verification and better phishing attempts, and performs open-source research to estimate the difficulty of compromising an organization, as well as the potential benefits. For instance, an organization involved in military research would both possess more valuable data and present a harder target than a small military supplier company.

3.2.1.2 Response

To head off attempted targeting of users, an organization can **allow disclosure of fictional information**[9] by creating and posting false user information publicly on social media sites and can **publish true network information** that will generate alerts on attempts to compromise publicly exposed users. EEDI that **exposes fictional systems**

---

[8] Charles Croom, "The Defender's 'Kill Chain'," *Military Information Technology*, Vol. 14, No. 10, 2010. http://www.kmimediagroup.com/files/MIT_14-10_final.pdf The author, Lieutenant General Charles Croom (Ret.) is Vice President of Lockheed Martin Information Systems and Global Solutions.

[9] Phrases shown in boldface are techniques originally presented in Table 2.3.

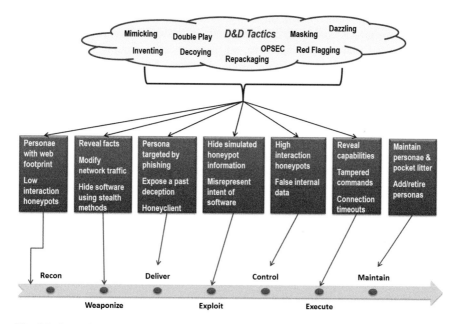

Fig. 3.3 Deception tactics for kill chain phases

can be correlated in order to characterize the reconnaissance strategies of a given actor group. For example, if a fake social media profile that only existed on a honeypot machine later receives "friend" requests, the adversary has exposed part of its recruitment tradecraft.

Organizations can influence how an actor perceives the difficulty of successfully compromising their network by **keeping deceptive security operations a secret** while **revealing technical deception capabilities**. In concert, these techniques can lead adversaries to underestimate the defender's capability. Even though they may develop detectors matched to the revealed technology, they are more likely to declare success when interacting with unknown deception capabilities.

3.2.2 Weaponization

3.2.2.1 Attack

The malicious actor then uses reconnaissance results to build and test exploits and malware that target a given user or system. If the target information is valuable enough the attacker may develop working exploits for previously unknown vulnerabilities. For example, a phishing email might be designed to target a specific application on the victim's computer. The patch level and configuration determine whether or not to expend effort on devising a zero-day exploit. If adversaries choose not to exploit an application, they may disguise an executable to look like a document; opening it would pass control directly to the malicious code. Development of exploits and malware is expensive, so many attackers simply reuse publicly known vulnerabilities. Adversaries evade detection by combining obfuscated unpackers with encrypted payloads.

3.2.2.2   Response

Unlike the other kill chain phases, the weaponize stage offers defenders no opportunity for direct action. However, a full defensive deception plan could corrupt the adversary's weaponization phase by influencing the attacker to assemble detectable or ineffective payloads. For example, the defender may want adversaries to use ineffective payload obfuscation methods, while encouraging them to deploy expensive zero-day vulnerabilities. Weaponized malware typically contains an exploit, an initial implant, and some sort of legitimate looking disguise. Although identifying incoming zero-day vulnerabilities is a hard problem, intrusion attempts may be exposed by other properties such as poorly concealed implants, recycled phishing attempts, contact with known bad servers, or unique C2 protocols. To support this goal, the defender reveals networks of currently patched systems throughout the reconnaissance and post-exploit stages. The defender's incident response plan permits detectable payload obfuscation methods that are not bundled with a known exploit to apparently succeed (e.g., engagement with honeypots) or partially succeed (e.g., obtain a response to a phishing email, but fail in network exploitation). Over time, the defender's plan will reward additional investment in exploitation.

Defenders can also intentionally lure the adversary by presenting a series of vulnerabilities to ascertain the attacker's weaponization skills. Information on the speed at which the attacker weaponizes malware, as well as the tools used to build the weapons, is very valuable to the defender's detection methods. Later on, during the delivery, exploit, and control stages, defenders can **hide detection software using stealth methods** to prevent weaponized tools and exploits from evading security systems. In the reconnaissance and execute stages, they can **modify network traffic** to report different versions of application software in service of the deception plan. They may also **allow disclosure of real files** to detect repurposed malicious versions of those files. As an example, the defender could mark a leaked internal memo to trigger a security alert if detected within inbound email.

3.2.3   Delivery

3.2.3.1   Attack

In this phase of the kill chain, malicious actors deliver their weaponized malware to the defender's systems and attempt to exploit external applications. Most organizations first detect attacks at this phase, and filter malicious network traffic using firewalls and intrusion detection systems (IDSs). Antivirus software may detect malicious email attachments at the email gateway or when they are delivered to a target user's machine.

Intruders use deception by delivering a malicious payload in such a way that only the target organization would be successfully exploited. For example, web exploit frameworks frequently block IP addresses of security researchers from interacting with infected pages,[10] and may infect victims on a limited basis based on incoming redirection chains.[11] A malicious page may also limit the number of victims to prevent examination by anyone other than the intended target.

3.2.3.2 Response

A defending organization sees its cyber-D&D defensive labors from the reconnaissance phase bear fruit when, subsequent to **allowing disclosure of fictional information**, the fake users who are the subjects of the information are targeted by a phishing attack. The defender may also begin to see compromise attempts on applications intentionally revealed in the other kill chain stages. Defenders can deploy low-interaction honeypots, such as honeyclients or LaBrea, to collect delivery attempts on a wide scale.

3.2.4   Exploit

3.2.4.1   Attack

A successful exploit can occur through various techniques, including memory corruption of internal applications, exploitation of access control misconfigurations, and user execution of malicious attachments that propagate infections and establish attacker footholds.

3.2.4.2   Response

To lower the risk of a Windows system's being compromised, Microsoft's Enhanced Mitigation Experience Toolkit (EMET)[12] deploys several low-level technologies that prevent shellcode from launching its payload.[13] These mitigations come at the expense of compatibility with some legacy software, so each enterprise must make a judgment about using EMET use in its production network.

---

[10] http://blog.spiderlabs.com/2012/09/blackhole-exploit-kit-v2.html

[11] http://blog.spiderlabs.com/2012/05/a-wild-exploit-kit-appears.html

[12] Enhanced Mitigation Experience Toolkithttp://support.microsoft.com/kb/2458544

[13] On the Effectiveness of DEP and ASLR https://blogs.technet.com/b/srd/archive/2010/12/08/on-the-effectiveness-of-dep-and-aslr.aspx

As with other stages, **exposing fictional systems** to an intruder by standing up high-interaction honeypots to host initial malware can support the defender's deception plan. The defending organization can **misrepresent the intent of software** to simulate a successful exploit, enabling passive and active monitoring for the subsequent kill chain stages.

3.2.5   *Control*

3.2.5.1   Attack

To evade detection, initial malware installed by an exploit often has limited functionality, a small footprint, and no persistence across reboot. Once malicious actors can send commands to a machine in the target environment, they can install more feature-rich malware that will remain resident on the infected system.

3.2.5.2   Response

D&D success in the control stage follows from a holistic deception plan that encourages the adversary to present known C2 protocols. In this scenario, defenders can actively monitor and corrupt adversary communications because they have previously analyzed the communication mechanisms. Without a D&D plan to incentivize use of known C2 channels, defenders must wait and hope that the adversary's choice will at some point coincide with their capability. However, encountering new C2 protocols also presents defenders with an opportunity to enhance their picture of adversary tactics, techniques, and procedures (TTPs) and subsequently to develop new active monitoring capabilities.

Short-term D&D TTPs can be effective in shaping the adversary's concept of failure. One way to prevent malicious actors from succeeding in the control phase is by "blackholing" or **rerouting network traffic** to unresponsive IP addresses. Defenders may also **silently intercept network traffic** to identify malicious communication and remediate systems to the best of their ability for disallowed C2 channels. They can also **modify network traffic** to present a misleading view of the compromised systems, making intrusions seem low value.

3.2.6   *Execute*

3.2.6.1   Attack

With a reliable C2 channel and persistent malware, malicious actors begin gathering information about their environment. Depending on the system compromised and the type of intrusion, the attackers either take files in a smash-and-grab fashion or slowly siphon off information over a period of months. Generally the malware has access to local user credentials, possibly even to local administrator and system accounts. Malicious actors crack user passwords and enumerate machines in the compromised system's enterprise. They then compromise internal machines by repeating the chain from reconnaissance to exploit, using legitimate user credentials, or exploiting insecure applications.[14]

3.2.6.2   Response

During the execute phase defenders can present adversaries with high-interaction honeypots seeded with compelling pocket litter and passage material that support the defending organization's deception plan. These documents should be tagged for later identification and threat intelligence. Defenders may also **present misleading compromise details** that allude to the failed intrusion attempt or **selectively remediate intrusion** to escalate an actor's pace of operations. They may increase the attacker's lateral movement and exfiltration, which could help the defender to detect malicious behavior. This strategy does entail some risks, as data would leave the organization faster, and adversaries could become aware of the incident response team's efforts to remove them from the network.

   At this time during a deception operation, the defense may choose to **reveal technical deception capabilities** to deter further intrusion attempts, or may allow malicious actors to continue operating so that the defense can gather more information. Revealing deception capabilities is the first step in developing false deception indicators that integrate with a production environment. Sophisticated adversaries develop detectors to identify the revealed capability, just as malware authors increasingly deploy virtual machine detection to frustrate instrumented dynamic analysis. Once defenders understand the adversary's technical detectors, they can seed their production networks with features designed to produce false positives.

   To keep an actor's interest, a defender can **allow partial enumeration of fictional files** that pertain to identified collection requirements. The defender can also **expose fictional systems** that simulate additional services and tantalizing targets.

---

[14] Mandiant. M-Trends 2011.

3.2.7   Maintain

3.2.7.1   Attack

Malicious actors maintain long-term access by using stealth and redundancy. Modern malware creates network traffic that blends in with background noise,[15] or passively waits for commands.[16] Multiple pieces of malware with redundant C2 and varying connection schedules provide continued access even if network defenders partially remediate the infection. Malware frequently switches IP addresses and domain names of control nodes to evade blacklists. This results in pervasive compromise of an organization's network until a concerted remediation removes all traces of the intrusion. Furthermore, adversaries use their access to steal legitimate credentials, enabling them to access systems with the same methods as authorized users.

3.2.7.2   Response

Cyber-D&D planning can counter adversaries during the maintenance phase by employing the same strategies used to control prior stages of the kill chain: allowing known persistence methods to "succeed" while instrumenting those footholds with active monitoring. In the case of stolen credentials, defenders can move affected users to new accounts and let the old ones become high-interaction decoys. As with the well-understood initial C2 channels, defenders should create compatible decoy maintenance implants that provide the same interfaces for the adversary, but alert defenders once the implants are exercised.

3.2.8   Recursive Cyber Kill Chain

While the phases of the kill chain are typically shown as linear and sequential, as illustrated in Fig. 3.3, full campaigns may have several phases underway at any given moment.[17] The kill chain may also be recursive rather than linear, and disjoint rather than smoothly sequential.[18] Some descriptions and illustrations of the cyber kill chain concept suggest these recursive and circular features, as shown in Fig. 3.4.

---

[15] Inside an APT Covert Channel. http://www.hbgary.com/inside-an-apt-covert-communications-channel

[16] Hikit: Advanced and Persistent Attack Techniques. https://blog.mandiant.com/archives/3155

[17] Mandiant's (2013) Attack Lifecycle Model (p. 27) shows the Chinese "APT1" cycling among kill chain phases "Escalate Privileges, Internal Recon, Move Laterally, Maintain Presence."

[18] C.f., Mandiant (2010) and Mandiant (2013).

Fig. 3.4 Alternative representations of the cyber kill chain concept. (Attributed to Secureworks, http://www.rbijou.com/2013/03/15/examining-the-cyber-kill-chain/)

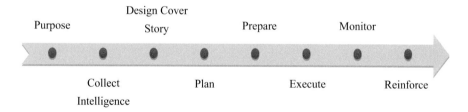

Fig. 3.5 Deception chain

3.3   Deception Chain

Defensive cyber-D&D teams need to plan against campaigns rather than incidents. Key to this strategy is allowing the adversary apparent success that is covertly under the control of defenders. This "success" reduces the adversary's incentive to innovate, and provides defenders with a channel to manipulate adversary action in pursuit of a deception goal beyond the integrity of their own cyber operations. To enable this strategy, we propose a "deception chain" that encompasses the phases of planning, preparation, and execution of cyber-D&D operations (see Fig. 3.5). Defenders can use this deception chain to develop adaptive and resilient courses of action (COAs) as defensive responses. The deception chain is based on the ten-step process for planning, preparing, and executing deception operations defined by Barton Whaley (2007c) and described in Chap. 2.

3.3.1 Purpose

Planners must have clear reasons based on their organizational goals for utilizing D&D. Thus, they must *define the strategic, operational, or tactical goal, the purpose of the deception, and the criteria that would indicate the deception's success.* Generally, the goals will primarily involve maintaining the security and surprise of the operation, with the secondary objective of facilitating speed in achieving the objective.

All deception effects have three goals in common. First, the deception must influence the adversary's perceptions and beliefs. This must then motivate the adversary to act; that is, to either take action *or* choose inaction based on those perceptions and beliefs. Finally, the defender should benefit in some way from the adversary's actions or inactions. The subtle point is that the deception planner should not seek to influence what the adversary *believes*, but what the planner wants the adversary to *do*. For example, the planner may wish to influence the adversary to believe that their strongest tools are actually their weakest so that the adversary decides to decrease strong tool usage. This could also slow the adversary's operations should the adversary opt to either find or create new tools. The defender would benefit, at least in the short-term, from the adversary relying on weaker tools and/or slowing their operations and giving the defender time to plan, prepare, and execute a follow-on deception operation when the adversary increases their activity armed with a new toolset.

3.3.2 Collect Intelligence

The deception planner must *define how the opponent is expected to react to the deception operation.* The deception objective generally must be to eliminate or delay the defender's reaction to the deception operation to enable network defenders to gain and maintain surprise and relative superiority as early as possible and until the objective is accomplished.

Deception planners must depend on intelligence to determine what the adversary will observe, how the adversary might interpret those observations, how the adversary might react (or not) to those observations, and how to monitor the adversary's behavior. This intelligence will help the defender to determine if the deception story is succeeding. For example, before reconfiguring its firewall in conjunction with the deception operation the defender must first know how that will affect the attacker's navigation through the cyber kill chain. That is, the defender needs to have enough intelligence about the attacker to know that such a reconfiguration will not prevent the attacker from cycling so far down the kill chain that the deception operation cannot achieve its goal.

3.3.3 Design Cover Story

The deception planner must *develop the D&D cover story or stories—the deception version of what the target of the deception should perceive and believe.* This step requires consideration of all the critical components of the operation, assessment of the opponent's observation and analysis capabilities, and development of a convincing story that "explains" the operation's components that the opponent observes, but misleads the opponent as to the meaning and significance of those observations. Generally, the most convincing cover stories are based on what the opponent already believes and wants to believe.

Full-scale planning up front is key to ensure the deception cover story is solid and fully backstopped. A solidly crafted story contains many dependencies, and backstopping is not trivial. Details matter and reality can impose many limitations. For example, Appendix B illustrates the complexity of constructing and maintaining false personae as part of a deception. Deception planners should always ask themselves: If adversaries are to believe this deception, what signs, indicators, etc., would they expect to see, and what signs, indicators, etc., would they expect *not* to see? The deception planner can then look for the incongruities in the planned deception. The planner must also keep in mind the dependencies and correlations between the cyber and kinetic worlds; the cyber deception should never allow misalignment.

Similarly, the planner must understand the big picture, which means knowing as much as possible about the "environment and events" in which the deception will be deployed: history, culture, and infrastructure. This applies to the adversary as well as to the physical and/or virtual locations for the deception. For example, an attacker may have established persistence on the defender's network, only accessing the network periodically over the course of several years, but shown a tendency to verify the existence of the same set of users and administrators. If a component of the cyber-D&D operation is to place the attacker in a synthetic environment, the defender must ensure that the environment includes this particular set of users. Defenders also benefit from knowing what channels are accessible to the adversary, as that knowledge will allow the deception planners to scope what the adversary can and cannot perceive and thereby what should and should not be part of the deception story.

The deception planner must *decide what is to be hidden to support the deception story* (the EEFI and NDDI), *and what must be created and revealed to support it* (the EEDI and NEFI). The deception operator must then align each of the critical components of the operation with the denial and OPSEC operations that will hide the components, or with the deception operations that will create misperception and misunderstanding.

3.3.4 Plan

The deception planner must *analyze the characteristics of the real events and activities that must be hidden* to support the deception cover story, identify the corresponding signatures that would be observed by the opponent, and explicitly *mask, repackage, dazzle,* or *red flag* those signatures to hide them from the opponent (see Table 2.4). The planner must design and prepare specific denial methods for each critical component of the operation that must be hidden (see Table 2.5), and must integrate the denial methods with the overall operation's security and OPSEC plans and preparations. Everything cannot be protected, nor should it be. Deception planners must work within the organization to determine what *has* to be protected in order to achieve the deception objective.

The deception planner must also *analyze the characteristics of the notional events and activities that must be portrayed and observed* to support the deception cover story, identify the corresponding signatures that the adversary would observe, and explicitly *mimic, invent, decoy,* or *double play* the appropriate signatures to mislead the adversary (see Table 2.6). The deception operator scripts the specific events that will be displayed to the adversary, the specific observations that the adversary will be allowed to make, and the manipulations of the adversary's sources that will be used to convey the deception story. These deception steps must be coordinated with the operational planning. The simulations should be as realistic and natural as possible; as far as possible (consistent with the security and OPSEC plans), they should allow the adversary to observe real operational events that support the deception cover story (see Table 2.7).

History has shown that deception is most successful when it closely aligns with the truth. A deception plan should take advantage of non-essential truths that can be used to cover the EEFI and NDDI and enhance the believability of the EEDI that support the cover story. To the extent possible, the deception planner needs a theory of mind for the adversaries, covering what they know, believe, expect, and desire. This information should come from the collect intelligence phase of the deception chain. The deception planner also needs to have an understanding of general human cognitive limitations, heuristics and biases, and stereotypes in order to exploit the combination of these characteristics with the EEDI and the cover story.

3.3.5 Prepare

The deception planner must *design the desired effect* of the deception operation and must also *explore the available means and resources to create the effect* on the adversary. In this step, the planner must coordinate with other operators regarding the timing and phasing of the notional and the real equipment, staff, training, and preparations to support the deception cover story. For example, the cyber-D&D operation might require the setup of one or more servers, increased network monitoring and/or logging, or coordination with operational network defense units to avoid disrupting their ongoing operations. Constraints or resource conflicts may arise between deception operations and real operations, forcing the deception planner to return to phase three to redesign the cover story to fit the constraints and available resources.

3.3.6   Execute

If the deception and real operational preparations can be synchronized and supported, the deception planner and other operators must *coordinate and control all relevant preparations so they will consistently, credibly, and effectively convey the deception cover story.* That is, in this step deception planning ends and *deception operations control* begins. Since real as well as deceptive operational units and activities are typically used to "sell" the deception effect to the adversary, the operational staff controls overall ongoing activities, while allowing the deception controllers to "fine tune" the execution of operations to reinforce the deception effect and conceal the deception methods.

Execution could, for example, entail defender engagement with the adversary in a sequence of move, countermove actions. These actions could be very dynamic and rapid, or they could unravel slowly over an extended period of time. Execution could also entail passive observation and logging as an adversary moves through an appropriately designed and pre-rigged synthetic environment.

3.3.7   Monitor

The deception controllers must *monitor and control the deception operations and the real operational preparations they cover.* That is, the deception controllers monitor both friendly and adversary operational preparations, and carefully watches the observation channels and sources selected to convey the simulation signatures to the opponent. The deception controllers must ensure that the targeted channels and sources remain open to the adversary, that these channels convey the planned deception simulations, and that the adversary observes them. The deception controllers monitor operational preparations *to ensure the notional effects are conveyed as planned while the deception methods remain hidden from the adversary's observation.* The deception controllers must deal with any operational mistakes and leakage in the dissimulations, while using intelligence to monitor the adversary's reactions to the deceiver's real and deception operations.

3.3.8   Reinforce

If the operational deception simulations seem not to be "selling" the cover story to the adversary, the deception controllers may need to *reinforce the story through additional simulations, or convey the simulations to the adversary through other channels or sources.* The deception controller must design the simulations and the monitoring of the adversary so that, if the adversary has observed the cover story, the adversary's actions or reactions will signify unambiguously that the cover story has been accepted. Similarly, the deception controller must aid intelligence to monitor the adversary and note if the adversary's actions, as required by the deception plan, take place on schedule. If feedback about the adversary indicates problems, the deception controllers may need to continue to reinforce the real and deceptive activities that support the overall deception cover story, or the deception planners may have to revisit the first phase of the deception chain and plan another deception operation.

3.3.9   Recursive Deception Chain

Much like the cyber kill chain, the deception chain is naturally recursive and disjoint. Deception operations require continual reexamination of the objectives, target, stories, and means throughout the planning, preparation, and execution phases. Deception planners must be prepared to respond to the dynamics of the adversary as well as friendly situations. For example, if the D&D planning team receives additional information about the adversary's TTPs during the preparation phase, the team may revisit the prior two phases to determine whether the cover story will still hold and/or whether the planned D&D TTPs will be sufficient to achieve the deception goal.

   It is important to note that each phase within a single kill chain instance may require its own deception chain. This could be due, for example, to different or evolving organizational goals at different stages of the cyber kill chain. To use an example involving industrial espionage,[19] during the reconnaissance phase the defending organization may seek to convince several nation-state actors that it has no connection to defense industrial base (DIB) activities surrounding a particular military program, and thus direct the attackers to targets outside the organization. During the delivery phase, however, the defender discovers that several staff members supporting the program have been targeted by the same spear phishing email and malware. Through analysis the defender determines that the attackers have become aware of its involvement in the program due to an exploit of another DIB member. In response, the defender may set a new goal of ensuring that the attackers believe they have access to the defender's program-related activities (e.g., plans, intellectual property, designs, budgets, etc.) so that the attackers take actions (or inactions) that benefit the defender. These could include slowing down the adversary's tactical or strategic responses to program activities given the overwhelming complexity of exfiltrated program materials that require highly skilled engineering and scientific review, or cause the adversary to invest a greater expenditure of

---

[19] This fictional scenario is described in detail in Chap. 4.

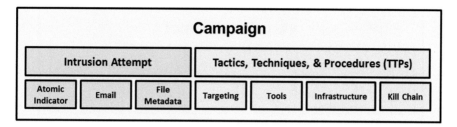

Fig. 3.6 Intrusion Campaign (The MITRE Corporation (2012b). Threat-Based Defense: A New Cyber Defense Playbook. http://www.mitre.org/work/cybersecurity/pdf/cyber_defense_play-book.pdf)

resources to acquire unnecessary intellectual property in order to compete with the defender's falsely revealed technological advances.

In the event that the deception operation is successful, (i.e., the deception goal(s) was achieved) there will be a need to either terminate the operation or return to the first phase of the deception chain to continue the deception with another purpose. For example, if the goal of collecting adversary intel on TTTPs has been met, then deception planners must determine a means for removing adversary access to the deception environment in which they had been operating. This means could be as simple as making it appear as if a system had been patched, thereby eliminated the exploited vulnerability. Similarly, if sufficient adversary intelligence on TTPs has been collected, but the adversary is demonstrating a specific exfiltration interest, deception planners may need to develop a new deception operation associated with providing the adversary false, but actionable, material targeted to the specific interest demonstrated. The inherently recursive nature of the deception chain supports the various forms a deception operation can take as it reaches the end of its lifecycle.

3.4 Intrusion Campaigns

One of the key elements of a threat-based approach to cyber defense is an understanding of the threat building blocks: intrusion attempts, TTPs, and intrusion campaigns (MITRE, 2012a, b). In its broadest sense, an intrusion campaign is a framework that combines all the related information about a particular intrusion into a set of activities (see Fig. 3.6).[20] It consists of a series of intrusion attempts combined with the attacker's TTPs. Within that construct, an intrusion attempt consists of a series of attack steps with associated discrete atomic indicators, such as email, and file metadata used by an attacker attempting to compromise an endpoint (see Fig. 3.7).

---

[20] The MITRE Corporation (2012b). Threat-Based Defense: A New Cyber Defense Playbook. http://www.mitre.org/work/cybersecurity/pdf/cyber_defense_playbook.pdf

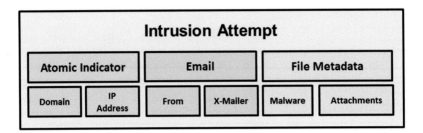

Fig. 3.7 Intrusion attempt. *Source*: Gilman (2013)

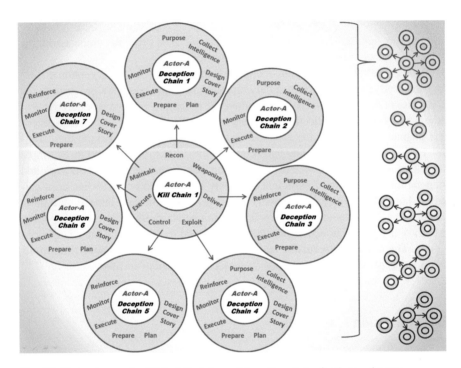

Fig. 3.8 Notional campaign TTPs: kill chains and deception chains for three red actors

TTPs consist of the targeting, tools, techniques, infrastructure, and kill chain activities used by the adversary to conduct a series of related intrusion attempts. These kill chain activities also include all of the defender's associated deception chain activities. Figure 3.8, using the notional industrial espionage campaign as an example, shows the kill chains and deception chains for three adversary actors based on their TTPs: Actor-A (orange), Actor-B (green), and Actor-C (brown). The close-up in the figure shows kill chain 1 and its corresponding seven deception chains for Actor-A.

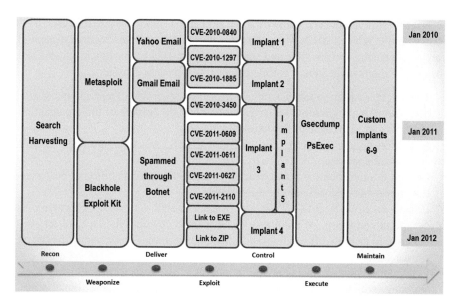

Fig. 3.9 Notional campaign over 2 years

Analysis of successful compromises is necessary for future network defense, but a synthesis of unsuccessful intrusions is necessary to identify intrusion campaigns. Longitudinal analysis of multiple intrusion attempts and TTPs, as shown in Figure 3.9, leads to the identification of commonalities and overlapping indicators, allowing defenders to define and recognize campaigns. Campaign analysis can then determine adversary patterns and behaviors, TTPs, and methods of operation in order to evaluate adversary capabilities, doctrine, objectives, and limitations. Building on this knowledge, campaign analysts can attempt to understand adversary intent and potentially determine the adversary's interest(s), such as technologies, individuals, information, external business relationships, and the like.

Organizations can use the campaign analysis results to plan and execute defensive security measures, which could include deception, to adaptively ensure resilience. An intrusion campaign could include several deception chains, each of which would address the defender's operational or tactical goals based on its assessment of the attacker's operational and tactical goals from the attacker's corresponding kill chain activities. Defenders can also use intrusion campaigns to assess the attacker's strategic goals, and use these findings to shape the strategic goal of a deception campaign.

An intrusion campaign could involve a single organization or coordination across multiple organizations if, for example, the indicators suggest a joint strategic goal in the underlying intrusions. If multiple organizations are involved, the deception campaign must present all intruders with a consistent set of actions aligned with the strategic goal of the intrusion campaign.

History (see Barbier 2007; Crowdy 2008; Holt 2007; Huber 1988; Macintyre, 2012; Rankin 2009; Whaley 2010a)[21] suggests that a few basic patterns recur in deception campaign planning, preparation, and execution. Cyber-D&D campaign managers, like their counterparts in the kinetic world, may therefore have to consider:

- The single most important lesson of history for deception campaign and operation planning, preparation, and execution is that the leaders of the organization must play an active role in deception campaigns.
- Deception organizations are not "one size fits all," but units are tailored to fit each specific system.
- Deception sophistication is independent of technological capability, while deception may overcome technological inferiority.
- Effectiveness of deception TTPs and operations will vary over the course of a deception campaign, so readiness and flexibility to reinforce and bolster successes, and to blow-off or cool-out failures are essential in managing deception campaigns.
- Deception campaign planners and managers must work within a bureaucratic structure, which requires that they know and understand organizational allies, friends, and colleagues as well as they do their opponents.
- Deception, operations, and operations security planning, preparation, and execution must be coordinated smoothly over the course of the deception campaign. The closer and smoother this coordination, the more successful the deception campaign.
- Guilefulness capabilities (i.e., skill at deception) between any two opponents are apt to be asymmetric at a given time.
- Differences in guilefulness between opponents can be crucial for determining the outcome of the conflict. When all other factors are equal, the more deceptive and guileful side will always win.
- Guilefulness and deceptiveness (i.e., the ability to deceive) can be learned, but are difficult to maintain without organization commitment to support deception campaigns.
- Deception campaign planners and managers must not only know their organization's goal for each deception operation in the campaign, but they must also sell their operational and campaign plans to their organization's leadership and staff.

---

[21] Appendix D summarizes historical analyses and intelligence estimates of the components of strategic deception capabilities.

Chapter 4
Cyber-D&D Case Studies

The goal of deploying deception to detect hackers is to change the underlying economics of hacking, making it more difficult, time consuming and cost prohibitive for infiltrators to attack a web application. … By putting a deceptive layer of code all over the web application, invisible to normal users, one creates a variable attack surface that makes the attacker detect themselves through their behavior. Once a hacker touches one of the deceptive "tar traps," they identify themselves and are immediately prevented from attacking the site.

Edward Roberts (2012) "Deception and the art of cyber security," *scmagazine.com*, February 28, 2012. www.scmagazine.com/deception-and-the-art-of-cyber-security/article/229685/

[Edward Roberts, *director of marketing at* Mykonos Software]

To highlight the benefits and challenges associated with cyber-D&D and explore aspects of operational implementation, we present two case studies: one based on accounts of the Stuxnet intrusion that damaged Iran's uranium enrichment facilities and the other a notional depiction of an espionage-motivated intrusion. The Stuxnet cyber-sabotage case showcases extensive use of offensive cyber-D&D at the technique, tactical, operational, and strategic levels. The fictional case study illustrates how elements of cyber-D&D can be used defensively against APT attempts at cyber espionage.

4.1 The Stuxnet Campaign

The Stuxnet attack on Iran's uranium enrichment facilities presents a unique example of offensive cyber operations in the real world.[1] It represented the first documented successful cyber campaign designed to cause physical destruction through

---

[1] Several sources were essential to investigating the D&D aspects of Stuxnet: Nicolas Falliere, Liam O Murchu, and Eric Chien (2011) W32. Stuxnet Dossier, ver. 1.4, February 2011. http://www.symantec.com/content/en/us/enterprise/media/security_response/whitepapers/w32_stuxnet_dossier.pdf Kim Zetter (2011) "How Digital Detectives Deciphered Stuxnet, the Most Menacing Malware in History," *Wired*, July 11, 2011. http://www.wired.com/threatlevel/2011/07/how-digital-detectives-deciphered-stuxnet/ David E. Sanger (2012b) *Confront and Conceal: Obama's secret wars and surprising use of American power.* Crown: New York; and Sanger's reports on Stuxnet in the *New York Times*. Ralph Langner (2013) *To Kill a Centrifuge A Technical Analysis of What Stuxnet's Creators Tried to Achieve.* Hamburg: The Langner Group, November 2013. http://www.langner.com/en/wp-content/uploads/2013/11/To-kill-a-centrifuge.pdf and TED

© Springer International Publishing Switzerland 2015
K.E. Heckman et al., *Cyber Denial, Deception and Counter Deception*,
Advances in Information Security 64, DOI 10.1007/978-3-319-25133-2_4

cyber attack. The attack had tactical, operational, and strategic objectives, all of which depended, in part, on successful use of cyber-D&D.[2] Retrospective analysis discovered documentation and details of Stuxnet's technical and tactical D&D components, their operational employment, and the extensive operational capabilities needed to research, engineer, plan, deliver, and exploit the Stuxnet weapon and its D&D capabilities. Analysts also derived descriptions of Stuxnet's operational employment over time, including operations that exploited both Stuxnet's D&D capabilities to remain covert and Stuxnet's ability to release itself into the wild with minimal physical effects but maximal effects on the global cyber security environment.

The Stuxnet campaign, possibly launched as early as June 2008 and certainly by June–July 2009, was a malicious targeted cyber attack against the centrifuge facilities of the Iranian government's uranium enrichment program at Natanz, 150 miles south of Tehran, which had begun operations in February 2007.[3] Natanz has two underground multi-story production halls with floor space for 50,000 centrifuges; by mid-2009 Iran had about 8000 centrifuges in one hall enriching uranium to nuclear reactor fuel levels. Natanz operations were under observation and inspection by the International Atomic Energy Agency (IAEA).

The attack against Natanz combined several cyber weapons: Stuxnet and precursor attacks by the Duqu worms (and probably the related Flame[4] and possibly

(2011) *Ralph Langner: Cracking Stuxnet, a 21st-century cyber weapon.* Mar 2011. http://www.ted.com/talks/ralph_langner_cracking_stuxnet_a_21st_century_cyberweapon.html Jon R. Lindsay (2013a) *Stuxnet and the Limits of Cyber Warfare.* University of California: Institute on Global Conflict and Cooperation, January 2013. http://www.scribd.com/doc/159991102/Stuxnet-and-the-Limits-of-Cyber-Warfare (a version published in *Security Studies*, V. 22-3, 2013. https://78462f86-a-6168c89f-s-sites.googlegroups.com/a/jonrlindsay.com/www/research/papers/StuxnetJRLSS.pdf)

[2] In this section we make no connection to the terminology or framework presented earlier for two reasons. First, we lack the reference materials to establish these connections without introducing much speculation. Second, forcing these connections would detract from our purpose: describing how the Stuxnet attack used deception.

[3] While Stuxnet has received (and continues to receive) extensive reporting, we could find no analyses focused on the D&D aspects. A November 2007 U.S. National Intelligence Estimate concluded Tehran had decided not to restart a nuclear weapons program. Office of the Director of National Intelligence (2007) "Iran: Nuclear Intentions and Capabilities," November 2007, http://www.dni.gov/press_releases/20071203_release.pdf.

[4] On Stuxnet, see Falliere, O Murchu, and Chien (2011) W32. Stuxnet Dossier, ver. 1.4, February 2011. On Duqu, see http://www.symantec.com/connect/w32_duqu_precursor_next_stuxnet Symantec's 2012 description of the Flamer weapon linked it to Stuxnet: "Highly sophisticated and discreet, the Flamer threat contains code that is on par with Stuxnet and Duqu in complexity. It appears to be the work of a well-funded group targeting Eastern Europe and the Middle East. The primary functionality of Flamer is to obtain information and data. The threat is not widespread. The overall functionality includes the ability to steal documents, take screenshots of users' desktops, spread through removable drives, and disable security products. When combined with the complexity of the code, the identified targets, and the possible link to recent threats … Flamer becomes a very noteworthy threat." http://www.symantec.com/outbreak/?id=flamer

Gauss[5] virus weapons). Stuxnet, Duqu, Flame, and Gauss were all probably elements of a covert operation named "Olympic Games" that damaged over 1000 centrifuges at Natanz.[6] The campaign included sophisticated intelligence and D&D tactics and techniques as well as the Stuxnet cyber weapon that specifically targeted the physical destruction of centrifuges performing uranium enrichment at Natanz. It sought to achieve strategic, operational, and tactical objectives, not only slowing the Iranian nuclear enrichment program but also affecting the strategic environment surrounding Iran's potential to acquire a nuclear weapon capability.[7] By 2010 over 100,000 copies of Stuxnet had spread "in the wild" (although Symantec determined that more than half the infected systems were Iranian). At that point, cyber forensic experts alerted the world to the new unique cyber weapon, and began to analyze it.

The *New York Times* account of Stuxnet[8] exposes a targeted intrusion lasting several years, continually disguised using D&D to avoid detection or eventual attribution (see Fig. 4.1).

The Stuxnet case shows the benefits of a complex and sophisticated D&D campaign planned, organized, and coordinated with other cyber resources, and reveals how cyber-D&D TTPs reinforce and augment other cyber techniques. The case also reflects some of the consequences and issues of using cyber-D&D TTPs.

---

[5] Symantec recently reported a "… complex espionage malware named Gauss … preliminary reports suggest the highest concentrations of W32.Gauss appear in the Middle East. … Gauss is similar in design and function to W32.Flamer… Stealing credentials for banking, email, IM, and social networking accounts, Communicating with a command-and-control server, Propagating through USB drives to steal from other computers, … may also intercept communication with financial institutions—not a typical target for cyber espionage malware of this complexity." Symantec, "Complex Cyber Espionage Malware Discovered: Meet W32.Gauss," Updated: 13 Aug 2012. http://www.symantec.com/connect/node/2416861

[6] "Normally Iran replaced up to 10 % of its centrifuges a year, due to material defects and other issues. With about 8700 centrifuges installed at Natanz at the time [summer 2009], it would have been normal to decommission about 800 over the course of the year. But when the IAEA later reviewed footage from surveillance cameras installed outside the cascade rooms to monitor Iran's enrichment program, they were stunned … workers had been replacing the units at an incredible rate…between 1000 and 2000 centrifuges were swapped out over a few months." Zetter (2011) "How Digital Detectives Deciphered Stuxnet, the Most Menacing Malware in History," *Wired*. See also Sanger (2012b) *Confront and Conceal: Obama's secret wars and surprising use of American power*; and Lindsay (2013) "Stuxnet and Limits of Cyber Warfare," *Security Studies*, v. 22-3, pp. 365–404.

[7] The Symantec and Langner analyses show conclusively that Stuxnet targeted the Natanz facility, and only the Natanz facility, specifically the two types of programmable logic controllers (PLC) units controlling the cascades and arrays of Natanz centrifuges. Lindsay (p. 383) wrote "The details in Stuxnet's code match hand-in-glove with the details known about Natanz from IAEA inspections;" "Stuxnet and Limits of Cyber Warfare," *Security Studies*.

[8] Source: Guilbert Gates for *The New York Times* http://www.nytimes.com/interactive/2012/06/01/world/middleeast/how-a-secret-cyberwar-program-worked.html

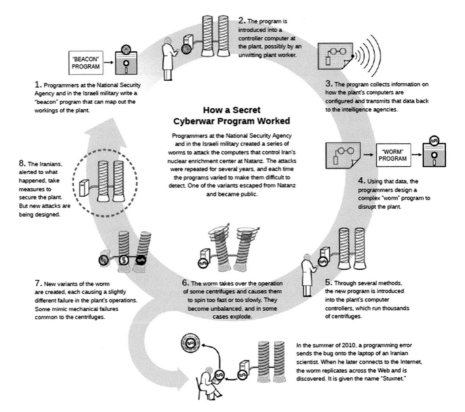

Fig. 4.1 How a secret Cyberwar program worked. *Sources*: Stuxnet Virus Opens New Era of Cyber War, Posted by NorAm Intel Group on August 9, 2011, http://noramintel.com/stuxnet-virus-opens-new-era-of-cyber-war/ and Guilbert Gates for The New York Times http://www.nytimes.com/interactive/2012/06/01/world/middleeast/how-a-secret-cyberwar-program-worked.html

4.1.1 Tactical Cyber-D&D

The tactical objective of the Stuxnet attack was to target and infect the computers of the Iranian centrifuge operators with specific logic control software, infect removable drives (thereby leading the operators to carry the Stuxnet worm across their air-gap defenses), and infect isolated networks of computers connected to the centrifuge process logic controllers (PLCs).[9] Stuxnet captured the PLCs and either changed

---

[9] Sanger (2012b) wrote: "It had already occurred to the Iranians that the computer systems running the centrifuges at Natanz were huge targets. But they solved that problem in the same naïve way that many American corporations, power stations, or even the U.S. military once relied on in a more innocent age: they made sure to not connect them to the Internet. Instead, they were surrounded by what engineers call an "air gap," meaning that the only way to get at the computers was to get inside the plant and work on them directly … the only way … the malicious software itself, would leap the air gap would be with the help of scientists, engineers, and others who had access to Natanz … the engineers at Natanz work on program updates on their laptops, and then connect them directly to the controllers." David E. Sanger (2012b) *Confront and Conceal: Obama's secret wars and surprising use of American power.*

the operating pressure controls inside the centrifuges or made the centrifuges (which spin at the speed of sound) speed up and slow down, causing them to fly off their bearings.[10] The sabotaged centrifuges were physically weakened, and many crashed, destroying themselves and adjacent centrifuges and equipment in the Natanz uranium enrichment arrays and cascades ("centrifuge forests") and possibly at other covert Iranian facilities. The Stuxnet weapon carefully concealed the pattern of the physical destruction, and issued misleading control signals indicating operations were normal so that Iranian operators would misattribute the damage to the complex cascade controls and unreliable centrifuge designs.[11]

The Stuxnet worm collects data from the centrifuge network, rides back to web-connected computers on removable media, and sends data back to the attackers. The PLC-infecting worm uses a variety of cyber-D&D techniques: it changes the pattern and locus of crashes it causes, hides its presence from defensive software, and eventually erases itself.

Symantec's "Stuxnet Attack Scenario"[12] showed how D&D techniques designed into Stuxnet concealed how the software propagated and replicated, bypassed behavior-blocking and host intrusion-protection software, avoided security products that Stuxnet identified as non-bypassable, hid Stuxnet files copied to removable drives, sought and reached the targeted Siemens Step 7 PLC software and hid the malicious Step 7 PLC code changes, randomly shifted which peripheral devices connected to the PLCs were sabotaged, blocked peripheral alert outputs that could warn operators of the sabotage, spoofed monitoring systems to indicate that the sabotaged frequency converters were operating normally,[13] blocked controller codes that prevented operators from gracefully shutting down the sabotaged systems, maintained connection to the attacker's C2 server, updated the malware via covert peer-to-peer connections, effected damage surreptitiously, uninstalled itself, avoided links back to the attackers, and may have left false flags in the code, possibly deceptively misleading indicators, pointing to other than the real attackers.

---

[10] "The primary payload's 2-month loop appears to be designed to introduce chronic fatigue in the cascades rather than to simply break them in one violent shock. The secondary payload periodically opens and closes valves (in contrast to the primary sequence that speeds and slows rotors), apparently also to achieve chronic fatigue rather than catastrophic failure." Lindsay (2013b) "Stuxnet and Limits of Cyber Warfare," *Security Studies*, p. 384. See also David Albright, Paul Brannan and Christina Walrond (2010) "Did Stuxnet Take Out 1000 Centrifuges At the Natanz Enrichment Plant?" Institute for Science and International Security, 22 December 2010. http://isis-online.org/uploads/isis-reports/documents/stuxnet_FEP_22Dec2010.pdf

[11] Langner (2013) *To Kill a Centrifuge A Technical Analysis of What Stuxnet's Creators Tried to Achieve;* Lindsay (2013b) "Stuxnet and Limits of Cyber Warfare," *Security Studies*.

[12] Falliere, O Murchu, and Chien (2011) *W32. Stuxnet Dossier*, p. 24.

[13] "For weeks before the attack happened, the bug recorded the electronic signals indicating that the centrifuges were operating normally. Then it played those back just as the computer worm was taking control, spinning the centrifuges to enormous speeds, or slamming on their brakes. The plant operators were clueless. There were no warning lights, no alarm bells, no dials gyrating wildly. But anyone down in the plant would have felt, and heard, that the centrifuges were suddenly going haywire. First came a rumble, then an explosion." Sanger (2012a) *Confront and Conceal: Obama's secret wars and surprising use of American power*.

Albright's ISIS report[14] assessed the tactical effects:

... by August 2009, there were two fewer cascades being fed with uranium hexafluoride and
two more under vacuum but not enriching. In November 2009, the number enriching had
decreased further to six cascades, with 12 cascades under vacuum. Some type of problem
likely accounted for the decrease in the number being fed with uranium. Sometime between
November 2009 and late January 2010, module A26 suffered a major problem with at least
11 cascades directly affected. The cascades being fed with uranium may have likewise suffered excessive breakage and operational difficulties. ... Stuxnet at a minimum appears
intended to disrupt operations and increase the number of centrifuges that fail while carefully
disguising the malware's presence from the operator. ... Stuxnet's effects may also be more
subtle, disrupting operations without destroying all the centrifuges in the plant. (pp. 2–5)

Albright, et al. provide data based on IAEA reports showing the kilograms of
Low Enriched Uranium (LEU, i.e., reactor fuel grade) per month. The number of
Natanz centrifuges being fed UF6 feed stock both leveled off in August 2008 and
stayed relatively flat through November 2010. On November 23, 2010, Ali Akbar
Salehi, head of Iran's Atomic Energy Organization, confirmed that malware had
attacked Iran's nuclear sites, "One year and several months ago, Westerners sent a
virus to our country's nuclear sites." Iranian President Mahmoud Ahmadinejad
admitted at a November 2010 press conference that a cyber attack had affected
Iran's centrifuges: "They succeeded in creating problems for a limited number of
our centrifuges with the software they had installed in electronic parts."[15]

4.1.2 Operational Cyber-D&D

The operational D&D objective of Stuxnet was to lead the Iranians to misattribute
the causes of the centrifuge sabotage to accidents, engineering problems, and poor
design, and to slow or shut down enrichment operations themselves as they investigated the centrifuge crashes. Because Stuxnet spread itself and also reported back
on the machines it had infected, cyber forensic experts estimated Stuxnet might
have been designed to covertly seek out and report back on clandestine Iranian
enrichment facilities.

Lindsay[16] described the operational D&D ploy against the Natanz operators:

... for Stuxnet to chronically degrade enrichment at Natanz, the worm had to stay hidden
while it sabotaged the ICS [industrial control system] over the course of several months.
Otherwise it would have been discovered and neutralized too early. Stuxnet remains hidden
via a "man in the middle" attack, inserting itself between [the Siemens Step 7] SIMATIC
software and the PLCs in order to send modified commands to the PLC as well as disguise
feedback back to the SIMATIC operator. Thus Stuxnet can mask alarms of breaking centrifuges. SIMATIC operators would thus have received deceptive feedback that centrifuges

[14] Albright, Brannan and Walrond (2010) "Did Stuxnet Take Out 1000 Centrifuges At the Natanz
Enrichment Plant?" Institute for Science and International Security (ISIS).
[15] "Iran says cyber foes caused centrifuge problems," Reuters, Nov 29, 2010.
[16] Lindsay (2013) "Stuxnet and Limits of Cyber Warfare," Security Studies, p. 384.

were spinning normally while they were actually speeding up and slowing down, and generating alarms. This devious ploy resembles a Hollywood movie heist in which a loop tape
distracts the guards while the burglars make off with the loot. (p. 384)

Sanger's (2012)[17] description of the Stuxnet attack underlines the key role played
by D&D at the operational level:

> When the centrifuges first began crashing in 2008 at the Natanz [Iran, uranium] enrichment
> center, […] the engineers inside the plant had no clue they were under attack. That was
> exactly what the designers of the world's most sophisticated cyberweapon had planned. The
> idea … was to make the first breakdowns seem like random accidents and small ones at that.
> A few centrifuges—the tall, silvery machines that spin at the speed of sound to purify ura-
> nium—raced out of control, seemingly for no reason. … blow apart, forcing the Iranians to
> shut down the whole plant and spend weeks figuring out what went wrong. 'The thinking
> was that the Iranians would blame bad parts, or bad engineering, or just incompetence,' …
> A mechanical failure seemed entirely plausible. …"if you do it this way, they won't see it'
> … 'The most elegant cyberattacks are a lot like the most elegant bank frauds,' … 'They work
> best when the victim doesn't even know he's been robbed.' (p. 174-191)

Planning to trigger such a response to the few apparently random accidents
required intelligence about the Iranian nuclear scientists and engineers operating the
centrifuge forests. The use of the Duqu and Flame cyber weapons probably helped
gather the necessary intelligence on how these scientists operated the centrifuge
facilities, how the centrifuge plants were constructed, and how the operators
responded to various problems. This intelligence would also produce information
about the Iranian defenses, enabling the cyber-D&D planners to manipulate the
Iranians into bypassing their own air-gap defenses and carrying the Stuxnet weapon
from the web-connected world to the isolated centrifuge controller networks.
Intelligence on the Iranian target made the cyber-D&D effects possible, which, in
turn, made the Stuxnet attack possible.[18]

To obtain information on the PLCs used for the Iranian centrifuges, and how to
attack them across the air gap, Stuxnet attackers apparently designed the stealthy,
self-destructing reconnaissance malware called Duqu. Symantec described Duqu[19] as:

> … a threat nearly identical to Stuxnet, but with a completely different purpose. Duqu is
> essentially the precursor to a future Stuxnet-like attack. Duqu was written by the same

---

[17] Sanger (2012) *Confront and Conceal: Obama's secret wars and surprising use of American power.*

[18] For example, it is apparent that the Stuxnet operational D&D was based in part on intelligence regarding Iranian centrifuge incompetence and problems with the centrifuge design itself. Sanger's (2012b) account described: "The British, the Indians, the Pakistanis, the South Africans, and many others had mastered the art of enriching uranium in far less time, oftentimes in only 3–5 years. The Iranians, in contrast, had been at this project for decades, and screwed up many of the most basic steps. Part of the problem was that they had bought an outdated, poor [centrifuge] design from Abdul Qadeer Khan, the rogue Pakistani metallurgist … The design … had developed a reputation …[of] periodic, random explosion. Bad ball bearings could cause a catastrophic failure. So could a tiny blip in the electrical system. But the Iranians were determined to keep them running until they could design and build a better one on their own." Sanger (2012b) *Confront and Conceal: Obama's secret wars and surprising use of American power.*

[19] http://www.symantec.com/connect/w32_duqu_precursor_next_stuxnet

authors as Stuxnet, or those that have access to the Stuxnet source code … Duqu's purpose
is to gather intelligence data and assets … in order to more easily conduct a future attack …
Duqu tracked how many days it was on each machine, only staying for 36 days. Then, it
would delete itself.

Insiders in the Olympic Games operation told Sanger[20]:

The intent was that the failures should make [Iran's leaders] feel [the Natanz operators]
were stupid, which is what happened…They overreacted, and that delayed them even more.
We soon discovered they fired people. (p. 275)

4.1.3 Strategic Cyber-D&D

Strategically, the Stuxnet operation had long-term, continuing goals, according to
Sanger's account.[21] The goals included testing the "Obama Doctrine," which posits
that adversaries can be effectively confronted through indirect methods (such as
cyber attacks cloaked by D&D).[22] The operation also sought to impel Iran to slow
or abandon its uranium enrichment operations by plaguing the operations with
problems, and ultimately threatening Iran with repeated covert and overt attacks.
Further objectives were to demonstrate capabilities to seek out and attack secret and
better protected enrichment sites (e.g., Qom) as well as Natanz, pressure Iran to
continue nuclear talks with Western nations and end economic sanctions by delay-
ing Iran's nuclear successes, and dissuade Israel from launching a bombing raid on
Iranian nuclear facilities.[23]

Sanger[24] summarized the strategic objectives of the stealthy Stuxnet attacks,
noting that:

---

[20] Sanger (2012b) *Confront and Conceal: Obama's secret wars and surprising use of American power.*

[21] David E. Sanger (2012a) "Obama Order Sped Up Wave of Cyberattacks Against Iran," New York Times, June 1, 2012. http://www.nytimes.com/2012/06/01/world/middleeast/obama-ordered-wave-of-cyberattacks-against-iran.html and Sanger (2012b)*Confront and Conceal: Obama's secret wars and surprising use of American power.*

[22] Sanger (2012b, p. 279) quoted a Stuxnet insider on the covert and overt strategic utility of the Stuxnet attack: "The thinking was that the longer it could stay unattributable, the better…But we had to be ready to work in an environment where the Iranians knew exactly who was doing this to them, to make the point that we could come back and do it again." Sanger, *Confront and Conceal: Obama's secret wars and surprising use of American power.*

[23] Sanger implies the Israelis may not have been entirely dissuaded. Despite the success of Stuxnet, in November 2010 two key Iranian nuclear scientists (Majid Shahriari and Fereydoon Abbasi) were targeted in simultaneous car bomb attacks in Tehran, and a year later a huge blast 30 miles west of Tehran wiped out Iran's main missile-development site, along with Iran's newest long-range missile, killing 17 people, including General Hassan Tehrani Moghaddam, leader of Iran's most advanced missile developments. David E. Sanger, *Confront and Conceal: Obama's secret wars and surprising use of American power.*

[24] Sanger, (2012b) *Confront and Conceal: Obama's secret wars and surprising use of American power.*

The intent of the operation was twofold. The first was to cripple, at least for a while, Iran's nuclear progress. The second, equally vital, was to convince the Israelis that there was a smarter, more elegant way to deal with the Iranian nuclear problem than launching an airstrike that could quickly escalate into another Middle East war. (p. 263)

By crashing over a thousand centrifuges, and disrupting enrichment operations, the Stuxnet attacks significantly delayed Iranian enrichment operations by an estimated 1–5 years, and thus disrupted Iran's potential development of nuclear weapons. Cyber-D&D significantly aided the attackers to achieve its strategic goals over several years in a continuous campaign. The Stuxnet attackers demonstrated the feasibility of using a complex, multi-phase cyber-D&D campaign of covert and clandestine[25] cyber attacks for sabotaging physical facilities and overcoming Iranian defenses and responses through deceptive cyber techniques and tactics. The D&D campaign succeeded in prompting misattributions of the causes of the centrifuge crashes by hiding attack code, causing the Iranians to take actions that further degraded enrichment operations, and avoiding attribution and thus direct Iranian retaliation.

Cyber-D&D plans and operations, and full integration of cyber-D&D capabilities with other cyber activities (e.g., reconnaissance, targeting, weapons design, and exploitation) were essential to the success of the Stuxnet attacks in gaining these strategic objectives. Symantec noted that "Stuxnet has highlighted that direct-attack attempts on critical infrastructure are possible and not just theory or movie plotlines. The real-world implications of Stuxnet are beyond any [cyber] threat we have seen in the past."[26]

The Stuxnet attack and Olympic Games operations also likely demonstrate that meaningful cyber attacks on physical infrastructures are probably only possible with the resources of a cyber-sophisticated nation-state. As Langner summed up in his TED talk: "the leading force behind [Stuxnet] is the cyber superpower. There is only one, and that's the United States—fortunately, fortunately. Because otherwise, our problems would even be bigger."[27]

---

[25] By "covert" we mean that the program was secret, i.e., not overt. By clandestine, we mean the program was "black," i.e., designed to be deniable, unacknowledged, concealed by OPSEC, protected by deception cover stories, and operated as if the Stuxnet attack never existed. Existence of code that was designed to erase all evidence that Stuxnet, or associated weapons, ever existed, indicated the clandestine nature of the Stuxnet attacks.

[26] Falliere, O Murchu, and Chien (2011) W32. Stuxnet Dossier, ver. 1.4, February 2011.

[27] TED (2011) *Ralph Langner: Cracking Stuxnet, a 21st-century cyber weapon.* Mar 2011. Lindsay (2013b) summarized the extensive resources necessary for reconnaissance, infiltration, designing, engineering, testing, deploying, operating, and fully exploiting a Stuxnet weapon in an Olympic Games-type operation: "what the unique ICS [Stuxnet] attack payload actually shows is that precision-targeted effects carry formidable requirements for specific intelligence and engineering expertise. There is still no general purpose round for cyberwar after Stuxnet. …Barriers to entry for targeted, destructive ICS attack will thus remain prohibitive for all but states with long-established and well-funded cyber warfare programs." Lindsay (2013b) "Stuxnet and Limits of Cyber Warfare," *Security Studies*, pp. 385-9.

4.1.4 Benefits of Stuxnet Cyber-D&D

Many benefits of cyber-D&D in the Stuxnet case are clear, although some of the D&D benefits essential to the Stuxnet attack (e.g., D&D to keep the attacks covert and clandestine) would also be beneficial, but perhaps not essential, for defensive cyber-D&D. The benefits included an overall cyber-D&D campaign plan that produced effective intelligence collection on Iranian capabilities and vulnerabilities. That plan, in turn, was weaponized to exploit Iranian systems. Intelligence provided detailed information on the specific PLCs to be targeted, identified defenses and vulnerabilities in the Iranian enrichment control infrastructures, and supported incorporation of D&D capabilities into Stuxnet to prevent detection by defensive systems in the Iranian infrastructure cyber defenses.

Intelligence and D&D capabilities supported each other. Intelligence provided essential details for deception capabilities (e.g., blinding and spoofing the control systems), while the D&D capabilities of the software enabled covert and clandestine collection on the target during the campaign.

The Stuxnet D&D campaign built upon and exploited the Iranians' knowledge of earlier attempts to sabotage nuclear enrichment equipment, and the ability of the malware to hide itself from detection and defenses. This accentuated the deception effects of the malware attacks—making the centrifuges and their controllers seem responsible for the "accidents"—as the Iranians disassembled large numbers of working centrifuges to detect the causes of the problems.

Detailed intelligence collection on how the centrifuge PLCs were programmed and controlled enabled the Stuxnet software designers to create cyber-D&D capabilities that allowed the malware to "jump" and "re-jump" undetected through the air-gap defenses, seeking the enrichment targets at Natanz, or other possible clandestine Iranian locations, but essentially harmless to other systems. The software concealed its capability to hone in on and hide in removable media.

Detailed intelligence collection on engineering designs, control systems, and operational procedures enabled complex D&D capabilities to be incorporated into the Stuxnet software to change times, targets, and modes of attack against the centrifuges. Engineering denial capabilities (e.g., self-erasing capabilities) into the Stuxnet software supported the strategic requirement for covert and clandestine operations.

Stuxnet D&D capabilities prevented identification and attribution of the malware even after it was compromised and analyzed. Furthermore, variations built into the Stuxnet malware operations and self-defense from detection enabled the Stuxnet campaign to continue even through a deception compromise, when an early version of the malware re-jumped the air-gap and escaped over the web into the world.

4.1.5 Challenges of Stuxnet Cyber-D&D

Stuxnet cyber-D&D also had several obvious, challenging consequences. Some of these cyber-D&D consequences and risks have special significance because Stuxnet was an offensive operation, but these challenges may still have implications for cyber-D&D in defensive operations.[28] Most notably, despite careful design of the Stuxnet malware to target only the software associated with specific PLCs, Stuxnet escaped via the web and roamed globally, seeking similar targets. Whether this was simply a mistake, or was intended as a subtle form of cyber force projection, is still debated. Although Stuxnet and associated malware included several self-destruct capabilities, once it had escaped from the Iranian organizations to which it was targeted, the software lacked the ability to terminate itself in some situations (badly patched systems). As a result, it was detected and captured, and was successfully analyzed and reverse engineered (some pieces remain encoded and mysterious) by cyber defense organizations such as Symantec and Langner.

While so far no nation or organization has attempted to exploit the Stuxnet escape by creating counter-propaganda—for example, by attributing disasters in hospital systems to the malware—the Stuxnet designers appear not to have built a concealed but foolproof or controllable self-destruct capability into the malware. This apparent overlooking of some escape vectors, and the otherwise benign character of Stuxnet (lethal only to Iranian centrifuge installations), have led some to speculate that global release of Stuxnet, intended or not, is analogous to sending the Great White Fleet to circle the globe: it projected cyber power, and indirectly provided deterrence. Similarly, because the cyber-D&D campaign planning for the Stuxnet attacks apparently did not anticipate its escape, the planners developed no deception cover stories and backup plans to discredit the revelation of the malware's unique attack and D&D capabilities, or to deal with counter-propaganda attempts to attribute accidents to the malware. Given the risks of detection by the Iranians, or accidental escape, Stuxnet lacked backup D&D capabilities, such as false flag clues and explicitly engineered but notional vulnerabilities and weaknesses that could be triggered by discovery to mislead Iranian defenders.

Strategically, Stuxnet risks changing the rules and opening the playing field for cyber attackers to use complex sophisticated malware against physical infrastructures. It also reduces the legal and diplomatic justifications for "cyber arms control," although the carefully engineered precision of Stuxnet's attack, proliferation, and D&D capabilities all indicate to some observers (Edinger, 2013; Foltz, 2012) that 'the lawyers were involved.'

---

[28] The general arguments in this section are explored in greater length in Lindsay (2013b) "Stuxnet and Limits of Cyber Warfare," *Security Studies*; Thomas Rid (2013) "Cyberwar and Peace: Hacking Can Reduce Real-World Violence," *Foreign Affairs*, November/December 2013. http://www.foreignaffairs.com/articles/140160/thomas-rid/cyberwar-and-peace; and Harald Edinger (2013) *Stuxnet And the Treatment of Cyber Attacks under International Law.* JHU SAIS Bologna Center, January 2013. See also Andrew C. Foltz (2012) "Stuxnet, Schmitt Analysis, and the Cyber "Use-of-Force" Debate," *JFQ*, v. 67-4, 4th quarter 2012. http://www.ndu.edu/press/lib/pdf/jfq-67/JFQ-67_40-48_Foltz.pdf

4.2   APT Espionage

To illustrate an attack with radically different goals from the Stuxnet campaign, we present a hypothetical APT espionage scenario.[29] Constructing a detailed scenario like this for a specific intrusion campaign might help defenders think through their planned strategic deception campaign, their technical defense for each phase of the attacker's kill chain, and their approach for each phase of the deception chain. This exercise might also help defenders to consider both the opportunities as well as what could go wrong, and to begin thinking through some potential outs, blow-offs, cool-downs, and other mitigations for blow-back and unintended consequences.[30]

This hypothetical scenario involves a targeted attack by an APT actor[31] to obtain national intelligence, specifically the design of a (fictitious) next-generation weapon system called the "X-20." In the interest of simplicity, the storyline involves only three parties: (1) the Department of Defense (DoD) program management office (PMO); (2) the Federally Funded Research and Development Center (FFRDC) supporting the X-20 PMO, a Defense Industrial Base (DIB) member; and (3) the APT actor. Adopting the terminology used in wargames, the PMO and FFRDC constitute the Blue forces, while the APT is the Red force. The PMO staff includes the program manager (PM), who is directly responsible for overall coordination and management of PMO OPSEC, security, and cyber-D&D. The PM is the Cyber-D&D Controlling Officer (CDDCO).

In the deception scenario, the PMO has established an X-20 defensive cyber-D&D control team, staffed by PMO and FFRDC personnel. This team manages the development of the fictitious X-20 cover story. Three contractor teams (A, B, C) are designing competitive prototypes: X-20-ALPHA, X-20-BRAVO, and X-20-CHARLIE, respectively. Like any major government acquisition, the development

---

[29] This is a fictional use case scenario. Any similarity to real events or people is completely coincidental.

[30] See Sect. 6.1 for a more detailed exploration of this topic.

[31] In this case we mean state actors actively engaging in cyber-war techniques, such as China. The U.S. Defense Department (Department of Defense, 2012) stated "Authoritative writings and China's persistent cyber intrusions indicates the likelihood that Beijing is using cyber network operations (CNOs) as a tool to collect strategic intelligence." A recent strategic assessment (Spade 2011) concluded "The People's Republic of China is one of the world's leading cyber powers and is working steadily with the intent to develop the capacity to deter or defeat the United States in and through cyberspace... [with] known and demonstrated capabilities for offensive, defensive and exploitive computer network operations." See also, Krekel, Adams, and Bakos (2009, 2012). In 2013 Mandiant published "APT1: Exposing One of China's Cyber Espionage Units" (http://intel-report.mandiant.com/Mandiant_APT1_Report.pdf) describing specific tactics, techniques, and procedures (TTPs) of a leading APT, which Mandiant identified as the 2nd Bureau of the People's Liberation Army (PLA) General Staff Department's (GSD) 3rd Department, which is most commonly known by its Military Unit Cover Designator (MUCD) as Unit 61398. In this fictional case, we adapted variations of the APT1 TTPs that Mandiant described. See also, Mark A. Stokes, Jenny Lin and L.C. Russell Hsiao (2011) *The Chinese People's Liberation Army Signals Intelligence and Cyber Reconnaissance Infrastructure*. Project 2049, November 11, 2011. http://project2049.net/documents/pla_third_department_sigint_cyber_stokes_lin_hsiao.pdf

occurs as a multi-year project, going through various phases from requirements definition to design, prototyping, and testing. The X-20 PMO is currently evaluating the three competing design prototypes. The APT wants to obtain these designs and the test results from the prototype evaluations in order to identify the best design and use it to advance Red's own weapons programs. The APT uses the kill chain phases[32] to gather the desired intelligence information, and employs several cyber attack tactics and techniques at each phase.

The PMO and FFRDC are keenly aware of the interest among various adversary states in the X-20 information and the rumors that the X-20 prototype developments and tests have generated. To protect the X-20 program from cyber threats, the PMO has directed the cyber-D&D team to develop a deception campaign. This campaign will include several cyber-D&D operations, based on the deception chain presented in Chap. 3, at various phases of the cyber kill chain. At the strategic level of this deception campaign, Blue's goal is to protect X-20 EEFI by luring Red actors into controlled cyber environments, isolating them, thwarting their attacks by making them believe their attacks are succeeding, and analyzing their attack tactics and techniques. This will help Blue to craft better cyber defenses without compromising the X-20 program's EEFI.

4.2.1   Assumptions

In this scenario, the PMO has approved the use of defensive cyber-D&D to enhance OPSEC and security for the X-20 program. The FFRDC and the PMO have public extranet and private intranet connectivity, as well as secure networking for classified communication and information processing. The APT has the ability to infiltrate both the FFRDC and PMO public and private networks and can penetrate the private networks, steal credentials, and masquerade as legitimate users. The APT has not compromised the PMO and FFRDC secure networks, but use of these networks is tightly controlled by operational and intelligence security restrictions.

The scenario also assumes that the APT may execute multiple kill chain phases simultaneously, or may iterate phases multiple times. Similarly, the Blue deception chain phases are not necessarily linear. Within a given APT kill chain phase, Blue may plan, prepare, and execute multiple deception chain phases simultaneously, iterate a subset of deception chain phases multiple times, or cycle past some deception chain phases.

---

[32] APT typical kill chain consists of initial reconnaissance, initial compromise, establish foothold, a recursive cycle comprisingDOUBLEHYPHENescalate privileges, internal reconnaissance, move laterally, maintain presence—and complete mission. Mandiant (2013) APT1: Exposing One of China's Cyber Espionage Units. http://intelreport.mandiant.com/Mandiant_APT1_Report.pdf

4.2.2   Reconnaissance Phase

4.2.2.1   Red Actions

In the initial reconnaissance (recon) phase Red wants to gather as much intelligence as possible on the X-20 program, the people associated with it, and the prototype designs and test results. These inputs will shape Red's selection of whom to target, their selection of intrusion tactics, their evaluation of their own tactics, and the believability of stolen data.

Red tactics include using popular Internet search and social networking sites such as LinkedIn, Google, and Facebook to harvest email addresses, home computer addresses, and personal and other organizational information about individuals and companies associated with the PMO, the FFRDC supporting the PMO, former employees of the FFRDC, contractors associated with the X-20 program, open source publications and public relations information produced by these people and organizations, and journalists covering the X-20 development. Red follows this human intelligence reconnaissance with more technical network reconnaissance that collects data on the PMO and FFRDC networks. Red sends spear phishing emails to specific individuals; the messages contain either a malicious attachment or a hyperlink to a malicious file. Red also creates webmail accounts using the names of real people familiar to the recipient, and sends emails that induce recipients to download a malicious ZIP file that installs a custom Red backdoor. These technical reconnaissance activities reveal information about protocols used by the PMO and the FFRDC, open ports, internal network topology, versions of operating systems and application software, etc. Red provides the output of such reconnaissance activities to its malware assembly and attack teams.

4.2.2.2   Blue Actions

Anticipating such reconnaissance activities, Blue observes Red's reconnaissance probes, and proactively conducts a cyber-D&D operation designed for the reconnaissance phase. Blue creates obvious real and fake persona targets likely to be known to Red and scans emails for indicators of spear phishing and other attempts to create initial compromises.

Purpose. Blue's primary goals are to subvert the Red actors by causing them to select incorrect targets, commit to ineffective intrusion tactics, confirm fictional "successes" of their campaign, or question their real successes. Achieving the reconnaissance stage goals is essential because many of the deceptive technologies require a substantial commitment of resources. Blue must induce Red to commit their efforts to deceptive targets and to use methods that Blue can detect and manipulate. Failure to guide Red's targeting and TTPs places Blue in a reactive posture where they must engage Red with fewer tools and more unknowns. For example, the target resource may have genuinely valuable information, Red's tools may be undetectable, or Blue may be unable to monitor Red's tools even if they know about them.

Blue's secondary goals include creating a better model of Red's reconnaissance tradecraft and developing methods for corrupting it. This tradecraft superiority would enable Blue to achieve its primary goals, which in turn would set up Blue's resource commitments later in the kill chain.

Collect Intelligence. Blue knows that Red follows the cyber kill chain phases to obtain access and information and escalate privileges, and that Red employs several cyber attack TTPs at each phase. Blue also knows that Red can infiltrate both the FFRDC and PMO public and private networks. Blue assumes that Red can steal credentials from the FFRDC and PMO private networks and masquerade as legitimate users. Based on cyber-intelligence analysis, Blue knows that Red has not compromised the PMO and FFRDC secure networks.

Blue anticipates setting up a honeynet, and expects that upon gaining access to it, Red will continue to return for more information on the progress of the X-20 program. Blue monitors the Red connections and communications from its backdoor footholds to the Red command and control servers. Blue also monitors Red's activities to identify the beachhead backdoors for simple reconnaissance and the standard backdoors for more extensive Red communications and control of Blue's systems. Given Red's continued access to misleading information, Blue expects to begin the process of influencing Red decision making.

Design Cover Story. The X-20 cover story covers all aspects of the (supposed) current status and evolution of the X-20 program. This story conceals the real breakthrough elements of the X-20 designs (i.e., the EEFI), and reveals X-20-ALPHA as the best design (one EEDI element) by associating the various X-20 prototype designs with misleading evaluation data. For example, the worst prototype designs are associated with notional good evaluations and tests, and vice versa.

The storyline calls for the X-20 program to evolve over time, bringing new elements and actors into the PMO and FFRDC, while some actors exit in a naturalistic fashion. For example, as the X-20 reaches the test phase, Blue will create a notional Test Manager role and corresponding user identity within the PMO. These personae are additional EEDI elements.

Plan. Blue D&D also develops system-level setups that support the cover story. For example, the CDDCO creates fake or modified user profiles and fictitious identities for various personnel involved in the program, placing these on public and social networking sites. The CDDCO also establishes associated fictitious email accounts on Gmail and Yahoo. These Blue D&D-controlled identities are mostly associated with the development of the notional "X-20-ALPHA, the best X-20 design."

Prepare. Using the D&D principle that a good D&D plan makes Red work hard to piece together the story, the CDDCO commissions extensive public relations stories by the FFRDC, X-20 contractors, the PMO, and DoD. The PMO's cyber-D&D team creates triumphal, but vague, stories of X-20-ALPHA successes expressly to "explain" any actual leaks or compromises of real EEFI detected by the PMO cyber security and OPSEC efforts. Additionally, the D&D team builds program setbacks, test failures, and the like into future leaks, associating these problems with the (truly) more successful X-20 designs. Contractor security personnel and executives are briefed into the PMO cyber-D&D operational plans, and specific offsetting public relations efforts are jointly developed to offset possible negative publicity that might harm public corporate interests.

Execute. Specific decoy network segments (honeynets) host fake PMO servers within the PMO and FFRDC networks. These servers store both false and innocuous real X-20 documents, requirements, design specifications, evaluation reports, program test schedules, and the like that collectively support the cover story. The honeynets alert Blue to Red attempts to escalate privileges, conduct internal reconnaissance, move laterally, and install mechanisms to maintain presence. Email chains by fake users, propagated by various shadow servers, reinforce and corroborate the cover story.

Blue specifically sets up targets (e.g., servers that supposedly host sensitive design documents on X-20-ALPHA) and lock these down to deceive Red into believing that Blue considers these servers secure, playing on known APT tendencies to view a locked-down server as having highly valuable contents. Blue rigorously shields the honeynet from real PMO and FFRDC users but also carefully simulates such traffic for Red to observe.

Monitor. Blue sets up appropriate trackers to observe how quickly and closely Red follows the new cover story elements and new personae. Links into the accounts of fake or modified user profiles and fictitious personnel identities engineered by the PMO D&D team allow Blue to monitor Red reconnaissance. Blue also attempts to leverage these accounts as the targets for social engineering activities that Red believes will lead to system breaches in the PMO and FFRDC networks. Blue plans to intercept, redirect (to honeynets), and monitor the tactics Red uses to maintain presence: for example, by installing new backdoors on multiple systems or by using captured and exfiltrated legitimate VPN credentials and log-ins to web portals.

In sum, Blue D&D creates a decoy version of the X-20-ALPHA team and activities to tempt Red. Blue wants to make it easy for Red to read what the CDDCO wants the attacker to read, and to force Red to expend considerable effort on understanding the "big picture" by assembling its reconnaissance collections into the cover story. Blue systematically "lures" and keeps Red on the honeynet, so that Red constantly returns for more information on X-20-ALPHA progress.

4.2.2.3 Benefits

First of all, D&D can systematically influence adversary decision making during this phase. Unlike a mid-stream reactive injection of D&D techniques, early incorporation allows for D&D planning and scripting at the program level to attract the interest of Red's decision makers. Early D&D gives Blue the opportunity for "active" deception by enticing Red decision makers to follow up on the information gathered about the X-20-ALPHA design.

Second, early D&D provides Blue with valuable information on Red's social engineering and technical skill sets, giving Blue significant lead time to protect infrastructure and prepare appropriate responses. In sum, this early response allows Blue to assess the maturity of Red's cyber attack skill set.

4.2.2.4 Challenges

While incorporating D&D right from the beginning of the kill chain is ideal, it also poses challenges for the participating organizations. The D&D actions at the program and technical levels must be coordinated from an organizational perspective. Such coordination can only occur with support from top management of both the PMO and the FFRDC, and (to a far lesser extent) of the PMO's contractors. At the program level, creating deceptive (i.e., fake) public user profiles, fictitious identities, and email accounts and maintaining related information and communications requires significant planning, coordination, and consultation with employees and corporate counsel. The organizations must seek consent from employees before setting up fake profiles and must keep the employees apprised. The PMO and FFRDC must take special care to ensure that the D&D activities do not damage employee and public corporation reputations.

Blue must coordinate the technical D&D to synchronize with the overall D&D plot. The PMO and FFRDC must isolate systems, data, and communications supporting D&D activities from the corresponding real elements of X-20 program to avoid cross-contamination.

4.2.3 Weaponization Phase

4.2.3.1 Red Actions

Based on the Blue characteristics, gaps, and vulnerabilities that Red observes during the reconnaissance phase, the Red malware designers and attackers create appropriate exploits to break in and establish a foothold on specific PMO and FFRDC systems relevant to the X-20 program. For example, Red reconnaissance activities yield information on the operating system and database system versions used, the internal topology of the FFRDC network, and the location of critical directory and file servers. Creating the appropriate weapon(s) involves multiple steps that take advantage of the different vulnerabilities. Red builds weapons using a combination of third-party tools as well as custom code based on the degree of sophistication and expertise required.

4.2.3.2   Blue Actions

Purpose. Blue does not act directly in the weaponization stage. Nevertheless, Blue's deception effects begin to have their impact at this stage. Blue wants Red to commit resources to the false targets and marked documents presented in the reconnaissance and execute stages. Furthermore, Blue wants to detect the results of Red's weaponization choices at some subsequent stage. Actions that enable detection could include delivering a technically sophisticated cyber weapon to a false user, bundling a technically sophisticated weapon with an intentionally leaked document, applying an exploit known to Blue's IDS, or selecting corruptible C2 protocols with known signatures. If Blue cannot detect Red's weaponization choices, the defender has lost control of the deception.

Collect Intelligence. At the program and cover story level, Blue expects Red to leverage existing technology available online and to use so-called "exploit markets," cultivating agents in both communities. Blue is aware of some of the technology and techniques that Red may use in the attack.

As part of the program-level deception before the reconnaissance phase, Blue leaked reports that similar exploits caused havoc on Blue's networks. This story was part of the EEDI; in reality, Blue allowed honeypot systems under its control to be compromised to conceal Blue's true network vulnerabilities. Red believes the leaks and develops exploits against the honeypot systems.

Prior to the reconnaissance phase Blue also interacted with elements of the exploit development community that provides exploit capabilities to Red, and shopped for defenses for the honeynet vulnerabilities. Blue's interest in certain defenses attracts Red's attention and influences Red's choices of weapons. Blue thus steers Red toward attack tools that Blue can detect and defend against. Blue's shopping reinforces the D&D cover story that previous exploits against Blue using these tools had succeeded. Blue's leaks and shopping hide the true nature of Blue vulnerabilities from Red.

Prepare. Blue sets up decoy target systems (e.g., servers, routers) "deep" in the PMO and FFRDC networks, with varying vulnerability exposures (i.e., attack surfaces).

Execute. The Blue D&D team feeds leads and leaks about X-20-ALPHA successes into the decoy systems in order to observe Red's attack efforts.

Monitor. Observations provide Blue with feedback on the success of the various D&D efforts during the reconnaissance phase. The efficiency and specificity with which Red exploits particular vulnerabilities give Blue more information about Red's intent and sophistication. For example, Blue can answer questions such as: How customized was the weaponization to exploit a particular vulnerability? How much effort was expended to create it? Did Red show the level of attack effort on the topics and systems intended by the D&D efforts?

4.2.3.3   Benefits

D&D at this phase allows Blue to influence the actual attack its systems will face. Using foresight, as well as intelligence on Red, gives Blue a greater opportunity to prepare defenses and to adapt the D&D apparatus to sustain the ruse that Red's weaponization has succeeded. As Red outsources exploit development, Blue's anticipation of APT activity in this market and deceptive shopping for defenses lead Red to buy exploits that Blue can easily detect and that work on Blue's honeynets but not on Blue's real networks.

Blue has substantial potential for long-term manipulation of Red's weaponization supply chain. To capitalize on that capability at this phase, Blue makes strategically deceptive purchases before the Red attack kill chain begins. In sum, D&D allows Blue to gather insights into Red's overall intentions, technical sophistication, resources, and risk tolerance. D&D also allows Blue to predict possible future moves by Red, deflect attacks, and enhance defenses in anticipation of specific attacks.

4.2.3.4   Challenges

The overhead involved in setting up a honeynet (i.e., decoy) infrastructure presents a challenge at this stage. It requires a two-pronged approach. First, at the program level, the D&D team must align the honeynet and decoys with the overall cover story. Second, these "targets" must evolve rapidly to keep pace with Red's moves and to continuously entice Red to remain active on the honeynet. Careful and systematic planning is needed to ensure that the attack surfaces of the various honeynet and honeytoken components yield to Red as required by Blue's D&D campaign.

At this stage Blue must answer questions such as: What vulnerabilities (i.e., attack entry points) must Blue set up for each decoy component? How will Blue manage the attack surface configurations and how will the information gathered from the attack surface exploitations be documented and shared to promote institutional improvements by the D&D and IT infrastructure teams? Depending on the size and number of the honeynets and honeytokens, the PMO and FFRDC may need D&D management tools to control the attack surface configurations and record their efficacies for subsequent outcome analysis and tool optimization.

Another challenge in this phase involves managing the apparent resemblance and fidelity of the honeynets and honeytokens to their real-world counterparts. Success depends on Blue's OPSEC and security awareness of how much Red already knows about Blue's networks. The more information that has been revealed to Red or compromised during the reconnaissance phase, the more realistic the Blue honeynets and honeytokens must be to fool Red. Conversely, if Red has little specific intelligence on Blue's networks, the honeynets and honeytokens need only be generally realistic. Overall, these decoys must have enough fidelity to make them enticing and believable to Red, but such realism must be simulated very carefully so as not to permit Red insight into Blue's real systems, operations, or EEFI.

Because Red may gain intelligence on the real Blue networks, the Blue D&D planning includes fallback operations to convince Red these windfalls actually pertain to the Blue decoys. By generating even more, but innocuous, information leaks on the real networks, Blue prompts Red to view these intelligence windfalls as coming too easily, and therefore very likely too good to be true. Blue checks on whether this ploy actually does steer Red away by pushing out more and more innocuous information until Red shows diminished interest in and collection of this worthless and possibly deceptive information. Blue can reinforce Red's suspicions of the "too good to be true" systems and information by operating key elements of the real networks in very unrealistic ways that Red can detect.

Blue's careful risk versus benefits analysis before and during setup of the honeynets and attack surfaces will pay large dividends if real leaks and compromises should occur, and the "too good to be true" ploy is needed to steer Red back to the honeynet. In short, as much as Blue must be prepared to make the deceptive honeynets seem real to Red, Blue must also be prepared to make the real networks, should they become exposed or vulnerable, seem false and deceptive.

4.2.4   Delivery Phase

4.2.4.1   Red Actions

At this stage Red has likely committed to a delivery mechanism because weaponization is such a specific undertaking. During the weaponization stage Red must foresee its alternatives in the delivery phase. A failed delivery phase becomes a reconnaissance phase for Red.

Red can employ various weapon delivery mechanisms, depending on connection modalities, access control setups, and characteristics of the user populations. For example, with regard to connection modalities, some systems are always connected to the public-facing Internet, while others may be connected in limited ways and for very specific purposes, such as remote repair diagnostics. Yet others may be completely air-gapped and isolated from the public network. For some systems, the incoming traffic filtering and admission control policies may be based on layer 3 and source IP addresses, while deep packet inspection may be the norm in other environments. As for user populations, some environments may have a large user community with public profiles, diverse levels of security awareness training, and variable susceptibility to social engineering and phishing attacks, while other environments may have very small populations and no public digital footprint.

The information that Red gathered during the reconnaissance phase on the Blue user populations and the target systems allows Red to determine appropriate delivery methods. Delivery may then occur through the open Internet, through flash drives, maintenance laptops, phishing emails, or other mechanisms.

4.2.4.2   Blue Actions

Purpose. The delivery phase gives Blue its initial opportunity to react to Red's weaponization phase. If Blue's deception effect is working, Red will increasingly attempt to deliver its attacks by detectable methods. The achievable goals depend on Red's choices:

- Red may be detectable because the targeted resource is fictional or because Blue has stocked it with marked documents. If Red delivered a high-sophistication cyber weapon, then Blue has an opportunity to assess exploit and implant sophisticated tools of its own and to develop new signatures and active monitoring methods. Subsequent application of the signatures will give Blue a fuller picture of Red's access.
- Red may be detected because the technology has known signatures. The resource targeting sheds light on Red's reconnaissance methods.
- Red's weapon may target one of Blue's prepared fictional resources. Blue should ensure that the attack secures Red "control" under Blue's active monitoring capability. This advances the later stages of Blue's deception plan.

Upon detecting the Red activity, Blue should choose the level of Red "success" that best suits its deception goals. For example, Blue may want delivery to appear successful—perhaps by sending an email reply or simulating a website visit from the target—but fail to exploit and establish control. If the attack targets a fictional resource, Blue may permit the exploit and control stages to proceed. Other delivery attempts are met with flat-out failure while Blue takes the time to analyze new information.

Collect Intelligence. Blue monitors the fake user profiles set up earlier and analyzes activity to determine if these users received more spear phishing emails. Cyber security (CyberSec) and OPSEC monitoring indicate that Red spear phishing indeed targets personnel associated with the X-20-ALPHA program, guided by information Red gathered during the reconnaissance phase.

Execute. Blue engages Red by actively responding to Red's collections. For example, for some Red emails requesting the user to open a document, the targeted Blue recipient (i.e., a fictional D&D persona) replies to Red, complaining that the document crashed and requesting Red to retransmit. Red becomes uncertain about the effectiveness of the weaponization. Blue uses such openings to spread the EEDI.

Reinforce. Blue allows Red to install weapons on Blue D&D-controlled network segments, followed by public PMO actions noting only a few of the actual installations. This increases Red's confidence that other installations were undetected. The PMO emphasizes that release of any data about the X-20-ALPHA's successes is highly damaging and that all personnel must redouble their security awareness. The CDDCO then lets Red continue to exploit the apparently undetected Red installations. Blue thus reinforces successful deceptions by increasing Red's confidence in the delivered weapons, and uses Red's actions and reactions to gauge Red's interest in particular topics, organizations, and people.

Purpose. As Red is lured toward particular aspects of the EEDI, Blue uses Red's interest to shape future deception story elaborations and effects.

Prepare. Using feedback from Red actions, Blue manipulates Red's beliefs about the success or failure of specific delivery methods, and sets up controlled channels to feed Red the EEDI though weapons that Red comes to believe are working undetected.

To guard against Red weapons Blue has *not* detected, Blue could generate deception traffic describing Blue's ploy of leaving certain compromised accounts open and available to adversaries so misleading information can be leaked. This ploy risks pushing Red off the Blue-controlled deception channels, but also reduces Red's confidence in information it gained from Red weapons Blue may not have detected.

4.2.4.3 Benefits

Detecting the diverse delivery methods Red uses yields enormous benefits for Blue. First, Blue obtains vital information on Red's technical sophistication and the range of Red's attack vectors. This information can be fed back to Blue's D&D teams to help them fine-tune attack surfaces on the honeynets and honeytokens, as well as proactively help Blue close vulnerabilities on its real infrastructure.

4.2.4.4 Challenges

Blue's ability to detect the delivery methods employed by Red presents the main challenge in this phase. Red's social engineering attacks open up many delivery vectors, and technology seldom detects such attacks. For example, basic reconnaissance on an employee though a social networking site may reveal hobbies and personal email addresses on Gmail or Yahoo. As an example, hacking into these inboxes may reveal that an employee is shopping for rare coins, and checks personal email on his FFRDC work machine. A Red phishing email from a prospective seller of rare coins could then include links to pictures of the coins. When the employee clicks on the links, zero-day exploit code (i.e., code not recognizable by virus scanners or IDSs) is loaded onto his machine. Most corporations cannot monitor such sequences.

Similarly, Red may attack a machine not connected to the Internet through a maintenance laptop used by service vendor personnel. The FFRDC or PMO may not have control over the security risks posed by the vendor's laptop. Therefore, Blue must thoroughly review operational and procedural cyber security from an information flow perspective and then both reduce the number of attack vectors and control their effectiveness.

Blue may also need to supply Red with deception information to the effect that Blue is leaking deceptive information through apparently compromised but actually Blue-controlled accounts. While this may make Red disbelieve some of the deception cover story, it may also make Red disbelieve information obtained through Red weapons that Blue was unable to detect. Making this trade-off poses a decision challenge to the cyber-D&D team and the CDDCO (i.e., the PMO).

4.2.5   Exploit Phase

4.2.5.1   Red Actions

Even more than in the delivery phase, Red has committed to actions it cannot reverse. By the time Blue is interpreting the cyber weapon's code, the exploitation attempt will have succeeded or failed. Some failures may have Red-detectable side effects, in which case Red can fold the results into its reconnaissance efforts. Red's primary goal is to progress into the control stage. One type of exploit may be sophisticated enough to autonomously sense its environment and activate under the right conditions; for example, Stuxnet propagated whenever external hard drives were connected to the Stuxnet-infected Internet-connected systems.

4.2.5.2   Blue Actions

Purpose. Blue's two complementary goals at this phase largely resemble its objectives in the delivery stage: usher Red into Blue's prepared deception environments and learn more about Red's technical sophistication in order to improve Blue's detection capability. This includes understanding failure side-effects in order to control Red's potential lessons learned. Exploits are among the most expensive and fleeting portions of offensive cyber technology and Blue may be able to stall Red by prompting unwise expenditure of limited zero-day exploits against false targets.

Plan. Blue adapts its D&D TTPs to the sophistication and degree of autonomy exhibited by the weapons delivered. In the autonomous case, the fake servers and systems on the honeynet present ideal conditions for the weapons to launch. For the Red exploits that communicate with an external C2 server, the D&D management team generates the right responses and interaction dynamics in the Blue honeynet environment. These range from "low-interaction" to "high-interaction" honeypots. Low-interaction honeypots take less Blue effort to construct and maintain, and can withstand a minimal level of Red scrutiny. Examples of low-interaction honeypots include low-fidelity emulated malware clients. When Red explores them Red discovers EEDI or innocuous information, or the clients simply disconnect after a short period, leaving Red uncertain about what happened. High-interaction honeypots— depending upon their fidelity—withstand Red's higher levels of scrutiny, but consume substantially more Blue D&D resources.

Execute. Blue issues CyberSec alerts on the networks, designed to make Red believe its weapons caused unintended disconnect problems.

Reinforce. Blue D&D feedback induces Red to increasingly favor weaker tools over stronger ones.

Execute. Blue deliberately guides Red into the X-20-ALPHA honeypot environment, which is connected to Blue's intranet.

Monitor. Blue monitors Red actions and exploitations. Blue's high-interaction honeypot requires extensive planning and maintenance to look and feel "live" and behave like the legitimate environment that Red expects to find. Blue must therefore plan, prepare, and execute a recursive deception operation, or simulation, to emplace Blue personae, computers, documents (so-called "pocket litter"), emails, and user activity.

Execute. The simulation gives Blue ad hoc opportunities to interact with Red, keep Red unaware of the deception, and completely control the information available to Red.

Monitor. During this phase, Blue closely monitors Red exploits to assess the adversary's sophistication, efficiency, and other behavioral dynamics, such as infection and spread patterns of the malware used.

Reinforce. Blue continuously updates the pocket litter and other ephemera in the honeypots and on the honeynets to keep Red coming back for new materials to collect.

4.2.5.3 Benefits

The benefits of D&D at this phase stem from the opportunity to interact with and directly modulate Red's beliefs and attack steps, making Red reveal its intent and attack methods. By carefully selecting which of Red's exploits seemingly succeed, Blue influences Red's attack behavior.

4.2.5.4 Challenges

This phase presents many challenges. First, Blue must be careful in signaling which of Red's exploits succeeded. The wrong choice may compromise elements of the deception or frighten away the attacker. Blue intelligence on Red's past behavior and likely beliefs regarding the probabilities of delivered exploit success is invaluable for designing D&D techniques, judging Red's actions and reactions, and managing interactions with Red. Blue's modulation of the successes or failures of the delivered exploits must be consistent with the attack surfaces of the honeynet and constituent honeytoken systems and data. Through apparent successes and failures of Blue defenses, Blue must tempt and entice Red to keep coming back for more.

Depending on the composition and intent of the Red team, after initially signaling the success of Red's exploit Blue may make Red's subsequent exploits more difficult (e.g., by changing attack surfaces to reinforce Red's belief that the deeper target systems will be more difficult to attack). Alternatively, Blue may make some attack surfaces seem to become easier to exploit. This would encourage Red to reinforce its efforts, and would channel the attacks into the areas of the controlled honeynet environment that will expose Red to the key elements of the EEDI and the Blue cover story. The overall D&D strategic plan guides this D&D signaling and manipulation, with the aid of various analysis frameworks, including game theory.

Just as the Blue cyber-D&D defenders must make the honeynets seem very realistic, Blue cyber-D&D must be prepared to make the real PMO and FFRDC networks seem unrealistic if Blue suspects they have also been successfully attacked by Red.

4.2.6   Control/Execute Phase

4.2.6.1   Red Actions

In this phase, the previously installed exploits settle into routines. An exploit moves around the infected system or network and establishes the foundation needed to execute the Red mission of intelligence collection and exfiltration. Some exploits probe deeper to establish additional footholds (i.e., beachheads) across the Blue network, creating additional electronic reconnaissance points, and amplifying and expanding the attack from multiple attack points.

Red takes advantage of these opportunities and installs additional tools and malware. Red exploits one of these vulnerabilities to break into the Active Directory server and enumerate user accounts and log-in information such as user identities. Using a password cracker tool, Red obtains user passwords, logs in, and masquerades as one or more legitimate users. Red executes opportunistic smash-and-grab attacks to copy and steal targeted information, or uses stealthy moves to exfiltrate the X-20 prototype design and evaluation data.

4.2.6.2   Blue Actions

Purpose. Just as with the delivery and exploit phases, Blue should connect Red with the primary cyber deception environment under appropriate monitoring. Upon successful transition into the control stage Red reveals hop-points for its C2 infrastructure, enhancing Blue's ability to develop threat indicators.

Most importantly, the execute stage is where most of Blue's X-20 prototype D&D unfolds. Most of the deception effects at the other kill chain stages enable the Blue D&D team to exert control in the cyber domain, but have little to do with the D&D plan for the X-20 prototype. Red achieves its mission goals during the execute state, which gives Blue its primary opportunity to deceive Red about X-20. While some deception information can be pushed through public channels, Red will value the information it gathers at this stage because it has expended non-trivial resources to acquire it. Blue populates the deception environment that Red has managed to infiltrate with conventional D&D information products (EEDI) designed to shape Red's thinking about the X-20 prototype.

As Red reaches the limits of the deception environment, Blue should appear to remediate the intrusion before Red becomes aware of the simulation.

Execute. Blue lures Red toward X-20 prototype EEDI by updating the pocket litter, personae, etc., to offer Red better sources of information and reinforce Red's confidence in their exploits.

Monitor. Blue closely monitors and controls these exploits.

Design Cover Story. Blue changes Red's future behavior by suggesting Blue will greatly strengthen its security posture by adding new security features in response to apparent leaks regarding the success of the X-20-ALPHA.

Prepare. The supposed future security features are already in place, but unknown to Red. Blue changes Red's behavior toward the EEFI by increasing security on information that Blue knows Red has already obtained.

Monitor. Blue also changes Red's behavior toward the EEFI by monitoring external information that Red will probably collect (for example, newspaper articles covering the X-20 story) to make the information Red already has or will collect seem to confirm the EEDI.

Plan. Blue evolves the EEDI to improve the cover story that the X-20-ALPHA has achieved significant success.

Execute. Blue also leaks reports to open source news media, knowing that Red monitors these sources, and uses them to "confirm" its collections and estimates. In addition, Blue leaks information about future Blue defensive efforts to influence Red to stick with weaker exploits.

Monitor/Reinforce. Blue conducts obvious "incident response" and monitors activity to reinforce the Blue D&D fictions about which Red exploits have been detected, causing Red to infer that other exploits remain hidden from Blue. Blue "helps" Red to reveal other TTPs for penetrating Blue networks as Red tries to reinforce and exploit its access.

Prepare. Blue also manipulates the Red C2 link by technically and semantically watermarking the documents Red exfiltrates to enable subsequent tracking and tracing. Some documents actively report their locations; others passively record locations or otherwise report their location to Blue.

4.2.6.3 Benefits

This phase presents the richest and most powerful opportunities for Blue D&D. Prior attack phases primarily involved Red's conducting reconnaissance and establishing footholds, but the control/execution phase is when Red executes the attack steps.

Red tactics and techniques reveal the source of the attack and the potential damage it could cause, as well as the expertise, risk tolerance, and resourcefulness of the Red team. Therefore, D&D at this phase is crucial to analyzing Red's execution patterns, gaining insights into Red's unique attack tactics and techniques, and, most important, planting the EEDI in Red's path to make Red confident that it has pieced together the real story through its exploits. Thus, cyber-D&D at this phase, when Red operates on Blue's real or synthetic networks, yields immense benefits.

Red must conduct this core execution phase of its cyber attack on Blue's terrain. Blue D&D efforts make this foothold in Blue's systems appear to be a Red success, while in fact Blue uses the favorable environment to manipulate Red into collecting more and more of the cover story EEDI. Much like operations against a known and monitored insider, Blue carefully controls the information Red sees, and how and when Red sees it. Blue reinforces and extends the EEDI, and measures its success by monitoring Red actions and reactions.

This phase represents the control point that allows Blue to evaluate D&D successes and reinforce them, offset weaknesses, and determine which D&D and other defensive tactics succeeded in previous kill chain phases. Blue has excellent opportunities for "active" deception, delivering EEDI that will filter back to Red decision makers. Blue deceives Red strategically as to the success of the X-20 program and tactically about the success of its tools and efforts in previous phases of the kill chain. Based on Red reactions to information collected during this phase, Blue builds a more complete picture of Red's D&D and counter-D&D capabilities.

4.2.6.4   Challenges

This phase also confronts Blue with technical and programmatic challenges. From a technical standpoint, the Blue D&D team and the CDDCO must have the tools and expertise to quickly reverse engineer and analyze Red's implanted exploits, and craft appropriate system responses in a timely fashion. This requires a high degree of readily available expertise. EEDI-related decoys may be of multiple types, including fake files, servers, and events. The formulation and placement of EEDI demand careful planning and coordination across multiple systems.

Further, Blue may have to expend significant resources on deceiving Red in this phase. Blue must maintain 360° situation awareness and must not open itself to attack from other hostile parties. Blue leaks should be carefully constructed not to reveal EEFI or information that would compromise D&D EEDI to third parties. Given the pervasive nature of cyberspace, this may be extremely difficult. Because any active deception program may experience leaks and compromises of EEFI, Blue runs the risk of being found out during this phase, but offsets this risk with minimization and backup D&D plans to deny perception or undercut understanding of any mistakes. Blue prepares for a situation in which Red discovers the deception by readying itself to dismiss these compromises as intentional leakages from the Blue D&D plan. If Blue makes real leaks look too good to be true and too easy to be real, while offering compelling alternatives via the D&D EEDI and cover story,

Red will reject the compromised true information. At the PMO level, the evidence and success that Red sees must be consistent with the cover story that Blue has assembled and offered, which reflects Blue's best understanding of Red's beliefs, behaviors, and intentions.

4.2.7 Maintain Phase

4.2.7.1 Red Actions

In this phase Red maintains the access it has acquired in the Blue structure, believing it has achieved its intermediate goals. Red seeks to entrench its presence on Blue systems and install further weapons for future exploitation. Red continues to spread weapons throughout the Blue networks to segments that it can now access, and sustains its efforts to gain access to additional Blue segments.

In this maintenance mode, Red's exploits become very stealthy. Red maintains a very small digital footprint in persistent and volatile memory and only communicates to the outside world very sparingly. Finally, Red iterates back to continue activities from previous phases of the kill chain. For example, Red may return to additional reconnaissance of deeper parts of Blue's networks, and deliver additional exploits.

4.2.7.2 Blue Actions

Purpose. Blue's goal for the maintain phase is to enhance its ability to control Red's interactions with Blue cyber resources, rather than directly advance the X-20 deception effects. In particular, Blue seeks to present a mix of resources that Red can corrupt in order to maximize Red's exposure of tools, permit successful compromise within planned limits, and move corrupted machines to the deception network. Blue also wishes to replace well-understood Red implants with compatible ones that alert Blue to their usage and analyze new implants to develop compatible replacements and active monitoring techniques.

The maintain phase is a microcosm of reconnaissance/exploit cycles. Red does not have time to develop new exploits; the Red team will need to use what it already has. Each exposure represents an expenditure of a scarce resource, and Blue can make significant threat-intelligence gains by eliciting maximal deployment. New detection and corruption methods feed Blue's superiority in its own networks.

Monitor/Reinforce. The Blue D&D team and the PMO CDDCO continue to update the EEDI available to Red, keeping the content adequate to maintain the Blue D&D cover story. Blue sustains the cover story as long as possible, while minimizing "collateral damage" that might be caused by false or misleading information that results from the cover story's reaching genuine X-20 stakeholders. For example,

Blue maintains information within the D&D information channels available to Red that sustains Red's belief that the X-20-ALPHA was the most successful prototype design, while ensuring that the actual prototype design selected will eventually become publicly identified as the X-20-ALPHA design. The differences between the cover story and the real versions—in other words, the EEFI design details that were altered when fed to Red in the course of the deception—remain secret, as do the existence of the Blue D&D and the D&D cover story.

Monitor. As part of these maintenance activities Blue updates and maintains personae and pocket litter, and realistically adds or retires personae as needed. The Blue D&D team maintains cover story cast members, settings and scenery, dialogue, and other elements for future sequel D&D operations.

Execute. As more information on the selection of the actual successful prototype becomes public, Blue D&D passes to Red a glut of real but nonessential information (NEFI) to keep Red hooked on the Blue cyber intelligence sources. This material can include real documents that are no longer sensitive, such as source selection for a contract that is already awarded, or are totally fake but wholly consistent with real and public documents. Creating meaningful fake documents to engage Red demands substantial Blue D&D team involvement, since cover story creation and maintenance cannot be effectively automated with current technology.

Prepare. Blue strips all sensitive EEFI from real documents and makes them available to Red, using a process similar to the sanitization of documents under "freedom of information" requests, but maintaining an appearance of pre-sanitation realism.

Monitor. Blue forces observe future Red reconnaissance and other operations to determine how Red used the stolen design information. Elements built into the D&D cover story should prompt Red to take various actions regarding the stolen design that allow Blue to verify the extent to which Red fell for the cover story. For example, Blue should monitor Red manufacturing processes and industry to see if Red appears to be using stolen intellectual property.

Design Cover Story. At some point, Red may discover that the X-20-ALPHA design is in fact inferior or unworkable, and may suspect it has been deceived. Blue's cyber-D&D cover story should anticipate such suspicions, and include follow-on ploys to "cool out the mark."[33] For example, Red engineers might discover the X-20-ALPHA design's stealth characteristics are infeasible. However, Blue has already planted tidbits of deception information that Red is now led to piece together, suggesting the X-20-ALPHA has extraordinarily secret breakthrough capabilities that made stealth shortcomings less important and expensive stealth unnecessary—hence the "superiority" of the X-20-ALPHA prototype. In this way, Blue sets Red chasing another layer of the deception chimera.

---

[33] Erving Goffman (1997) "On Cooling the Mark Out: Some Aspects of Adaptation to Failure," in Charles Lemert and Ann Branaman eds. (1997) *The Goffman Reader.* Oxford UK: Blackwell.

4.2.7.3 Benefits

Cyber-D&D at the maintenance phase enables Blue to influence Red for the long term, possibly even at the strategic and program levels for follow-on activities. Blue has the opportunity to modulate the timing, frequency, and intervals between X-20 program activities seen on the honeynets so as to evaluate Red's agility. For example, Blue could introduce several bursts of activity followed by long periods of inactivity, indicating that the X-20 program is on hold. This gives Blue the opportunity to assess Red's techniques for varying degrees of stealthiness and for long-term reconnaissance, among other factors. Blue should avoid revealing the deception, and instead slowly reduce Red's access, while allowing Red to continue to believe it has compromised the security of Blue's sensitive intellectual property.

At this stage, Blue has excellent opportunities to direct future Red reconnaissance and planning by injecting EEDI that suggests a follow-on project to the X-20 that is consistent with the cover story, thus diverting Red completely from other, legitimate Blue programs. Blue should feed Red information of real value, just not the EEDI secret design data. With Blue's compromised network as a seemingly reliable source, Red should come to trust it over other public or private information. This opens the door to numerous strategic D&D opportunities as the real X-20 program winds down.

4.2.7.4 Challenges

At the program level, Blue must refresh all aspects of the cover story and thus maintain the appearance of a "live" program. At the technical level, Blue must understand and keep up with Red's diverse, stealthy, long-term maintenance modes. With their very small footprints, Red's exploits may evade many detection mechanisms. Blue thus must remain vigilant and continuously develop smart radar-like tools for keeping pace with Red's evasion techniques. Blue D&D ploys to increase Red uncertainty and force Red to stay agile will reduce Red's ability to burrow in and stay hidden.

Another Blue challenge is making certain that Red has been completely isolated from Blue's real networks when the X-20 D&D effort ends. Thus, Blue sanitization procedures for systems must screen all basic input/output systems (BIOS), firmware, and software layers to ensure they are free of Red's exploits. Equally challenging is to develop methods by which Blue can safely capture and quarantine Red's exploits for future analysis.

Chapter 5
Exercising Cyber-D&D

If deception can be used to attack, can it also be used in cyber defense? Today, it's not clear how thoroughly cyber security professionals embrace this well-established military tactic beyond lip service that deception is a good idea. Traditionally, security professionals have been mired in a mindset of fortifying perimeter defenses, creating impervious walls, relying on defensive signatures and valiantly, or vainly, attempting to passively keep attackers from stealing data.

Edward Roberts (2012) "Deception and the art of cyber security," *scmagazine.com*, February 28, 2012. www.scmagazine.com/deception-and-the-art-of-cyber-security/article/229685/

[Edward Roberts, director of marketing at Mykonos Software]

This chapter examines the components necessary to conduct operational Red/Blue team exercises that incorporate cyber-D&D. As an example, we describe a research experiment referred to as SLX II in which Blue network defense personnel used cyber-D&D against a Red threat actor. This experiment demonstrated the value of adding D&D TTPs to traditional CND and the importance of cyber intelligence. The inclusion of D&D TTPs led to the successful neutralization of the attacker's compromise of the defender's operational planning communications.

5.1 Incorporating D&D in Red/Blue Team Exercises

Cyber operational exercises, whether wargames or other types of simulation exercises,[1] pit human cyber defenders against cyber attackers. Cyber-D&D tends to be interactive, involving actions by cyber defenders in anticipation of and in response to cyber adversaries attacking the defended network. These exercises allow cyber defenders to practice their cyber defensive capabilities against skilled adversaries in a controlled environment. Since the use of cyber-D&D in static and active cyber defenses is relatively new, testing cyber-D&D tools, tactics, techniques, and procedures (TTPs) can demonstrate the strengths and weaknesses of cyber-D&D in controlled environments before they are used against real cyber adversaries in the wild. Exercising cyber-D&D TTTPs via cyber wargames also provides a useful mechanism to explore areas for further research and development of cyber defensive measures.

---

[1] For simplicity, we will refer to all such exercises as wargames.

© Springer International Publishing Switzerland 2015
K.E. Heckman et al., *Cyber Denial, Deception and Counter Deception*,
Advances in Information Security 64, DOI 10.1007/978-3-319-25133-2_5

Recently Kott and Citrenbaum (2010)[2] described the traditional uses of wargames in business and military operational and decision analyses. Uses include exploring likely outcomes and unanticipated effects of different plans; identifying possible reactions and counteractions; characterizing the evolution of market and environmental attitudes; identifying alternative plan implementations; exploring possible actions, reactions, and counteractions of opposing forces; and estimating likely outcomes of the operational plan. Traditionally, military wargames have focused on forces, weapons, movements, and fires, while business wargames focused on marketing, investments, revenues, and profits.

A cyber wargame exercise in a simulation environment known as a sandbox enables organizations to better understand how either to utilize cyber-D&D TTTPs or prepare to counter an adversary with a D&D capability. Like kinetic wargames, cyber wargames have one or more objectives. These objectives can vary from testing the utility of a new network defense tool, or the efficacy of recent modifications made to the network sensor infrastructure, to evaluating the skills of the organization's cyber intelligence analysts so that future training can be appropriately developed.

Cyber wargames are organized around a scenario that is intended to simulate reality and be relevant to the challenges an organization is likely to face. Scenarios can range from using collaborative cyber mission systems, to conducting a multinational military operation (Heckman et al. 2013), to assuming an adversary already has credential access to the organization's network and is attempting to establish persistence and exfiltrate sensitive information while engaging in defense evasion. The scenario should permit a clear end to the exercise while ensuring sufficient gameplay to achieve the wargame's objectives.

Most cyber wargames include players divided into three teams: Red, White, and Blue. The Red team represents adversarial elements, such as malicious cyber attackers with hands-on-keyboards, cyber intelligence analysts, or the head of a nation-sponsored organization that manages or hires such attackers and analysts. The Blue team represents friendly elements, such as computer network defenders, cyber intelligence analysts, or the head of an organization undergoing a cyber attack.

The organizers make specific team assignments on the basis of the scenario. When a cyber wargame involves D&D, the scenario requirements determine how many Blue cyber-D&D teams will play defensively, and how many Red cyber-D&D teams will play offensively. D&D team(s) should interact closely with their operational team counterparts (e.g., Blue for the Blue cyber-D&D team) to ensure continuity

---

[2] Some recent wargame examples are described in David S. Alberts, Reiner K. Huber, and James Moffat (2010) *NATO NEC C2 Maturity Model*, Washington, DC: DoD Command and Control Research Program. The Joint Chiefs of Staff (2006) *Joint Publication 3-13 Information Operations*, Washington, DC: Department of Defense, recommends wargaming plans and courses of action for information operations. Wargaming by DoD may be less frequent than suggested by doctrine and history, e.g., regarding the 2008 Russian invasion of Georgia a U.S. Army War College analysis concluded "U.S. intelligence-gathering and analysis regarding the Russian threat to Georgia failed. … No scenarios of a Russian invasion were envisaged, wargamed, or seriously exercised;" p. 72, Ariel Cohen and Robert E. Hamilton (2011) *The Russian Military and the Georgia War: Lessons and Implications*. ERAP Monograph, June 2011, Carlisle Barracks PA: Strategic Studies Institute, U.S. Army War College.

and informed team play. For example, a Blue cyber-D&D team can benefit greatly from close interaction with a Blue player representing a cyber intelligence analyst, since intelligence is a key component in planning and executing defensive cyber-D&D operations.

The White team provides overall game control, which includes enforcing the rules of engagement and ensuring that Red and Blue make continual progress. The White team also manages requests for information (RFIs) from the teams, and provides the teams with stimulating injects. White stimulates both teams on a turn-by-turn basis or intermittently as required by the scenario, using injects tailored to encourage Red and Blue play likely to fulfill the objectives of the wargame. Injects can include the results of actions taken by the team receiving the inject or those taken by the other team that, in reality, would be visible to the team receiving the inject, as well as scenario activities that stimulate game play. The White team must also monitor the actions and interactions of the Red and Blue players with their respective teammates. White solicits updates from the teams regarding their situational awareness and current plans, as well as an assessment of the other team, such as their capabilities, objectives, and plans. White also enforces the "lanes in the road," i.e., the roles assigned in the wargame for Red and Blue players.

White simulates those elements of the cyber environment that are impractical to replicate in the sandbox cyber wargame environment. For example, White might provide both the Red and Blue operators with simulated cyber intelligence on the other team. In addition, White adapts and modifies the cyber environment sandbox as needed to facilitate the continuation of wargame play. For example, White might play the role of a high authority and require Blue to use cyber-D&D TTTPs against the Red opponent.

Wargames can be played synchronously, with direct dynamic interaction between Red and Blue, or asynchronously, with Red playing the game under White oversight, and Blue later playing with White.[3] However, given that deception is fundamentally psychological, synchronous play works better in games that involve D&D. The Red and Blue teams are humans interacting in a cyber environment, and if D&D is used the scenario should be designed to afford such psychological interplay. The scenario should also allow direct interaction: that is, direct communication between the Red and Blue players. For example, a Red player masquerading as an authorized user of an instant messaging (IM) system might send a Blue player a phishing link in an IM. In general, however, the Red and Blue interaction is more likely to be indirect, mediated by the technical elements of the cyber environment. For instance, Blue sets up sensors that are triggered when Red players engage with the cyber environment or interacts with Red indirectly when baiting the Red players with honeytokens or vulnerable assets that Blue knows will attract Red's interests. However, if the objectives of the wargame do not lend themselves to an experimental design that allows synchronous play, cyber-D&D can still be employed in asynchronous play, perhaps by incorporating some of the manhunting principles described in Sect. 6.3.

---

[3] In asynchronous play, Red and Blue are playing the equivalent of mail chess, but with many moves at a time.

Cyber-D&D wargames are difficult to replicate because exposure to and uncovering of D&D will necessarily affect team behavior in subsequent exercises. That is, once deception is "out of the bag," it is almost impossible to prevent this knowledge from influencing future actions. As such, cyber-D&D wargames allow less scientific control of variables than pure experiments; on the other hand, they offer more control and more measurement opportunities than observations in the wild. Relative to observations in the wild, wargames also provide greater opportunities to collect and measure Red and Blue behaviors and interactions. Just as experimental study of Internet threats has yielded valuable insights and tools for monitoring malicious activities and capturing malware binaries (Dacier et al. 2010), wargames create opportunities for control and manipulation to better understand offensive and defensive interactions, such as the use of cyber-D&D.

Exercise leaders should be aware of potential unintended consequences, particularly if the exercise will expand beyond the sandbox and into the wild, or will involve unwitting participants.[4] For example, the exercise's Red team may attack the enterprise network, and the unwitting Blue cyber defenders would follow their standard incident response process and begin sharing threat indicators with trusted partners across the community. This example has the unintended consequences of not only falsely alerting others, but also potentially damaging the trusted relationship among the sharing partners as well as trust in the data being shared. Thus, exercise planners should take great care to alert all appropriate stakeholders well in advance of the exercise.

This does not imply that an exercise cannot have unwitting participants; however, the exercise leaders may need to develop some creative solutions to erect "Chinese walls" in order to inform participants appropriately. Continuing from the example above, perhaps the White team could direct the subset of Blue defender(s) responsible for sharing indicators to confer with a fully witting supervisor during a time window surrounding the exercise before pushing threat indicators to the community. With some careful planning and consideration, an organization should be able to benefit from running exercises without undue concerns about potential unintended consequences.

5.2 Example: SLX II Exercise Parameters

In January 2012, The MITRE Corporation, an organization that operates several Federally Funded Research and Development Centers (FFRDCs), performed a real-time, Red/Blue team cyber-wargame experiment (Heckman, et al. 2013)[5] that

---

[4] See Rein, L. and Yoder, E. (2014). Gone phishing: Army uses Thrift Savings Plan in fake e-mail to test cybersecurity awareness, *The Washington Post*, March 13, 2014; and Jowers, K. (2008). Phishing scam turns out to be an inside job. *Army Times*, April 1, 2008.

[5] This experiment was conducted with two MITRE Innovation Program (MIP) research teams: Strongarm and Countering Cyber-Deception. The authors of this book constitute the Countering Cyber-Deception MIP team; MIP team members Stech and Heckman participated in this exercise. For more information about MITRE, see http://www.mitre.org

blended cyber-warfare with traditional mission planning and execution, including D&D tradecraft. The cyber-wargame tested a dynamic network defense cyber-security platform being researched in a MITRE activity called Blackjack, and investigated the utility of using D&D to enhance the defense of information in C2 systems.

The cyber-wargame used a military scenario that involved a planned Blue attack on an extremist group's compound. Blue planned and executed the scenario using a C2 mission system: in this case an instance of the web-based application MediaWiki. The wargame took place from January 23 to January 26, 2012 (referred to as T1 through T4), beginning with one day of experimentation planning on January 20, 2012 (referred to as T0).

The cyber-wargame was designed to validate two hypotheses:

Hypothesis 1: A CND tool known as Blackjack would deny Red access to real information on the real Blue C2 mission system.

Hypothesis 2: Traditional D&D techniques would deny Red access to real information on the real Blue C2 mission system, and instead provide the adversary with access to false information on a fake Blue C2 mission system.

5.3   Example: SLX II Exercise Design

Meeting the exercise goals required the Red team to compromise Blue credentials, gain access to the Blue C2 mission system, and be discovered by network defenders, who in turn would have to respond in coordination with their D&D planners. Blue CND incorporated two approaches: Blackjack policy-filtered content as the primary experimental approach and entirely independent content as a backup approach in the event the primary failed.

The real C2 mission system was operated and managed according to the defender's practice of CND, whereby the defender focused on detecting the adversary's penetration by monitoring and analyzing its border boundary. The border boundary took the form of an Apache HTTP (HyperText Transfer Protocol) server configured as a reverse proxy that would first receive and process every HTTP client request to the C2 mission system. The defender's monitoring consisted of analyzing the Apache server's access logs. Web browser clients would remain unaware of the Apache server's existence; thus, interaction with the proxy would lead either adversaries or approved users to believe they were directly accessing the real C2 mission system. The client would continue to make ordinary requests for content; the reverse proxy would then decide[6] where to send the user's request downstream to be processed: either directly to the real C2 mission system or to the Blackjack CND tool. Requests were processed on the basis of the user's certificate and the proxy's configuration.

---

[6] The reverse proxy was in place for all communication as a load balancer. Such a load balancing reverse proxy could make decisions about which backend content provider should be used based on several factors, such as geographic location, server load, network load, etc. In this experiment, the load balancing reverse proxy simply used userID as the decision criterion.

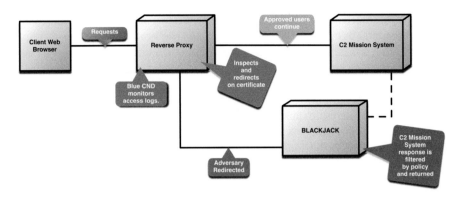

Fig. 5.1 Technical architecture for blackjack policy-filtered content

That is, approved user requests continued on to the real C2 mission system, whereas adversary requests were redirected to Blackjack, as shown in Fig. 5.1. After processing the request, the server returned the response of the downstream system as if it were the originator.

The primary experimental approach used Blackjack's policies to filter the responses returned from the C2 mission system in order to deny and deceive the adversary. The assumption underlying this approach was that adversaries would be unaware of the reverse proxy configuration. As a result, they would effectively be "Blackjacked," as each of their requests would be sent to Blackjack, which in turn would make a request of the C2 mission system. Before returning the content of the response to the proxy, Blackjack would apply policy to the content and rewrite it in order to deny and deceive the adversary. This assumption would hold if the configuration introduced no discernible delay in responding to a client's request. If this assumption did not hold, and Blue CND detected a delay, they would deactivate Blackjack, and commence experimentation with the backup approach.

Upon discovering that the adversary had penetrated the C2 mission system, Blue CND instantiated a fake Blue C2 mission system wiki. Authorized Blue users, including Blue D&D and mission personnel,[7] continued to work from the real Blue C2 mission system. Blue CND made a copy of the real C2 mission system from the moment the adversary's presence was detected and used this clone as a baseline for the fake C2 mission system that the Blue D&D team would operate to further deny and deceive the adversary. This approach leveraged essentially the same reverse proxy as the Blackjack policy-filtered content approach, but instead of sending the

---

[7] The "entirely independent content" approach operated like a secure compartmented back channel, or a special access program, with "need-to-know" access granted only to a very small number of essential users. Blue D&D hinted to Red at the existence of this back channel through compromised e-mail accounts, and used "leaks" via those accounts to reinforce elements of the Blue D&D cover story (e.g., actual covert infiltration of special forces into the terrorist country to lase the terrorist compound for what these forces believed would be a kidnap mission, part of the Red-compromised COAs), while communications within the backchannel allowed for real mission execution (e.g., tasking and execution orders to carrier-based aircraft carrying laser-guided munitions).

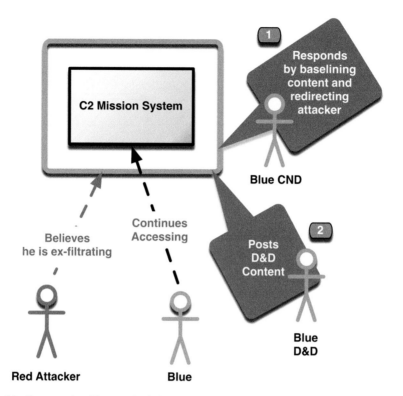

Fig. 5.2 Conceptual architecture for independent content

adversary's requests to Blackjack, the reverse proxy sent Red's requests to the fake C2 mission system, while sending approved user requests to the real C2 mission system. Each system serviced the requests, processed them on the basis of the information in the respective wikis, and responded through the proxy, which in turn sent the response on to the client, whether the requestor was an adversary or an approved user. Through this approach, Blue attempted to trick Red into believing that the fake C2 mission system wiki content was real. Some of the Blue operators placed real information on the fake wiki to maintain this deception, while other Blue operators continued producing and consuming real information on the real C2 mission system wiki. Figure 5.2 shows the conceptual architecture for this approach; Figure 5.3 shows the technical architecture.

5.4 Example: SLX II Exercise Red/Blue Interplay

On T0, White brought the Blue C2 mission system wiki online. Red gained access to the real C2 mission system wiki and began exfiltrating information. Blue CND detected Red's presence via requests from a user with a known compromised

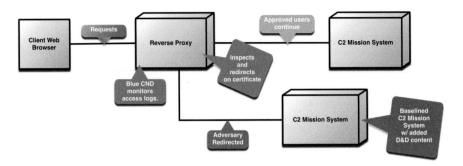

Fig. 5.3 Technical architecture for independent content

certificate. Given Red's access to the real C2 mission system wiki on T0, Blue CND responded on T1 by activating Blackjack. Shortly thereafter, Red observed both performance degradation and differences in wiki content depending on the credentials used for access. That is, by using one set of credentials that it had compromised without Blue CND's knowledge, Red had accessed the real C2 mission system wiki, and by using a different set of credentials which Blue CND knew had been compromised, Red was redirected and accessing the fake C2 mission system wiki. By the end of T1, Blue CND also observed a discernible delay in Blackjack's responding to an approved user, but postponed a response until late morning on T2. Given Red's access and exfiltration activities, Blue CND discovered a Red "signature," and used this to begin enumerating compromised accounts. At the end of T1, however, Blue D&D learned that the four military scenario COAs had been compromised by Red.

At the start of T2, Blue D&D briefed a new D&D plan. Blue CND assisted by providing current information on compromised accounts. Blue D&D used this input to ensure Red received deception information that supported the new cover story and mission plan. In response to the performance degradation observed on T1, Blue CND deactivated Blackjack, and instantiated a fake Blue C2 mission system wiki that hosted entirely independent content. To create a covering backstory for the compromised COAs, Blue D&D disseminated a set of email traffic via injects from the White team, which Red acted upon. Blue confirmed that Red's actions indicated belief in the Blue D&D cover story, including the creation of a fake double agent with the code name "Cotton Dollar."

During the late hours of T2, Blue conducted the military mission via a COA that Blue D&D had made available to Red. T3 dawned with a White inject reporting explosions in the country where the extremist group leader's compound was located. White later reported that the extremist group's compound had been destroyed; however, it was not yet known whether the leader was dead or alive. Red responded with a propaganda message.

To aid Blue CND, Blue D&D developed a plan to use the fake double agent Cotton Dollar as bait to discover which of four Blue user accounts were compromised, but did not yet execute it. Red provided White an assessment of its perception of Blue's intended COA, and Blue D&D confirmed Red's belief in the D&D cover story.

T3 ended with a White inject confirming the death of the extremist group leader, followed by a set of Blue D&D propaganda materials denying responsibility.

By the start of T4, Red knew Blue had carried out its military mission successfully, but still believed in the existence of Cotton Dollar. Blue D&D executed the Cotton Dollar extraction ruse planned on T3.[8] This was done by placing different extraction locations and times in four email messages, each of which was directed to one of the four Blue users whose account status was unknown. Via injects, White sent Red the fake email messages directed only to accounts that Red had compromised. Red then recommended actions to prevent Cotton Dollar's extraction, utilizing the unique extraction locations and times sent to each user. As a result of these spatial and temporal actions, Blue D&D assessed which email accounts were compromised. T4 ended with the White team's declaring the cyber-wargame complete, given the sufficiency of captured observables.

5.5   Example: SLX II Exercise Results

On the basis of the experimental results, the organizers rejected the first hypothesis, because; Blackjack was not effective at denying adversary access to real information on the real Blue C2 mission system. Blue CND activated Blackjack because of a tip that a particular certificate had been compromised; however, Red had previously compromised a number of other credentials without Blue CND's knowledge and had kept persistent access to both the authentic and fake Blue C2 wiki sites. Red then recognized that content and performance varied based on the certificate used to access the wiki, and could easily distinguish real information from false.

The Blackjack policy filtered content approach was fraught with problems in authoring policy, and discovering and removing telltale indicators of deceptive information became infeasible. Obvious indicators included wiki edit history, search indexes, lists of orphaned pages, and page rendering time. Dynamically rewriting the content received from the wiki was technically difficult, and the resulting output was not convincing. The deceit was revealed and Red exploited these shortcomings at time T1.

The exercise results supported the second hypothesis: traditional D&D techniques were effective in enhancing Blue CND's ability to deny adversary access to information on the real Blue C2 mission system. The backup approach created entirely independent content on another fake Blue C2 mission system. Coupled with traditional D&D techniques to create a covering backstory, this fake Blue C2

---

[8] Blue D&D used a version of the "knight's fork" chess move, when the knight threatens two pieces. Red had to react to the Cotton Dollar ruse and choose between two responses, both of which could benefit Blue. If Red chose to chase Cotton Dollar, Red exposed the accounts Red had compromised. If Red chose not to believe the Blue D&D ploy and not to ambush the Cotton Dollar locations, these locations would then be available to Blue for, e.g., real Blue forces extraction. Inasmuch as Red did not suspect Cotton Dollar was a deception, Red chose to cover the extraction points it knew about, thus exposing the accounts Red had compromised.

mission system increased the believability of the D&D story, and allowed Blue to carry out the military mission as planned.

Although the approach of using entirely independent content succeeded, it was vulnerable to the same technical problems as the Blackjack policy-filtered content approach. That is, if Red had again utilized a set of credentials without Blue CND's knowledge as it did on T1, Red would have been able to access the real Blue C2 mission system wiki. However, based on the experimental results, the D&D appeared sufficiently compelling that even if Red had gained access, the wiki still contained enough misinformation that Red would have been deceived as to Blue's real mission.

Chapter 6
Considerations, Adaptation, and Sharing

If the performer knows enough outs, he will never fail to bring a trick to successful conclusion.

Jerry Mentzer (1974) *Close-up Card Cavalcade.* First Edition: Jerry Mentzer.

Indocilis Privata Loqui.

The Magic Circle motto.

Adaptability and agility are essential in planning, preparing, and executing deception operations. Deception planners must be prepared to respond so that they can still achieve their goals even when it seems that everything is going wrong. This chapter brings together considerations for the cyber-D&D planner, covering the realities of utilizing cyber-D&D. Applying cyber-D&D poses risk and has the potential for unintended consequences. Cyber-D&D operations can be compromised, and even the best-laid plans can fail. Although the defender can gain advantages by using D&D in each phase of the kill chain, utilizing cyber-D&D TTPs always involves challenges and potential drawbacks. We review some of these to inform and encourage cyber-D&D cadres to explore these considerations early in the planning phases of cyber-D&D operations.

Further, defenders cannot always keep an adversary from breaking into their network. Defenders who discover that an adversary had gained access to their network become engaged in incident response. Thus, we explore how physical manhunting principles used in irregular warfare can be adapted to support Blue/Red network hunting with cyber-D&D.

Finally, we address concepts related to data sharing and standardization.

© Springer International Publishing Switzerland 2015
K.E. Heckman et al., *Cyber Denial, Deception and Counter Deception*,
Advances in Information Security 64, DOI 10.1007/978-3-319-25133-2_6

6.1 Risk, Unintended Consequences, Compromise, and Failure

At each phase, D&D planners must carefully consider the risks involved in using deception. The overriding consideration in risk analysis is the tradeoff between the risk taken and the possible benefits of the deception. The major determining factors include unintended effects and consequences, exposure of means or feedback channels (i.e., compromise), and deception failure.

The Deception Research Program (1980) developed a set of hypotheses, or maxims, relevant to deception and surprise.[1] These serve as a set of guiding principles that help deception planners to avoid unfavorable responses and failure. Deception Maxim 9, "The Monkey's Paw," posits that:

> Deception efforts may produce subtle and unwanted side effects. Planners should be sensitive to such possibilities and, where prudent, take steps to minimize these counterproductive aspects.

Prior to executing a D&D operation, deception planners should assess their plans to identify any potential unintended effects or consequences and, as possible, develop appropriate contingency plans. To minimize "blowback"—the unintended consequences of a covert operation that affect Blue and friendly populations—planners should prepare "blowoffs" and "coolouts."[2] During execution, deception operators must monitor the target for such unintended effects and be prepared to execute contingency plans. Deception planners cannot foresee all the possibilities during the planning phase; however, they should be sensitive to the possibilities.

Deception planners must assess the possible effects if the adversary responded differently than expected, as well as the risks of the adversary's not responding favorably. For example, a deception operation that utilizes false messages from incident responders or authorities with the intention of conveying to Red that their attack is succeeding in order to keep them on Blue's network might have the unintended consequence of frightening Red to the point where Red terminates the attack.

Deception planners must also determine the likelihood of compromise, and ultimately, the risks of failure. Barton Whaley's historical research (2010a, b) shows that deception rarely fails, and almost never fails completely. He also found that failed deceptions cause no more harm than no deception, and furthermore, that any deception, regardless of its maturity, is better than none at all. In analyzing these rare and very rare cases, Whaley (2010a, b) identified five general circumstances in

---

[1] See Appendix C for a list of the deception maxims and their application to cyber-D&D.

[2] Blow-offs and cool-outs are typically associated with confidence games (see Goffman, E. (1952), "On cooling the mark out: Some aspects of adaptation to failure." *Psychiatry*, 15 (4): 451–463.), but can be adapted for espionage. A blow-off is the means taken by the entity executing the covert operation to recuse itself from any or all activities attributed to the blow-back. A cool-out is the means taken to assuage a complainant, particularly one that is a blow-off target, in order to minimize the extent of the blow-back.

which deception fails: (1) design failure; (2) initiation failure; (3) transmission failure; (4) inept implementation; and (5) target detection of the deception.

On the basis of this analysis, Whaley (2010a, b) proposed three ways to minimize the chance of failure in a deception operation. First, Blue must anticipate the developing situation by considering and evaluating the various alternative hypotheses. Second, Blue must understand and act on the lessons learned from the failure of other organizations willing to share information about their experience. The benefits of developing trusted partnerships for such information sharing include broader knowledge not only about the specifics of a cyber incident, but also about the defender's operational deception response and its outcome(s).[3] Third, Blue must engage in a subtle psychological game that plays upon Red's ignorance regarding the maturity of Blue's deception capability maturity, whether low or high. Blue must appear to possess the capability maturity that best matches that of the adversary at hand. A cyber-D&D CMM helps Blue to assess an adversary's cyber-D&D capability as well as its own.[4]

Blue can overcome compromises and turn potential failures into advantages. For example, if sufficient resources are available, Blue can develop a new deception operation that leverages resources already compromised to reinforce the new deception story so that it will be more readily believed and accepted.[5] At a minimum, Blue can often ensure that Red becomes more confused about Blue's capabilities, intentions, and actions then it was prior to the compromises. Blue can then gain the advantage to maintain operational security while Red attempts to make sense of the environment and events.

More theoretically, deception planners and operators can follow Whaley's (2010a, b) Theory of Outs. The Theory of Outs is a practical set of guidelines for getting the deceiver "out" of all types of failed deception operations. Whaley presents five rules: (1) always preplan the Out; (2) tailor each Out to fit each deception plan; (3) the Out must be in place for execution before the deception operation executes; (4) gaming the Out can be effective to identify potential problems; and (5) always seek to minimize catastrophic consequences by building at least part of the Out into the deception plan and operation. Whaley (2010a, b) also captured 14 lessons learned from his analysis of deception failures, all of which harmonize well with the characterization of deception planning, preparation, and execution described in this book.[6]

---

[3] See Sect. 6.4 for a more detailed exploration of this topic.

[4] Chapter 7 describes this concept in detail.

[5] Chapter 5 of this book presents a case study of a cyber-wargame Red/Blue team exercise in which the EEFI was fully compromised, and thus Blue's military operation was a potential failure, but with an additional iteration through the deception chain, the cyber-D&D operation supported Blue in planning and successfully executing its military operation.

[6] Briefly, the lessons learned are: Know your commander's (or organization's) intentions and battle plans; know the desired enemy reaction; know the available deception assets (i.e., human and material) and their capabilities and limitations; communicate up (e.g., your commander), across (e.g., parallel staffs), and down (e.g., subordinate staffs) your deception capabilities; coordinate the deception plan with other planning and operational units whose cooperation is needed; provide

A common feature of successful deceptions is that they were designed to subvert the target's disbelief by requiring some participation from the target (i.e., either physical effort to obtain evidence or analytic effort to interpret it). This participation forces the target to "work for it"; that is, to invest labor and cost to piece together the "convincing truth" from the bits and pieces of "leaked" evidence and misinformation. As Lieutenant Colonel John Bevan observed during WWII, the resulting convincing truth is less likely to be readily dismissed: intelligence easily obtained was intelligence readily disbelieved.[7] This most likely occurs because of a human cognitive bias now referred to as the IKEA effect,[8,9] and to a method of social influence known as commitment and consistency.[10,11] That is, once the target has expended the labor to piece together "the convincing truth," it will become highly valued due to that expenditure. To compound this effect, once the target has become committed to this "convincing truth," the target will be committed to think and act accordingly, as predicted by the principle of commitment and consistency.

---

advance notification to the HQs of all friendly units that could be adversely affected by the deception operation if they fell for the deception; take advantage of the target's military doctrine, capabilities, intelligence standard operating procedure, and preconception in the deception plan; keep the deception plan simple so that one detected discrepancy does not unravel the whole deception operation; make plans within plans so that there are separate deception sub-plans for the lower level units; the deception plan must become operational in time to serve its purpose, though that timeline can be unexpectedly shortened in order to achieve surprise; keep the deception operation as brief as possible to minimize the likelihood of its detection; seek accurate and timely feedback as these are the only clues to whether the deception operation is succeeding or failing; fine-tune the deception operation based on the feedback received; and stay flexible by designing the deception plan to include at least one "out."

[7] Cave Brown, A. (2007) *Bodyguard of Lies: The Extraordinary True Story Behind D-Day*. Lyons Press.

[8] Norton, Michael I., Mochon, Daniel, and Ariely, Dan. (2012). "The IKEA effect: When labor leads to love," *Journal of Consumer Psychology*, 22 (3), 453–460.

[9] The IKEA effect occurs when consumers place a disproportionally high value on self-made products as compared to objectively similar products which they did not assemble. Empirical studies show that this effect occurs only when labor results in successful completion of tasks. That is, when experiment participants built and then destroyed their creations, or failed to complete them, the effect dissipated.

[10] Cialdini, Robert B., (1993). *Influence: The Psychology of Persuasion*. William Morrow and Company: New York.

[11] The principle of commitment and consistency deals with our desire to be and look consistent with our words, beliefs, attitudes, and deeds. Being consistent with earlier decisions reduces the need to process all the relevant information in future similar situations; instead, one simply needs to recall the earlier decision and to respond consistently with it, even if the decision was erroneous. People will add new reasons and justifications to support the wisdom of commitments they have already made. As a result, some commitments remain in effect long after the conditions that initiated them have changed. It should be noted that not all commitments are equally effective. Those that are the most effective are active, public, effortful, and viewed as internally motivated (i.e., uncoerced).

6.2   Benefits, Challenges, and Drawbacks of Cyber-D&D

A defender can gain advantages by using cyber-D&D in each phase of the kill chain, but must overcome challenges and potential drawbacks for utilizing particular techniques. The decision to use a given D&D technique should take all three factors into account. Cyber-D&D techniques are more effective when used in combination with psychology and with the results of past deception operations via an intrusion campaign framework to understand the mindset and motivations of a malicious actor.

Table 6.1 captures a set of cyber-D&D techniques that can be utilized at the different phases of the kill chain. The techniques labeled with asterisks were presented by Rowe and Rothstein (2004) and Rowe (2007); those proposed by the authors were first shown in Fig. 3.6 and are repeated in the table. In addition, the table summarizes the benefits and challenges of these techniques within each phase. Maintaining a table such as this during an actual deception operation enables a defending organization to progressively learn, adjust, and adapt its cyber-D&D capabilities.

Reconnaissance Phase: The defender can employ a number of cyber-D&D techniques that might provide opportunities to learn more about the attackers, such as their identity and their interests. These techniques must be deployed carefully to ensure that interactions are controlled and do not tip off the attacker. In anticipation of potential future attacks, the defender can develop a set of false personae with a corresponding public web footprint that can be used in cyber-D&D operations. Similarly, the defender can operate a low-interaction honeypot with fake public-facing services that can be scanned in anticipation of potential attacker interest in the defender's activities.

Weaponization Phase: The defender must invest in technical defensive and offensive capabilities to gain insight into the tools utilized by the attacker. This understanding will allow the defender to influence the design, execution, and after-effects of the attacker's weapons. Examples of cyber-D&D in this phase again include low-interaction honeypots in which the service banners have been modified to match known vulnerable versions. Attackers can then be sandboxed so that defenders can allow exploits to which the network is not vulnerable to "succeed." However, the defender could become susceptible to attacker deception and CD, which could pose significant long-term security costs.

Deliver Phase: The defender has its first opportunity to interact directly with the attacker and control the interaction environment by, for example, placing the attacker in a high-interaction honeypot and having a false, or real, persona click on malicious links in (spear) phishing emails. Another alternative is for defenders to give the impression that an attacker's email was successfully delivered to the intended victim by responding to the email with questions about the attachment.

The defending organization is limited in that it can only defend against known delivery vectors. Defenders can visit a drive-by download site with a honeyclient,

Table 6.1 Cyber-D&D techniques

Kill chain phase and description	Techniques	Benefits	Challenges	Possible drawbacks
Reconnaissance: The adversary develops a target.	• Set up a decoy site that parallels the real site[a] • Lie about reasons for asking for an additional password[a] • Lie about reasons for asking for authorization data[a] • Plant disinformation; redefine executables; give false system data[a] • Deliberately delay processing commands[a] • Pretend to be an inept defender or to have easy-to-subvert software[a] • Craft false personae with a public web footprint • Operate low interaction honeypots	• Lure attacker to honeynet, or other controlled environment • Conduct reconnaissance on attacker • Make attacker reveal identity • Provide misleading data and responses to manipulate weaponization and delivery phases	• Risk of accidental disclosure • Resistance from PR staff	• May alert attacker to defenses • May scare off attacker • May alert attacker to need for CD capabilities • Attacker may shift to more capable attack teams, tools, and techniques • Attacker may increase ISR on target organization
Weaponize: The adversary puts the attack in a form to be executed on the defender's computer/ network.	• Camouflage key targets or make them look unimportant; disguise software as different software[a] • Redefine executables; give false file-type information[a] • Associate false times with files[a] • Do something in an unexpected way[a] • Falsify file-creation times[a] • Falsify file-modification times[a] • Reveal facts regarding the enterprise and/or its network • Modify network traffic to reveal/ conceal activity • Hide software using stealth methods • Deploy low-interaction honeypots • Deploy sandboxes	• Cause misdesigns in attacker weaponization • Lead weapons to attack false targets • Cause weapons to reveal themselves • Cause weapons to misfire and attack the wrong targets • Create built-in appearance of weaponry successes	• Investment in tool reverse engineering • Visibility into adversary's offensive tool supply chain	• Attackers deploy deceptive weapons • Attackers develop double-barreled – decoy plus real – weapons • Attackers deploy weapons with ISR capabilities • Weapon designs include significant feedback and control

Deliver: The adversary puts in place the means by which the vulnerability is weaponized.	• Transfer attack to a safer machine such as a honeynet[a] • Transfer Trojan horses back to attacker[a] • Ask questions, with some intended to locate attacker[a] • Try to frighten attacker with false messages from authorities[a] • Plan an operation for any false persona targeted by spear/phishing • Expose a past deception • Confirm malicious email delivery expectations • Visit drive-by download site with a honeyclient	• Attacker targets a contained and controlled environment • Weapons backfire on attacker • Attacker inadvertently reveals identity • Attacker breaks off attack	• Limited to known delivery vectors	• Attacker develops stealthier delivery • Attacker deploys defenses • Attacks become more surgical and targeted • Attacker resorts to social engineering to reinforce weaponry
Exploit: The adversary executes the initial attack on the defender.	• Pretend to be a naïve consumer to entrap identity thieves[a] • Lie that a suspicious command succeeded[a] • Lie about what a command did[a] • Lie that you can't do something, or do something not asked for[a] • Swamp attacker with requests[a] • Send overly large data or requests too hard to handle to attacker[a] • Send software with a Trojan horse to attacker[a] • Induce attacker to download a Trojan horse[a] • Conceal simulated honeypot information • Misrepresent the intent of software • Allow malicious email to run in sandbox	• Attacker inadvertently reveals identity • Attack broken off due to DoS responses • Attacker exfiltrates booby-trapped materials • Attack fails to retrieve targeted information • Attacker vulnerable to deceptions attributing counterattack to insiders in attacker's operations • Attacker vulnerable to deceptive double agent information sources	• Investment in exploit reverse engineering • Implementation of host-based security suite	• Attacker invests in counter-attack defenses • Attacker double checks all exfiltrated materials for booby-traps, Trojan horses • Attacker re-doubles security operations • Attacker re-doubles counter-espionage efforts

(continued)

Table 6.1 (continued)

Kill chain phase and description	Techniques	Benefits	Challenges	Possible drawbacks
Control: The adversary employs mechanisms to manage the initial defender victims.	• Deploy a high-interaction honeypot with infrastructure • Systematically misunderstand attacker commands, for instance by losing characters[a] • Operate a high-interaction honeypot • Falsify internal data	• Attacker has false sense of control • Attacker misled by manipulated control • Attacker directed away from valuable targets • Attacker loses control	• Visibility into attacking organization's network traffic • Continuous development of protocol decoders	• Attacker seeks insider information to confirm control • Attacker increases investments in ISR • Attacker invests in counter-intelligence operations
Execute: Leveraging numerous techniques, the adversary executes the attack plan.	• Reveal technical deception capabilities • Tamper with the adversary's commands • Timeout the adversary's connections • Emplace honeytokens in defender-controlled environment	• Attacker activity detectable • Attacker exfiltrates tagged materials • Attackers reveal their identity and/or techniques • Attacker deterred from further engagement	• Selective remediation for purpose of escalating attacker's operations	• Attacker may be alerted to defenses • Attacker accelerates lateral movement and exfiltration
Maintain: The adversary establishes a long-term presence on the defender's networks.	• Maintain false personae and their pocket litter • Add/retire false personae • Allow partial enumeration of fictional files • Expose fictional systems that simulate additional services and targets	• Cause attacker to reveal node(s) in social network	• Ability to track adversary usage of stolen information • Provable removal of adversary	• Attacker may be alerted to defenses

Sources: Rowe and Rothstein (2004) and Rowe (2007)

[a]

but mature attackers will try to thwart these attempts by various means, such as developing stealthier delivery, more surgical and targeted attacks, and weaponry reinforcements such as social engineering.

This phase also presents an opportunity for the defender to expose a past deception in a way that makes the attacker disbelieve information gleaned from past intrusions. Malicious actors may doubt the authenticity of future intrusions, and be wary when interacting with supposedly compromised systems.

Exploit Phase: In controlling the interaction environment, the defender has the opportunity to make fictional material available to attackers, and attempt to convince them that they have succeeded by misrepresenting responses to their weapons. To do this, the defender must invest in exploit reverse engineering and must implement a host-based security suite. For example, defenders can allow a malicious email link or attachment to be run in an Internet-connected sandbox. The drawbacks of these D&D techniques are that they may tip off the attackers, who could respond by enhancing their counter-attack defenses, security operations, and counter-espionage efforts.

Control Phase: If defensive efforts in previous phases succeeded, the defender now controls the attackers weapons and approaches, although the attackers should believe that they are in control. In this phase, defenders can allow the result of an exploit to run in a high-interaction honeypot with infrastructure components. However, if prior defense efforts were not entirely successful and the attackers become suspicious, they might seek alternate means to confirm that they indeed have control. These actions may actually alert the defender and offer the defender a new deception channel to the attacker. Clearly, the defender must stay ahead of the attacker in this measure–countermeasure–counter-counter-measure competition.[12]

Execute Phase: Although neither Rowe and Rothstein (2004) nor Rowe (2007) identified cyber-D&D techniques applicable to this phase, the defense may choose to reveal technical deception capabilities to deter further intrusion attempts, or to confound attacker certainty and potentially gather more information on the attackers by allowing them to continue operating. The former approach has the drawback of requiring selective remediation, and could also result in the attackers' escalating their pace and potentially the amount of information exfiltrated. The latter could yield benefits in that the defender may gain valuable insight by allowing the attacker to continue operating. The defender may also attempt to tamper with the attacker's commands in order to mislead and cause confusion. The defender may also periodically timeout the attacker's connection to force a more desirable response, or scatter misleading or innocuous data and documents (i.e., honeytokens) around an environment controlled by the defender.

---

[12] These duals of measures–countermeasures are basic elements of electronic warfare; see, e.g., Sergei A. Vakin, Lev N. Shustov, and Robert H. Dunwell. *Fundamentals of electronic warfare.* Norwood MA: Artech House, 2001.

Maintain Phase: Again, the literature does not propose any cyber-D&D techniques applicable to this phase. However, the defenders could allow the adversary to keep operating in their controlled environment. In so doing, defenders would need to maintain the false personae and their respective pocket litter, and to add or retire false personae as appropriate to support the typical movement of staff in, around, and out of the organization.

The defenders can also allow partial enumeration of fictional files, or expose fictional systems that simulate additional services and targets that should be of interest to the attacker. This forces the defender to track the attacker's use of exfiltrated data; however, this process might reveal nodes in the attacker's social network. The biggest challenge in this phase is ensuring that the attacker and its tools have been removed from the network.

Defenders could use other D&D techniques, either physical or virtual, to reduce the benefits that the adversary can gain from the data already found and exfiltrated. For example, the defense could execute a deception operation with the goal of raising doubt about the data's accuracy or relevance.

6.3   Post Exploit Manhunting

Steps prior to a successful exploit offer opportunities to detect intrusion attempts, but it is not always possible to keep an attacker from exploiting the defender's network. If the defender finds an attacker on the network, the defending organization must understand the scope of the intrusion. Incident response and forensics deployed after an exploit are very costly; thus, to the extent possible, cyber defenders should be adaptive and seek lessons learned from other applicable domains. One promising approach involves the notion of "post exploit manhunting," which adapts physical manhunting techniques to a cyber defense process with cyber-D&D support.

Manhunting includes not only the ability to find a high-value target (HVT) or a person of national interest (PONI), but also the concept of tracking individuals until friendly forces can achieve a desired end-state: influence HVT behavior, apprehend the HVT, or, if the threat or situation demands, eliminate the HVT.[13] In manhunting, "The fugitive always wants to avoid capture, while the pursuer always wants to engage and capture the target – the pursuer must *confront* to win, whereas the fugitive must *evade* to win."[14] In cyber defense, the malicious actors want to avoid *detection* in order to execute their objectives (such as exfiltrate, establish persistence), while the cyber defender wants to detect, deny or redirect, observe, and potentially engage or deceive. Thus, the defender must *detect* to win, whereas the malicious actor must *evade* to win. Throughout this section we will use the term

---

[13] George A. Crawford (2009) *Manhunting: Counter-Network Organization for Irregular Warfare.* JSOU Report 09-7 Hurlburt Field FL, JSOU Press.

[14] Steven Marks, Thomas Meer, Matthew Nilson (2005) *Manhunting: A Methodology for Finding Persons of National Interest,* Monterey, CA: Naval Postgraduate School, p. 19.

hunter as an analogy for cyber defenders and the term PONI as an analogy for cyber adversaries who have, or are attempting to gain, access to the defenders' network.

Counterintelligence tools include both disruption and deception, which offset the inherent asymmetric advantages that the attacking side enjoys.[15] Regardless of the type of malicious actor—criminal, hactivist, APT—on the network, the defender probably has "control of the search space" (Marks et al., 2005, p. 15). That is, the defender owns the network and should therefore have an advantage in its active defense approach.

6.3.1 Elements Underlying Hunter Strategies

Manhunting strategies are defined according to three elements: detection, exposure, and maneuver. *Detectability* reflects both the PONI's visibility—that is, the size and strength of a signature left by the PONI—and the hunter's acuity, or ability to detect the PONI's signature. Visibility depends in part on whether the targets take stealthy measures and can successfully utilize them to achieve their objectives. For example, migrating into a common, benign process before launching a tool prevents the defender from detecting that a potentially malicious executable is running on a host. The defender's acuity is based in part on analyzing an adversary's pattern of life; that is, knowing what adversaries are likely to do and how they are likely to do it so that it can be quickly recognized. The defender can gain some sense of "normal" network behavior by conducting longitudinal analysis of activity on instrumented hosts, and developing a set of sensors that alarm when potential adversary signatures are observed. The hunter can only capture the prey when both occupy the same bounded region.

Given that the defender owns the network on which the adversary is operating, no physical boundaries or issues prevent the adversary's exposure to the defending hunters. However, the adversary's activities may only remain exposed for a limited amount of time. Given this, defenders could attempt to identify optimal hiding and detection locations to expedite their defensive response.

Maneuver is related to both the hunter's and the PONI's mobility. The PONI is either captured in a stationary state (for instance, hiding in a compound) or a dynamic state (for instance, moving to avoid capture via some means of transportation). The hunter can be stationary (e.g., in an ambush position waiting for the PONI to move into the "kill zone") or dynamic and actively tracking the PONI. These issues of fixed versus mobile are related to whether the adversary can move laterally and, if so, to identifying which hosts have been compromised so as to give the defenders a 'map' of the adversary's operating region. Likewise, the defenders must discover what protocols the adversary uses to move (for example, the Remote Desktop Protocol), why the adversary moves from one host to another, and how the

---

[15] Stokes, Mark A. and L.C. Russell Hsiao (2012) *Countering Chinese Cyber Operations: Opportunities and Challenges for U.S. Interests.* Project 2049 Institute, October 29, 2012, p. 3.

defenders might influence this movement. If a stationary hunter targets a mobile PONI, the hunter must be patient and confident in the ability to predict the PONI's movement patterns, and anticipate the PONI's avenue of approach.

Campaign analysis and cyber intelligence can yield great benefits in supporting the defender's predictions. The defender should 'think ahead' to the next potential engagement and predict what the adversary will likely do, and then take action during, or shortly after, the engagement in preparation.

Targeting PONIs depends on the hunter's ability to understand the effects of both social and physical terrain on the PONI's normative and adaptive behavior patterns. This calls for an understanding not only of the defender network, but also of the adversary: What does the adversary expect to see? How does the adversary perceive the defender's network, and what conclusions does the adversary draw? What and how will the adversary attack based on these expectations, perceptions, and understanding? Again, campaign analysis and close support from cyber intelligence analysts may help to fill in these gaps.

6.3.2   Hunter Strategies

The hunter has five basic strategies: still hunting and stalking, stand hunting, drive hunting, trapping, and calling. "As the name implies, *still hunting* means walking stealthily through an animal's habitat, stopping frequently—sometimes for long periods—to scan and listen for game" (Marks, et al., 2005). Still hunting allows both the prey and the hunter to operate in a mobile state. The hunter has to understand not only the terrain and the prey's normative behavior patterns, but also the prey's adaptive behavior patterns. *Stalking* is a variation of still hunting. "The difference between still hunting and stalking is that when stalking, you follow signs leading to a particular type of game or group of animals, or close the distance to game already spotted" (Hunting Strategies, 2005). In cyber security, the analogies to still hunting and stalking are covertly watching Red operate on the network in real time, perhaps in a honeynet, honeypot, or honeyclient.

In *stand hunting*, hunters analyze the terrain and the normative behavior patterns of the prey to determine the prey's likely avenue of approach. Next, the hunter places a stand or a blind in a location that provides excellent observation over the prey's paths, or game trails. The hunter remains fixed while the prey is mobile. This technique works best when the target is active in a given area and the hunter has enough time and patience to wait. Stand hunting is analogous to the defender's analysis of the adversary's pattern of life and campaigns. If the defender detects the execution of a sequence of particular commands within a specified time period, its confidence that it can distinguish the adversary's behavior from that of an authorized user may increase. Likewise, enumerating compromised credentials allows the defender to identify the adversary's area of activity. If those hosts are instrumented with sensors, then the defender can tag and track the adversary as the adversary operates.

In *drive hunting*, or flushing, the drivers push the prey to a point where the posters or hunters are positioned. The defender can use honeytokens or vulnerable assets to entice adversaries and "drive" them to a particular host, file, or persona that is being logged or otherwise observed by the defender.

Calling is the opposite of drive hunting in that it lures the prey out of a concealed or secure location by sending out false signals, whereas *trapping* means that the hunter baits or sets a trap and waits for the target to fall for the ruse. Calling requires active participation and presence by the hunter, whereas trapping does not. Calling in cyber security employs the same techniques used for drive hunting. The defender can also force the adversary to reveal itself by ensuring that the enticing honeytokens or vulnerable assets cannot be accessed via stealthy techniques. Forcing the adversary to resort to noisy behavior enhances the defender's detection capability. The defender can entrap the adversary by, for example, using host-based sensors to silently trigger alerts when the adversary attempts to use an Administrator tool that the defender made available to adversaries willing to work for access to it.

6.3.3 PONI Strategies

The PONI typically uses one of three general strategies to avoid apprehension: masking, maneuver, and disengagement. *Masking* reduces the PONI's visible signature. Signals can be masked through a number of different techniques, including noise and concealment. In a cyber attack, the adversary may attempt to operate in a stealthy manner so as to conceal its presence, or may attempt to mask its signals with noise by, for example, using bots for a distributed DoS attack.

Maneuver, or mobility, helps the PONI to move at a time, to a place, or in a manner that the hunter does not expect, and thereby optimize the ability to avoid capture. For example, the adversary could choose to access the defender's network after normal business hours, anticipating that the organization's defense and response capabilities would be minimal. The adversary may also attempt to penetrate the network via a trusted insider, on the assumption that the trusted insider would be less likely to trigger defenses than the adversary.

Disengagement allows the PONI to operate in areas not accessible to the hunter because of political, economic, legal, military, or geographic constraints and limitations. Although political, legal, and potentially economic constraints and limitations could prevent consequences from the adversary's activities, no clear constraints or limitations prevent the defender from *detecting* the adversary. That is, the only way the adversary can disengage is to leave the defender's network.

Finding and apprehending PONIs can be complicated by a PONI's possible deception operations. The PONI must choose how to conduct D&D operations. The PONI can control the observables the hunter sees or the hunter's focus. Since the PONI can only devote a limited amount of resources to misleading the hunter, it is to his advantage to control the hunter's focus rather than to control all of the observables. However, the PONI will most likely use a mix of the two strategies.

The best way to reduce the success rate of a PONI's D&D operations is for the hunter to understand his own biases, intelligence system, and decision-making process, and how the PONI is likely to manipulate these to his advantage. Similarly, in cyber defense, the defender can try to control all of the observables by, for example, making deceptive entities look real, or control the adversary's focus by, for example, influencing and manipulating where and what the adversary chooses to pursue, go to, or seek, for instance by adding more vulnerable assets near the adversary's areas of activity or luring the adversary to other decoys.

6.4 Standardization and Sharing

Organizations operating independently have more limited situational awareness of the cyber threat landscape than organizations that share cyber threat intelligence and information with other trusted organizations. Endsley and Robertson (1996) identified three levels of situational awareness: perception of the elements in the environment; comprehension of what that pattern of elements mean; and projection of what may happen next given the current pattern. Each of these is pertinent to the discussion of standardization and sharing of cyber threat intelligence and cyber-D&D data.

Numerous platforms exist for sharing such cyber threat intelligence and information; structuring this data via a standardized form increases its usability. Organizations must also structure and share offensive and defensive cyber-D&D data. Such sharing might foster an organization's ability to assess the effectiveness of its cyber-D&D operations and to increase the maturity of its cyber-D&D capabilities.

Threat-based active defense is driven by cyber threat analysis, which, much like traditional kinetic intelligence, ascertains an understanding of adversaries' capabilities, actions, and intent. However, no single organization has complete access to the range of timely, relevant information needed for an accurate analysis of the threat landscape. Sharing relevant cyber threat information among trusted partners and communities offers one solution, potentially enabling each partner to achieve a more complete and accurate situational awareness of the threat landscape. Sharing can also contribute to broader collaboration across organizations and can improve future operations and campaign analysis. The threat facing one organization today may be the threat another organization confronts tomorrow, particularly if both organizations fall within the targeting scope of a given adversary's campaign. Sharing may position the second organization advantageously to address the threat while it is still left of exploit.

Sharing can help focus and prioritize the use of voluminous, complex cyber security information. A standardized form of representation enables the widest possible community of partners to contribute and leverage the shared information. Standards provide better coverage, easier interoperability, efficiency, overall situational awareness, and enhanced security, allowing disparate entities to "speak" the same language. Standardizations can include a common taxonomy or a structured language template.

The ability to structure cyber threat information, yet maintain human judgment and control, can pose a challenge (Barnum, 2014). Organizations may wish to share information that is both human-readable and machine-parsable. This calls for structured representations of threat information that are expressive, flexible, extensible, automatable, and readable.[16] A similar need exists for structured representations of both offensive and defensive cyber-D&D TTPs and operational data.[17] Such standardizations may also form the basis for evaluation of D&D TTPs, D&D operations, deception chain phase elements, and their effectiveness.

Sharing models take different forms, such as hub-and-spoke, post-to-all, peer-to-peer, and hybrid models.[18] Likewise, a number of mechanisms enable sharing of actionable cyber threat information across organizational and product/service boundaries. Examples include the FBI's iGuardian, Financial Services Information Sharing and Analysis Center (FS-ISAC), Multi-State Information Sharing and Analysis Center (MS-ISAC), DoD/DHS's voluntary DIB Cyber Security/Information Assurance (CS/IA) Program, DoD's DIB Enhanced Cyber security Services (DECS), the Center for Internet Security's Multi-State Information Sharing and Analysis Center (MS-ISAC), and the office of Cybersecurity and Communications at the U.S. Department of Homeland Security's Trusted Automated eXchange of Indicator Information (TAXII). Some of these mechanisms define trust agreements and governance, while others simply enable organizations to share chosen information with chosen partners.

Engaging in an actual deception operation enables a defending organization to progressively learn, adjust, and adapt its cyber-D&D capabilities. Thus, in addition to sharing cyber threat information, organizations could benefit from sharing offensive and defensive D&D TTPs, ongoing cyber-D&D operations, and outcomes from completed operations. Participating in a trusted sharing program that includes standardized cyber-D&D data as well as cyber threat intelligence and information further enables an organization to build its capabilities in active threat-based cyber defense.

---

[16] One community-driven solution to this problem is the Structured Threat Information eXpression (STIX™) language, which extends indicator sharing to also include other full-spectrum cyber threat information (Barnum, 2014). STIX is a language for the specification, capture, characterization, and communication of standardized cyber threat information. Cyber threat information represented as STIX is shared through Trusted Automated eXchange of Indicator Information (TAXII™) services that allow organizations to share cyber threat information in a secure and automated manner (see http://stix.mitre.org/ and http://taxii.mitre.org/). STIX, TAXII, and the STIX and TAXII logos are trademarks of The MITRE Corporation.

[17] We are currently exploring the development of a structured cyber-D&D data solution via the STIX language (see https://github.com/STIXProject/schemas/pull/334/files).

[18] See, for example, The MITRE Corporation. (2012). Cyber Information-Sharing Models: An Overview. http://www.mitre.org/sites/default/files/pdf/cyber_info_sharing.pdf. Last accessed October 25, 2015.

Chapter 7
Countering Denial and Deception

> In principle it should always be possible to unmask a deception.
> R.V. Jones (1980) Intelligence and Deception, *Journal of the Royal Institution*, Spring, p. 142.

In this chapter we explore cyber-counterdeception (cyber-CD), what it is, how it works, and how to incorporate it into cyber defenses. We review existing theories and techniques of counterdeception and adapt them for usage by cyber defenders in conjunction with their deception chains and deception campaigns. In so doing we present a cyber-CD process model, then apply it to the Mandiant APT1 case. Our goal is to suggest how cyber defenders can use cyber-CD, in conjunction with defensive cyber-D&D campaigns, to detect and counter cyber attackers.

7.1   Defining Counterdeception

The term counterdeception was coined in 1968 by William R. Harris of the Center for International Studies at Harvard University.[1] McNair (1991) offered a "concept for counterdeception," that is, in assessing the actions and intentions of the enemy or adversary, "to effectively avoid falling prey to enemy deception efforts, a commander must accurately identify the enemy operation as deceptive, and avoid taking the action his opponent desires him to take."[2] Whaley (2006, 2007a) claims the term counterdeception is merely convenient shorthand for "the detection of deception." All definitions of counterdeception link it to the function of intelligence, that is, of understanding the behavior and objectives of the adversary, as contrasted with

---

[1] Whaley (2006) further wrote: "Counterdeception is … now standard jargon among specialists in military deception. This useful term was coined in 1968 by Dr. William R. Harris during a brainstorming session with me in Cambridge, Massachusetts." Harris's papers, while widely influencing other scholars of deception and counterdeception, are hard to come by. Epstein (1991) cites William R. Harris (1968) "Intelligence and National Security: A Bibliography with Selected Annotations." Cambridge MA: Center for International Affairs, Harvard University. Other relevant Harris counterdeception papers Epstein cited include "Counter-deception Planning," Cambridge MA: Harvard University, 1972; and "Soviet Maskirovka and Arms Control Verification," mimeo, Monterey CA: U.S. Navy Postgraduate School, September 1985.

[2] McNair, Philip A. (1991) *Counterdeception and the Operational Commander*. Newport RI: Naval War College.

© Springer International Publishing Switzerland 2015
K.E. Heckman et al., *Cyber Denial, Deception and Counter Deception*,
Advances in Information Security 64, DOI 10.1007/978-3-319-25133-2_7

denial and deception, which is the operational function of influencing the perceptions, beliefs, and behaviors of the adversary (e.g., Bennett and Waltz 2007; Gerwehr and Glenn 2002; Whaley 2006, 2007b).

Bennett and Waltz (2007) define counterdeception in terms of the defender's actions that counterdeception must support: "counterdeception is characterized [by]... awareness [of the adversary's deception capabilities and operations], detection and exposure [of specific deception techniques and tactics by the adversary], and discovery and penetration [of the adversary's deception intentions and objectives]." Bennett and Waltz define the purposes of counterdeception as determining the deceiver's real and simulated capabilities, and determining the deceiver's deception intentions:

> the purpose of counterdeception is to find the answers to two fundamental and highly interdependent questions. First, counterdeception must ... penetrate through the deception to discern the adversary's real capabilities and intentions, in other words, to answer the question: What is real? Simultaneously, analysts and decision-makers must determine what the adversary is trying to make them believe in order to consider the second question: What does the adversary want you to do? The answers to these two questions are absolutely essential to the success of one's own strategies, policies, and operations.

Unfortunately, Barton Whaley's (2007b) analysis of many historical cases of military and political deception reached a striking conclusion, that is, the odds overwhelming favor the deceiver, no matter how shrewd the victim: "the deceiver is almost always successful regardless of the sophistication of his victim ... it is the irrefutable conclusion of the historical evidence." But Whaley offers some hope for counterdeception: "the avoidance of victimization" by deception "requires [a] decisional model, specifically one designed to analyze the signals of stratagem [i.e., deception] ... To detect deception, one must, at the minimum, know to look for those specific types of clues that point to deception ... they are an essential part of the counterdeception analyst's toolkit."[3] We will describe one such counterdeception model in this chapter.

Gerwehr and Glenn's (2002) research echoes Whaley's recommendations on counterdeception: the counterdeception analyst must understand the strengths and weaknesses of the deceiver's methods, and identify ways to exploit specific weaknesses to detect corresponding indications of deception. They write: "[a] key finding ... is that different counterdeception methods can and should be applied toward different deception techniques. ... experimentation should be done to define these relationships. ... A body of thoroughly vetted experimentation and analysis is needed that clearly prescribes what sorts of counterefforts to employ to stave off particular types of deception." We return to the issue of experimentation and its role in developing counterdeception techniques at the end of this chapter.

---

[3] Bodmer et al. (2012) noted Chinese cyber deception in cyber wargaming (p. 82): "reports of the People's Liberation Army (PLA) advancing their cyber-deception capabilities through a coordinated computer network attack and electronic warfare integrated exercise." We found no references explicitly to cyber exercises of *cyber-counterdeception*.

7.2 Defining Counter-Deception

It is important to distinguish *counterdeception* from *counter-deception*. That is, *counterdeception* is the analysis of the actions and intentions of an adversary's denial and deception operations, typically by the defender's intelligence organization; while *counter-deception* is a deception operation run by the defender's deception organization to expose or exploit an adversary's deception operations. *Counterdeception* is necessary to engineer successful *counter-deception* operations; while conversely *counter-deceptions* can be useful tools for extending and amplifying the *counterdeception* analysis of the deceptive adversary.

Rowe (2004) described *counter-deception* as: "defending information systems, planning to foil an attacker's deceptions with deceptions of our own. ... Besides the intrinsic suitability of a deception, we must also consider how likely it fools an attacker."[4] Rowe (2006) uses the term "second-order deceptions" to mean what we term *counterdeception*: "recognition by an agent of one or more ... first-order deceptions. ... detection of deception affects perceptions about who participates, why they do it, and the preconditions they recognize."[5]

A recent U.S. government small business innovation research (SBIR) award (Wick 2012), titled "Deceiving the Deceivers: Active Counterdeception [sic.] for Software Protection," described a *counter-deception* system to deceive cyber attackers with decoys:

> To better protect [DoD operations and infrastructure] critical systems, we propose to design and build an "active counterdeception" software protection system... CYCHAIR consists of two complementary technologies. The first [provides] the ability to easily generate large numbers of reusable, extensible and highly reconfigurable decoys. These decoys serve multiple purposes: first of all, they serve to increase the adversary's workload while confusing them as to the manner and location of the real targets. Secondly, they serve as intelligence gatherers, recording all the adversarial interactions. These records are fed to the second piece of the system, an inference engine we call LAIR (Logic for Adversarial Inference and Response). These inferences can be used to automatically trigger dynamic reconfiguration of the decoys (to further frustrate and slow down the adversary), and used as recommendations to the human-in-the-loop for additional active responses to the attack.

---

[4] Rowe used the term *counterdeception*, we believe he meant what we term here *counter-deception*; Rowe, N. C. (2004) "A model of deception during cyber-attacks on information systems," *2004 IEEE First Symposium on Multi-Agent Security and Survivability*, 30–31 Aug. 2004, pp. 21–30. Rowe (2003) proposed a counterplanning approach to planning and managing what we term *counter-deception* operations; Rowe, N. C. (2003) "Counterplanning Deceptions To Foil Cyber-Attack Plans," *Proceedings of the 2003 IEEE Workshop on Information Assurance,* West Point NY: United States Military Academy, June 2003. A recent description of counter-deception, "a multi-layer deception system that provides an in depth defense against ... sophisticated targeted attacks," is Wang, Wei, Jeffrey Bickford, Ilona Murynets, Ramesh Subbaraman, Andrea G. Forte and Gokul Singaraju (2013) "Detecting Targeted Attacks by Multilayer Deception," *Journal of Cyber Security and Mobility,* v. 2, pp. 175–199. http://riverpublishers.com/journal/journal_articles/RP_Journal_2245-1439_224.pdf

[5] Rowe, N. C. (2006) "A taxonomy of deception in cyberspace," *International Conference on Information Warfare and Security,* Princess Anne, MD.

In other words, the use of decoys in CYCHAIR is a *cyber-counter-deception* (cyber-C-D) operation intended to counter stealthy and deceptive cyber attackers, while the LAIR component enhances the effectiveness of the defenders' deceptive decoys. The system provides secondary *counterdeception* elements (i.e., "intelligence gatherers, recording all the adversarial interactions") but the clear objective of this system is *counter-deception*.[6]

7.3   Applying Cyber-CD to Computer Intrusions

In some respects, cyber-counterdeception (cyber-CD) is not new. Attackers often use denial techniques to hide within innocuous code, which are typically detected by searching for known patterns of data within executable code. Assuming such signatures are shared among defenders, this acts as counterdeception to exploit known signatures of malicious code.

Cyber attacker cyber-D&D goes far beyond planting malicious code inside innocuous code. Attacker cyber-D&D tactics (see Fig. 2.1) are extensive, and complex (e.g., they may either reveal or conceal facts, or reveal or conceal fictions, or they may conceal facts and reveal fictions), so cyber defenders need considerable cyber-CD capabilities to detect these various tools and techniques using cyber-D&D in the attack.

7.3.1   Building a Tripwire

Additionally, cyber-CD must help defenders understand the attackers' possible intentions and objectives. If the cyber defenders also use cyber-D&D in the defense, the cyber-CD effort assists in shaping the defensive cyber-D&D plans and operations, as well as supporting the cyber defender generally. For example, to convince the cyber attacker that their offensive cyber-D&D tools, tactics, techniques, and procedures (TTTPs) are succeeding in deceiving the defenders, counterdeception might support what Whaley (2006) terms the counterdeception "triple cross," that is, detecting the adversary's deception, and turning the detected deception against the adversary, using defensive cyber-D&D TTTPs.

Recently, *The Economist* described a cyber-CD and defensive cyber-D&D operation to protect a bank from cyber fraud.[7] A U.S. bank created "Honey Bankers;"

---

[6] For a general analysis of denial techniques in cyber-*counter-deception* (cyber-C-D), see Yuill, Jim, Dorothy Denning, & Fred Feer (2006) "Using Deception to Hide Things from Hackers: Processes, Principles, and Techniques," *Journal of Information Warfare*. 5,3: pp. 26–40.

[7] *The Economist* (2014) "Banks and fraud: Hacking back--Bankers go undercover to catch bad guys," *The Economist*, April 5th 2014. http://www.economist.com/news/finance-and-economics/21600148-bankers-go-undercover-catch-bad-guys-hacking-back

non-existent bankers with cyber identities, with fake e-mail addresses and plausible biographies, with supporting biographical details on bogus bank web pages not linked to the rest of the bank's website. An attacker, using offensive cyber-D&D to conceal their own identity, sending a transfer request to one of these fictional "Honey Bankers" aliases, is thus exposed as a likely fraudster. The bank then blocks the sender's internet address, pending further investigation. The bank's defensive cyber-D&D tactic, the "Honey Bankers," also serves a defensive cyber-CD function, that is, by tempting fraudsters, the bank exposes them as something other than legitimate customers.

In short, cyber-CD provides the means and methods to identify the cyber-D&D TTTPs cyber attackers are using, and, having identified the possible use of cyber-D&D TTTPs, a defender will want to generate and investigate hypotheses to understand what the attacker's possible intent may be in using cyber-D&D. Because many of the cyber attacker's D&D tools and tactics are designed to be "lost in the noise" of normal operations of the cyber systems defending the enterprise, a key component of cyber-CD is maintaining high resolution characterizations of what constitutes normal operations (i.e., "the noise"), and even more detailed descriptions of anomalies, including known and suspected cyber attacks (i.e., "the signals" that must be detected and described), including detailed descriptions of prior use of cyber-D&D tools and techniques by attackers. That is, the defender must have an evidence-based representation of their baseline activity with the ability to detect anomalies. For instance, if legitimate customers rarely make one-way transfers to international recipients, the financial institution may wish to flag such transfers as anomalous pending additional verification. This type of detection and response is privy to an arms race between attacker and defender—the fraudster may then respond by relaying funds through intermediaries or intercepting the out-of-band authentication code.

7.3.2 Sharing Intrusion Data

Defenders are incentivized to share information to better detect attackers and intrusion methods. For example, Mandiant reported in 2013[8] on tactics used by advanced persistent threat (APT) actors including indicators and detection signatures. In Appendix C: The Malware Arsenal, Mandiant provided detailed technical information on offensive tools developed by the actors and operational details of intrusions against U.S. companies. The actors also leveraged public-key encryption to encrypt communications between clients and servers, using self-signed X.509 certificates.

Publication of a large amount of indicators on this actor group, via Mandiant's digital Indicators of Compromise, helped unaware victims detect this actor's operations in their network. Cyber-CD greatly benefits from the publication and

---

[8] Mandiant (2013) *APT1: Exposing One of China's Cyber Espionage Units.* http://intelreport. mandiant.com/Mandiant_APT1_Report.pdf and Appendices.

exploitation of detailed indicator data that cyber-CD can use to recognize and identify cyber-D&D TTTPs.

As described in the previous chapter, the STIX and TAXII systems, sponsored by the office of Cybersecurity and Communications at the U.S. Department of Homeland Security, offer mechanisms for defenders to share threat indicators in a structured format in a manner that reflects the trust relationships inherent in such transfers. Structured Threat Information eXpression[9] (STIX) is a community-driven language to represent structured cyber threat information. Trusted Automated eXchange of Indicator Information[10] (TAXII) enables sharing of information across organization and product boundaries to detect and mitigate cyber threats.

More complex defender cyber-CD methods, beyond recognizing and identifying indicators of cyber-D&D, are necessary for more complex cyber-D&D methods. For example, methods are needed to infer possible intentions and objectives of an adversary's cyber-D&D operation. To this end, it should be noted that cyber-CD plays a major role in the second step of the deception chain (i.e., Collect Intelligence) and secondarily in aiding the security of the other deception chain steps by, for example, supporting the defender to Plan, Monitor, and Reinforce the defensive cyber-D&D by furnishing information on the attacker's offensive cyber-D&D. That is, cyber-CD detects and describes the capabilities of the attacker's use of cyber-D&D. While a great deal more intelligence is collected about the adversary for the deception chain, for example, the attacker's general and specific beliefs about the defenders capabilities, cyber-CD is essential to defeating the attacker's use of cyber-D&D TTTPs.

7.4   Counterdeception Components

Several counterdeception theories have described methods and processes to implement these components. We describe one such counterdeception theory and suggest how it might be adapted to cyber-CD. We also describe the essential elements and necessary steps of counterdeception analysis. Counterdeception capabilities have been described by Bennett and Waltz (2007) and Whaley (2006, 2007d, 2012; Whaley and Busby 2002). Notably, neither Bennett and Waltz nor Whaley described the capabilities needed for cyber-CD.[11] Bennett and Waltz in their 2007 book,

---

[9] STIX and the STIX logo are trademarks of The MITRE Corporation. The STIX license states: The MITRE Corporation (MITRE) hereby grants you a non-exclusive, royalty-free license to use Structured Threat Information Expression (STIX™) for research, development, and commercial purposes. Any copy you make for such purposes is authorized provided you reproduce MITRE's copyright designation and this license in any such copy (see http://stix.mitre.org/).

[10] TAXII and the TAXII logo are trademarks of The MITRE Corporation. The TAXII license states: The MITRE Corporation (MITRE) hereby grants you a non-exclusive, royalty-free license to use Trusted Automated Exchange Indicator Information (TAXII™) for research, development, and commercial purposes. Any copy you make for such purposes is authorized provided you reproduce MITRE's copyright designation and this license in any such copy (see http://taxii.mitre.org/).

[11] Other than a few references to detecting deception in social engineering situations, we found no research on cyber-counterdeception, per se, in general searching of the scholarly literature.

Counterdeception: Principles and Applications for National Security, described both counterdeception functions and the components and capabilities of an organizational counterdeception system. The functional capabilities they describe are:

- Identify an adversary's deception operations;
- Negate, neutralize, diminish, or mitigate the effects of, or gain advantage from, the adversary's deception operation;
- Exploit knowledge of the adversary's deception;
- Penetrate through the deception to discern the adversary's real capabilities and intentions;
- Determine what the adversary is trying to make you believe--What does the adversary want you to do?

An organization must have a variety of counterdeception systems, Bennett and Waltz argue, to perform effective counterdeception functions. These counterdeception organizational system capabilities include:

- Fundamental counterdeception technical methods;
- System architecture to support counterdeception operations;
- Counterdeception planning and collection strategies;
- Counterdeception information processing systems for:

  - Analysis methodology and workflow,
  - Processing filters and knowledge bases,
  - Computational analytic support tools,
  - Analytic tool workflow;

- Counterdeception analysis, decision support, and production systems:

  - Deception analytic flow,
  - Considering alternatives analysis,
  - Deception warning;

- Counterdeception system performance & effectiveness measures.

Whaley's (2007d) *Textbook of Political-Military Counterdeception: Basic Principles & Methods* defines "counterdeception … as the detection of deception— and, by extension, the possible triple-cross of the deceiver…. Ideal counterdeception reveals the truth behind the lie, the face beneath the mask, the reality under the camouflage. Good counterdeception spares us from unwelcome surprises. This term may be extended to also mean 'triple cross' of the detected deceiver…the active measures to turn an opponent's deception back upon himself." Whaley (2012) also refers to counterdeception analysis as "incongruity analysis," and credits this label to the aforementioned William Harris.[12]

---

[12] Some (e.g., Bennett and Waltz 2007) would credit "incongruity analysis" to R. V. Jones, and his theory of spoofing and counter-spoofing. See Jones, R. V. (2009) *Most Secret War*. London: Penguin, pp 285–291: "the perception of incongruity—which my ponderings have led me to believe is the basic requirement for a sense of humour—[concluding]… the object of a practical joke [is] the creation of an incongruity."

Whaley notes the significant differences between the deceiver, weaving the web of deceit, and the counterdeception detective, unraveling the web, thread by thread:

> the analyst faced with deception [must] think more like a detective solving a mystery [and be able to] think … into the mind of a deceptive opponent …The mental process whereby … generally all deception planners… design deception operations is mainly or entirely linear and one-dimensional like a connect-the-dots game. Conversely … intelligence analysts [detecting deceptions] … solve the mystery largely using a process that is logically non-linear and three-dimensional, similar to solving a crossword puzzle.

Whaley differentiates the type of analytic thinking needed for counterdeception analysis from what he terms "conventional analysis:"

> Conventional analysts, by working from a mainly linear cause-to-effect deductive model, tend to quickly (and often prematurely) lock onto the most obvious cause. Conversely, abductive [counterdeception] analysts, engineering backward from an observed effect to discover its most likely cause, tend to explore alternative hypotheses before circling in on the one that most closely fits the evidence. Essential to this abductive process is that it is non-linear, cycling through successive feedback loops, which assure at least some open-minded analysis of the competing hypotheses (ACH). …Our two types of … analysts will differ in their reaction to deception. Whenever deception is present, the deductive type of analyst predictably tends to directly focus on the most obvious cause—just as the deceiver had planned. Conversely, the abductive analyst is better positioned to perceive those special telltale incongruities (anomalies or discrepancies) that always distinguish each real object and event from its simulation—its counterfeit…

Whaley describes counterdeception capabilities in terms of general principles, specific methods, operations for verification and falsification, and operations beyond detection and verification.

Whaley conceives of counterdeception as requiring the capability to apply several general principles to analysis. First, counterdeception analysis is largely the mirror-image of deception planning and execution: "the characteristics of the things hidden and displayed and categories of analysis are the same. The only difference…is that the process by which the deceiver plots a deception follows a different (although related) logical path than the process by which the [counterdeception] analyst unravels it." One consequence of this symmetry is that Whaley advocates counterdeception analysts should have experience in planning deceptions. McPherson (2010) makes this point emphatically for military units: "An effective cell brought together to identify adversary deception should be drawn from individuals who already understand how to operationally plan deception."[13]

Second, Whaley argues "the deception detective's job is, at least in theory, [easier than the deceiver's]." Whaley describes what he terms the 'counterdeception analyst's advantage' in terms of capabilities to detect the observable indications of simulation and dissimulation:

> Whoever creates a deception simultaneously creates all the clues needed for its solution. Moreover, every deception necessarily generates a minimum of two clues, at least one about the real thing being hidden and at least one other about the false thing being shown.

[13] McPherson, Denver E. (2010) *Deception Recognition: Rethinking the Operational Commander's Approach.* Newport RI: Joint Military Operations Department, Naval War College.

1) Whenever deceivers create a deception they simultaneously generate all the clues needed for its detection. These give the [counterdeception] detectives additional chances for discovering the [deception] operation.

2) Each of these deception-generated clues is an incongruity—an incongruous characteristic that distinguishes the false thing from the real one it seeks to replace.

3) Every deception has two fundamental parts. These are dissimulation (hiding) and simulation (showing). Dissimulation hides or conceals something real and simulation shows or displays something false in its place. In theory both hiding and showing take place simultaneously, even if one is only implicit.

Corollary 3a) Ideally, the deceiver should hide and show simultaneously.

Corollary 3b) If this isn't possible, at least always hide the real before showing its false substitute.

Corollary 3c) And if doing so, allow enough time for the thing being hidden to have plausibly reappeared somewhere else.

4) Each of these parts is incongruous with its previous reality. Thus every deception creates at least two incongruities. One represents a built-in inability to hide all the distinctive characteristics of the thing being hidden. The other represents an inherent inability to show all the characteristics of the thing being shown in its place. Each part, therefore, creates a decisive clue for the [counterdeception] detective.

5) Consequently, although the deceiver has only one opportunity to "sell" his deception operation, the [counterdeception] detective (analyst) has two chances to detect it, two clues that lead directly to a solution.

Whaley observes that there are actually many specific methods (he lists 20) that take advantage of the 'counterdeception analyst's advantage' and enable the detection of deception:

> There are dozens of specific theories, principles, and methods for detecting deception. Most tend to be overlooked by the great majority of political-military intelligence analysts—they have simply not yet been adopted by our analyst's teaching and training schools and courses. However, all have been adopted in one or more other disciplines, particularly by consistently successful analysts who deal more or less regularly with deception.

Simply detecting deception is insufficient for successful counterdeception, and Whaley stresses the need for capabilities to verify deception hypotheses, and to falsify alternative hypothesis (i.e., disprove the "reality" presented by the deceiver and prove it is not real). The capability to assess multiple alternative competing hypotheses is widely seen as a requirement for effective counterdeception analysis.[14]

---

[14] For example, Heuer, Jr., Richards J. (1981) "Strategic Deception and Counterdeception: A Cognitive Process Approach," *International Studies Quarterly*, v. 25, n. 2, June 1981, pp. 294–327. Whether or not deception is detected, assessing hypotheses regarding the adversary's possible courses of action against the evidence provides useful insights into adversary intentions: "The [counterdeception] cell would be tasked to … [look] at the data from the enemy's point of view. They would need to place themselves in the mind of the enemy, determine how they would develop a deception plan and see if evidence supports it. … The enemy may not be employing a deception plan, but the process will aid in exploring different enemy courses of action that may have been overlooked." Heuser, Stephen J. (1996) *Operational Deception and Counter Deception.* Newport RI: Naval War College, 14 June 1996. Bruce and Bennett (2008) wrote: "the failure to generate hypotheses increases vulnerability to deception…One key to Why Bad Things Happen to Good Analysts has been conflicting organizational signals regarding promotion of overconfidence ("making the call") versus promotion of more rigorous consideration of alternative hypotheses and the quality of information;" Bruce, James B. & Michael Bennett (2008) "Foreign Denial and Deception: Analytical Imperatives," in George, Roger Z. & James B. Bruce (2008) *Analyzing intelligence: origins, obstacles, and innovations*. Washington DC: Georgetown University Press.

Whaley notes "the cost may be prohibitive—economically, psychologically, ethically, socially, or politically—but it can be done." He describes several specific methods that provide help to test alternative hypotheses; providing verification and falsification capabilities, passive versus active measures, tripwires, traps, lures, and provocations.

Whaley (2012) recently proposed a set of four skills for detectives (i.e., intelligence and deception analysts) that must be used in sequence to solve any mystery: the ability to perceive incongruities; the ability to form a hunch or hypothesis that explains those incongruities; the ability to test the hypothesis to determine how closely it fits the current conception of reality; and the ability to weigh the relative merits of any alternative or competing hypotheses. If this four-step process successfully explains and eliminates all of the incongruities, then the mystery is solved. More likely, this process will uncover new incongruities, and the process iterates. Each cycle of this four-step process will produce either an increasingly close match with reality or an entirely new model of reality or a new point of view. The counterdeception model described below follows Whaley's four-step process.

Finally, Whaley stresses the need for actions before, during, and after detection of deceptions. Before and during detection of deception, he argues that anticipation of deceptions and proactive counter-measures can reduce susceptibilities and vulnerabilities to deceptions, and help to negate or counter-act the effects of deceptions. After deception detection and verification, the friendly side should consider using the detection as the basis for the "triple cross," that is, leading the deceiver to believe the deception has worked, while the deceiver's belief is actually being exploited by the friendly side.

Whaley observes that "these special actions require close and continuing liaison and coordination among the intelligence analysts, the planners, operations staff, and even the commander ... close institutionalized cooperation between intelligence and operations at the top... [and] direct liaison links across organizational hierarchies at all levels of intelligence analysts and intelligence collectors." These organizational liaison and coordination links require additional capabilities to effectively perform counterdeception. Cyber-CD capabilities need to be both psychologically and organizationally complex because cyber attackers use complex attack kill chains and intrusion campaigns and adapt cyber-D&D TTTPs to conceal them.

7.5   Applying Cyber-CD to Network Defense

Assuming cyber attackers will use both denial (or hiding) and deception (or misleading) TTTPs in their attack campaigns, cyber defenders must develop TTTPs to counter both of these. That is, defenders must develop capabilities for counterdenial, to reveal what is hidden, and for counterdeception, to determine what is actually real from what is false (i.e., the detection of deception). As Whaley (2007b) concluded from his analysis of many historical cases of military and political deception, the odds overwhelmingly favor the deceiver, no matter how shrewd the target

Table 7.1 Attacker's D&D moves versus defender's counterdenial and counterdeception moves

Attacker: Denial & Deception Moves	Defender: Counterdenial and counterdeception moves		
	2. Naïve—No Counterdeception and No Counterdenial	*4. Counterdenial Moves*	*6. Counterdeception Moves*
1. Unwitting— No Denial or Deception	*No advantage* No advantage	*Disadvantage: Suspects denial hiding that is not present* Advantage: Perceives unwarranted intrusiveness	*Disadvantage: Suspects deception that is not present* Advantage: Perceives unwarranted paranoia
3. DENIAL: Covering— Hiding	*Disadvantage: Misses denial hiding of critical information* Advantage: Conceals critical information	*Advantage: Perceives hidden critical information* Disadvantage: Critical information exposed	*Disadvantage: Suspects deception that is not present; misses denial hiding* Advantage: Conceals critical information; perceives unwarranted deception detection
5. DECEPTION: Misleading— Deceiving	*Disadvantage: Misled by deception* Advantage: Misleads <u>and</u> hides critical information	*Disadvantage: Misled by deception* *Advantage: Perceives what is hidden* Disadvantage: Critical information exposed Advantage: Misleads	*Advantage: Perceives what is hidden <u>and</u> is not misled* Disadvantage: Denial <u>and</u> deception fail; critical information exposed

of the deception. Table 7.1 shows this disparity conceptually. Unless the defender uses effective counterdenial and counterdeception TTTPs at the appropriate opportunities, most of the advantages accrue to the attacker (i.e., see the six light gray-shaded cells). But when the defender's counterdenial and counterdeception capabilities are appropriately matched against the attacker's use of D&D TTTPs, the advantages accrue to the defender (i.e., see the two dark gray-shaded cells).

7.6 A Cyber-CD Process Model

D&D TTTPs are difficult to detect because they exploit the victim's reasoning errors, cognitive limitations, and concomitant biases. The most important reasoning errors contributing to victims' susceptibility to deception are:

- Reasoning causally from evidence to hypotheses,
- Failure to entertain a deception hypothesis,
- Biased estimates of probabilities, and
- Failure to consider false positive rates of evidence.

The first two errors involve considering too few alternative hypotheses due to incomplete generation or premature pruning, which can involve misestimates of probabilities. The sources and effects of biases arising from mental estimates of probabilities are well-known.[15] Two biases are particularly debilitating for detecting deception: bias due to making conclusions that support preconceptions, assuming a piece of evidence is consistent with too few hypotheses; and mirror imaging—assuming an adversary is likely to choose a course of action that appeals to the observer.[16]

Two major analysis shortcomings impairing counterdeception analysis are poor anomaly detection (i.e., missing anomalies or prematurely dismissing anomalies as irrelevant or inconsistent) and misattribution (i.e., attributing inconsistent or anomalous events to collection gaps or processing errors rather than to deception). The first shortcoming results when analysts have insufficiently modeled the normal environmental patterns so that unusual events and anomalies can be detected and measured, and when there is a lack of familiarity with the indicators of D&D TTTPs so that the linkages between unusual and anomalous events and possible use of D&D TTTPs are missed.

To recognize deception, the analyst must consider the deceiver's alternative courses of action (COAs) and overcome biases that lead to inappropriately weighing evidence that seems to support one of only a few alternative COAs. The analyst must estimate the likelihood of these COAs as new evidence is received, while simultaneously considering the likelihood that evidence is deceptive.[17] The most promising techniques to reduce bias in probabilistic assessments is to require a subject to perform and document a systematic analysis of the evidence, considering on the one hand that the evidence is veridical, and on the other hand, that the evidence may be deceptive.

Stech and Elsäesser (2007) proposed a counterdeception process model (see Fig. 7.1), integrating a variety of counterdeception theories,[18] to help analysts avoid cognitive biases and increase deception success. This process model estimates the likelihoods of deceptive and veridical information by following four analysis processes sequentially, with possible recursion:

---

[15] Gilovich, T., D. Griffin, & D. Kahneman (2002) *Heuristics and Biases.* Cambridge UK: Cambridge University Press; and Dawes, R.M. (2001) *Everyday Irrationality: How Pseudo Scientists, Lunatics, and the Rest of Us Systematically Fail to Think Rationally.* Boulder CO: Westview Press.

[16] Heuer, Jr., R. J. (1981) "Strategic Deception and Counterdeception: A Cognitive Process Approach," *International Studies Quarterly,* v. 25, n. 2, June 1981, pp. 294–327; Elsäesser, C. & F. J. Stech (2007) "Detecting Deception," in Kott, A. & W. M. McEneaney eds (2007) *Adversarial reasoning: computational approaches to reading the opponent's mind.* Boca Raton FL: Taylor & Francis Group.

[17] See Fischhoff, B., (1982) "Debiasing," in Kahneman, D., P. Slovic, & A. Tversky, eds. (1982) *Judgment under Uncertainty: Heuristics and Biases.* Cambridge UK: Cambridge University Press, pp. 422–444.

[18] See Stech, F., and C. Elsäesser (2007) for review of the various counterdeception theories, "Midway Revisited: Detecting Deception by Analysis of Competing Hypothesis," *Military Operations Research.* 11/2007; v. 12, n. 1, pp. 35–55.

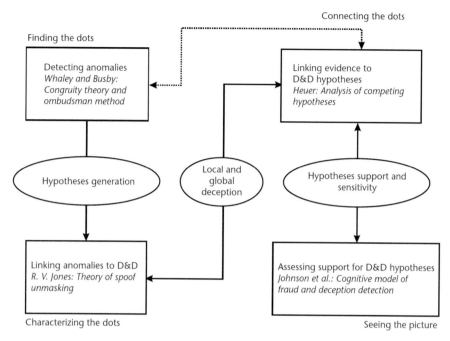

Fig. 7.1 Conceptual schematic for counterdeception analysis process. From Bennett and Waltz (2007), based on Stech and Elsäesser (2007)

Finding the dots: Detecting anomalies and inconsistencies between expectations about the evidence that will be observed and the actual observations.

Characterizing the dots: Linking anomalies to possible D&D TTTPs, and deceptive manipulations of the environment and evidence of possible adversary deception tactics.

Connecting the dots: Testing hypotheses about adversary D&D COAs against evidence of (global and local) D&D TTTPs and COAs without D&D. Assess sensitivity and support for alternative hypotheses and recollect evidence as needed.

Seeing the picture: Recommending actions to test the D&D hypotheses and exploit adversary D&D.

The first step of the process, *finding the dots*, addresses the detection of anomalies using techniques based on Whaley and Busby's congruity-incongruity and ombudsman theory—asking if the anomalies have possible D&D utility. Detection of anomalies (incongruities) is not necessarily evidence of deliberate deception, hence the importance of having a well-understood baseline of the "normal" (i.e., no D&D) operational environment, and the incidence of anomalies and incongruities from non-D&D causes, as well as from D&D TTTPs. Anomalies and incongruities in the absence of D&D may result from sensor malfunctions, unintentional distortion or corruption of data or information during transmission, atypical behavior of users in the cyber environment, or analytical errors. Deception often succeeds because the deception victim explains away anomalies and fails to attribute them to D&D TTTPs, so the first step is to find the anomalous dots and consider if they may be due to D&D.

The second step, *characterizing the dots*, involves linking anomalies to D&D TTTPs. The counterdeception process uses R. V. Jones's concepts of unmasking spoofs by examining anomalies through multiple information channels. D&D becomes harder and more detectable as more channels must be spoofed. D&D that is extremely successful in some channels may be very weak or even absent in others.

Between the second and thirds steps the counterdeception process shows "local and global deception." This is a key distinction in counterdeception analysis. A local deception represents D&D due to local conditions such as concealment of network traffic due to "local deception," (i.e., failures of local systems), rather than to "global deception," such as traffic masking and obfuscation created by an attacking adversary. Evidence of "local deceptions" will be sporadic, apparently random, widely distributed, and at best, weakly linked to various hypothetical adversary COAs; while "global deceptions" will have the opposite characteristics.

The third and fourth steps, *connecting the dots* and *seeing the picture*, use Heuer's analysis of competing hypotheses (ACH) to assess the likelihood that the observed anomalies are associated with a probable deceptive course of action (COA), and to evaluate the level of support for each identified D&D and no-D&D hypothesis. As support for hypothetical D&D COAs is found, the counterdeception analyst may wish to re-collect new information (i.e., finding new dots, indicated by the dashed line connecting the first and the third steps) in light of the possible adversary COAs and the indicators they suggest.

Stech and Elsäesser adapted Heuer's ACH for counterdeception; the most significant adaptations to Heuer's original eight-step outline for the analysis of competing hypotheses[19] are:

- Adding the "other" or "unknown" hypothesis to Heuer's step 1, that is, "Identify the possible hypotheses to be considered." This modification supports Bayesian analysis of the alternative hypotheses.
- Making sure that Heuer's step 2, "Make a list of significant evidence and arguments for and against each hypothesis," considers not only the case where evidence supports a hypothesis, $p(E|H_i)$, but also the likelihood of observing that same evidence if the hypothesis is not true, $p(E|\neg H_i)$.
- Specifically considering deception-related COAs in Heuer's steps 4, "Refine the ACH matrix," and 5, "Draw tentative conclusions about the relative likelihood of each hypothesis."
- Adding the concept of conducting operational "experiments" to Heuer's step 8, "Identify milestones for future observation that may indicate events are taking a

---

[19] Heuer, Jr., Richards J. (1999) "Chapter 8, Analysis of Competing Hypotheses," *Psychology of Intelligence Analysis,* Washington DC: Central Intelligence Agency. https://www.cia.gov/library/center-for-the-study-of-intelligence/csi-publications/books-and-monographs/psychology-of-intelligence-analysis/

different course than expected," in order to provide additional intelligence that would reveal evidence of deliberate deception.

The first two adaptations support the use of Bayesian belief networks to model the alternative COAs and to perform sensitivity analysis in order to analyze the diagnosticity of the evidence, part of Step 3 in Heuer's ACH. The last two adaptations support the comparisons of possible COAs, which might include D&D, or not; and to identify possible ways to react to the adversary to create operational experiments, which help identify possible adversary intentions and objectives.

Some suggestions for training intelligence analysts to detect deception are consistent with this model. Hobbs (2010), for example, recommended methods like this for use by IAEA analysts assessing inspections of nuclear facilities and evidence of possible deception.

7.6.1   Case Study

These analysis steps can be applied against an opponent apparently using deception to conceal their identity and operations, as in Mandiant's report on an intrusion group dubbed "APT1."

After alluding to APT1 as a prolific and well-resourced group of malicious actors with an overseas nexus since 2010, the company decided to publish documentation supporting their hypothesis that APT1 was an intelligence gathering unit under the Chinese military designated Unit 61398.[20] Comprising hundreds of victims and thousands of gigabytes of stolen intellectual property, the actors are accused of giving Chinese government-owned businesses advantages in negotiating and manufacturing that would not have been possible otherwise. The industries targeted by APT1 match industries China identified as strategic to growth, including four of seven strategic emerging industries that China identified in its 12th Five Year Plan.

7.6.1.1   Finding the Dots

This first step of the counterdeception analytic process involves collecting evidence and investigating provenance. Several indicators, or data points, were suggested as links between APT1 and a group of intrusion operators in Shanghai. The overwhelming majority of IP addresses in their "last hop" control infrastructure

---

[20] "2nd Bureau of the People's Liberation Army (PLA) General Staff Department's (GSD) 3rd Department, which is most commonly known by its Military Unit Cover Designator (MUCD) as Unit 61398." Unit 61398 functions as "the Third Department's premier entity targeting the United States and Canada, most likely focusing on political, economic, and military-related intelligence," Stokes, M.A., J. Lin, and L.C.R. Hsiao (2011) "The Chinese People's Liberation Army Signals Intelligence and Cyber Reconnaissance Infrastructure," *Project 2049 Institute,* 2011: 8, http://project2049.net/documents/pla_third_department_sigint_cyber_stokes_lin_hsiao.pdf

resolved to the same Chinese network provider, which happened to be geographically located next to a military installation. Observation of social media accounts for several actors indicate membership in a PLA unit operating out of that installation, with specialties in computer network intrusions.

7.6.1.2 Characterizing the Dots

This group was observed using both offensive deception to facilitate intrusions, and defensive methods to hide their location and identity.

Offensively, victims were sent spoofed emails with malicious contents and a plausible sender and subject line, with the intent of exploiting local vulnerabilities and installing malicious software. By creating new email accounts based on actual contacts the recipient likely knows, the actors were able to boost the likelihood of the target interacting with the message. Grammatically incorrect English phrases were common throughout these operations, indicating non-native speakers.

On a technical level, malicious software installed by the actors mimicked legitimate systems services and benign filenames, such as "svchost.exe." Malicious documents were crafted to fool mail scanning tools and appear legitimate, while including exploit code.

The actors leveraged a blend of publicly available software such as Poison Ivy and Gh0st RAT and custom tools to control remote systems. Incidental differences in configuration of public tools falls under "local deception," while usage of customized backdoors makes "global deception" possible. A network of proxies and compromised servers were used to hide the source of control servers, with inter-mediary Windows machines being used by multiple simultaneous actors over Remote Desktop.

Several tools implement covert communication methods that mimic legitimate Internet traffic such as chat clients and web services, increasing the cost of detection and chance of false positives by the defense. Since web communication is frequently allowed outbound without egregious filtering, the actors leveraged implementations of HTTP and SSL to tunnel control traffic. Further propagation on a victim's network was often accomplished by executing commands using stolen system administrator credentials and the psexec tool, commonly used for legitimate enterprise management.

7.6.1.3 Connecting the Dots

Evidence from satellite imagery, open sources, and captured actor activity appears to implicate APT1 as a Chinese state-sponsored operation.

From January 2011 to January 2013 there were 1905 instances of APT1 actors using Remote Desktop to log into control infrastructure from 832 different IP addresses. The vast majority of addresses were assigned to network providers in Shanghai, with registration in Pudong New Area of Shanghai.

Domains were largely registered to "Shanghai" with false contact information, suggesting a familiarity with the local region. Several APT1 actors used the password "2j3c1k" for authentication, likely a reference to the unit identifier for PLA 2nd Bureau, 3rd Division, 1st Section.

7.6.1.4   Seeing the Picture

The primary hypothesis is that the nature of APT1's targeted victims and the group's infrastructure and tactics align with the mission and infrastructure of PLA Unit 61398. The report concludes that the two groups are identical, based on the information shown in Table 7.2.

7.6.1.5   Hypothesis Validation

Mandiant proposed two alternative hypotheses in the report:
Either

- "A secret, resourced organization of mainland Chinese speakers with direct access to Shanghai-based telecommunications infrastructure is engaged in a multi-year, enterprise scale computer espionage campaign right outside of Unit 61398's gates, performing tasks similar to Unit 61398's known mission."

Or

- "APT1 is Unit 61398."

The counterdeception analysis process would recommend the counterdeception version of the ACH Matrix. That is, a single hypothesis "column" for APT1 = Unit 61389, another for APT1 ≠ Unit 61398, and a third for "Other Hypothesis." All evidence would be assessed with respect to its likelihood, or unlikelihood, of being observed if the given hypothesis were true, and also if the hypothesis were false, to assess diagnosticity of the evidence. For the "Other Hypothesis," all evidence would be treated as neither supporting nor ruling out "Other Hypothesis," to provide a neutral baseline against which to compare the other hypotheses. Then the overall likelihood of the two primary hypotheses can be compared to the neutral baseline "Other Hypotheses," to see if either hypothesis is strongly supported by the evidence.

Table 7.2 Characteristic comparison

Characteristic	APT1 (as directly observed)	Unit 61398 (as reported)
Mission area	Steals intellectual property from English-speaking organizations Targets strategic emerging industries identified in China's 12th Five Year Plan	Conducts computer network operations against English-speaking targets
Tools, Tactics, and Procedures (TTPs)	Organized, funded, disciplined operators with specific targeting objectives and a code of ethics (e.g., we have not witnessed APT1 destroy property or steal money which contrasts most "hackers" and even the most sophisticated organize crime syndicates)	Conducts military-grade computer network operations
Scale of operations	Continuously stealing hundreds of terabytes from 141 organizations since at least 2006; simultaneously targeting victims across at least 20 major industries Size of "hop" infrastructure and continuous malware updates suggest at least dozens (but probably hundreds) of operators with hundreds of support personnel	As part of the PLA, has the resources (people, money, influence) necessary to orchestrate operation at APT1's scale Has hundreds, perhaps thousands of people, as suggested by the size for their facilities and position within the PLA
Expertise of personnel	Some English language proficiency Malware development Computer intrusions Ability to identify data worth stealing in 20 industries	English language training pre-requisites Operating system internals, digital signal processing, steganography Recruiting from Chinese technology universities
Location	APT1 actor used a Shanghai phone number to register email accounts Two of four "home" Shanghai net blocks are assigned to the Pudong New Area Systems used by APT1 intruders have Simplified Chinese language settings Actor's location is the Pudong New Area	Headquarters and other facilities spread throughout the Pudong New Area of Shanghai, China
Infrastructure	Ready access to four main net blocks in Shanghai, hosted by China Unicom (one of two Tier 1 ISPs in China) Some use of China Telecom IP addresses (the other Tier 1 ISP)	Building network infrastructure with China Telecom in the name of national defense

Chapter 8
Capability Maturity Model

National Deception Program: One might hope that some sort of national deception program could be created based on a collection of traps strategically planted across national infrastructure components, tied together by some sort of deception analysis backbone. Such an approach is unlikely, because deception remains a poorly understood security approach, and infrastructure managers would be very hesitant to allow traps to be implanted in production systems. These traps, if they malfunction or do not work as advertised, could trick authorized users or impede normal operations.

Edward Amoroso (2011) *Cyber attacks: protecting national infrastructure.* Burlington MA: Elsevier.

… when there are limited seats at the strategy table, the cyberwarrior may be tagged to be the "deception rep." However, there is no reason to believe that a person trained in cyberspace operations is any more capable of being a deception planner than a tank driver or logistician would be.

Larry K. Wentz, Charles L. Barry, and Stuart H. Starr (2009) *Military Perspectives on Cyberpower.* Washington DC: Center for Technology and National Security Policy, National Defense University.

As cyber-D&D becomes a well-recognized, mainstream technique in cyber defense operations, a capability maturity model (CMM) can enable organizations to assess their readiness to conduct cyber-D&D operations. The systematic framework provided by a CMM enables organizations to implement a strategic cyber-D&D capability, assess the maturity of that capability over time, and estimate the capabilities of cyber adversaries.

In general, a CMM[1] is a collection of practices that help organizations to improve their processes in a specific domain. "Maturity" refers to the degree of formality and optimization of the processes used in an organization. As shown in Fig. 8.1, maturity levels range from ad hoc, unpredictable practices (Level 1), to formally defined process steps (Level 3), to process improvement optimization (Level 5).

---

[1] The first CMMs were created after study of data collected from organizations that contracted with the U.S. Department of Defense. These CMMs dealt specifically with Software (SW-CMM), Systems Engineering (SECM), and Integrated Product Development.

© Springer International Publishing Switzerland 2015
K.E. Heckman et al., *Cyber Denial, Deception and Counter Deception,*
Advances in Information Security 64, DOI 10.1007/978-3-319-25133-2_8

Characteristics of the Maturity levels

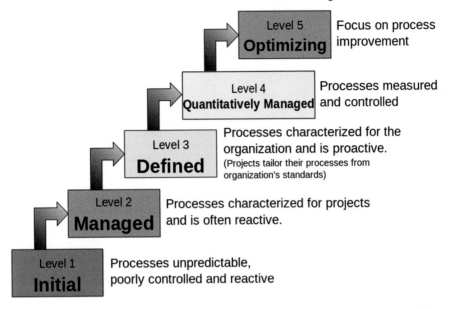

Level 5 Optimizing	Focus on process improvement
Level 4 Quantitatively Managed	Processes measured and controlled
Level 3 Defined	Processes characterized for the organization and is proactive. (Projects tailor their processes from organization's standards)
Level 2 Managed	Processes characterized for projects and is often reactive.
Level 1 Initial	Processes unpredictable, poorly controlled and reactive

Fig. 8.1 Maturity of processes in the capability maturity model. *Source:* Wikipedia—capability maturity model integration

8.1 Cyber-D&D Maturity Model Framework

This chapter describes a cyber-D&D CMM that provides a coherent blueprint to enable organizations to assess, measure, and increase the maturity of their current cyber-D&D operations, as well as offering a basis for developing specific cyber-D&D innovations. The cyber-D&D CMM we outline in this chapter takes a holistic view of the people, services, processes, and technology and techniques needed to achieve strategic cyber-D&D capabilities. This model can serve as a detailed and explicit framework for cyber-D&D capability development, and help organizations characterize cyber-D&D capability maturity for themselves and for their adversaries by providing explicit, observable, and often measurable indicators of specific cyber-D&D capabilities.

For example, the cyber-D&D CMM may reveal that an organization's deception capabilities are random and ad hoc, usually fail to mislead an opponent, can be readily anticipated and countered (thus failing to attain the deception objectives), and lack the ability to correctly characterize an opponent's response. Organizations with such immature capabilities should build expertise before attempting to engage in cyber-D&D. The cyber-D&D CMM provides a systematic basis for building such expertise. By contrast, mature deception capabilities are well understood by the deception operators in organizations at higher maturity levels; deception capabilities are repeatable,

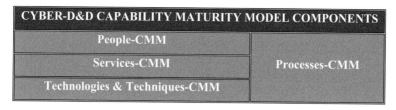

Fig. 8.2 Cyber-D&D capability maturity model components

customized to individual opponents, and not obvious. They also incorporate inter-domain data and anticipate the opponent's response to deceptions.

A cyber-D&D CMM also helps organizations to evaluate the cyber deception capabilities of opponents, and to estimate an opponent's future evolution toward mature capabilities. This chapter presents brief examples of cyber-D&D maturity drawn from real-world descriptions of cyber offensive and defensive deception capabilities.

To define a CMM for cyber-D&D, we focus on four capability categories: people, services, processes, and technology and technique (Fig. 8.2) and define each category at the five maturity levels. Together, the categories comprise an organizational model for a holistic set of enterprise-wide cyber-D&D capabilities.

The People capability category for cyber-D&D focuses on developing an effective cyber-D&D workforce, or a cadre of cyber-D&D practitioners who can develop, coordinate, and control cyber-deceptions. The Service capability model describes the maturity of cyber-D&D services provided by the deception organization to the target of the deception on behalf of the deceiver's organization. We use the term "servicing the deception target" much the same way as the U.S. Air Force describes "servicing the target," as in "aircraft servicing targets nominated for immediate attack."[2] The people who operate a cyber-D&D capability (People-CMM) and the cyber-D&D services (Services-CMM) used against adversaries on behalf of the defending organization comprise the two critical capability areas.

The maturity of the organization's capability to develop and deploy cyber-D&D technologies and techniques (Tech & Tech-CMM) determines the quality and innovative character of the organization's cyber-D&D tools by evaluating the technical skills and technology artifacts produced and used by the deception organization to deliver cyber-D&D activities. In support of these people, services, and technologies and techniques capabilities, the organization's process capability maturity determines the effectiveness of its overall planning, preparation, and execution of the cyber enterprise operational processes (Process-CMM). The Process-CMM describes the five maturity levels of organizational cyber-D&D processes, as applied across the other three CMM areas, and includes the tracking of cost, schedule, performance, and impact, as well as management support for conducting cyber-D&D operations.[3] We use these analyses in Table 8.1 to define basic elements of

[2] *Air Operations Center (AOC) Standard Operating Procedure (SOP)* Twelfth Air Force (12AF) Air Force Forces (AFFOR). http://www.fas.org/man/dod-101/usaf/docs/aoc12af/part05.htm

[3] Appendix D reviews historical and contemporary analyses to describe the components of a mature capability for national strategic denial and deception.

Table 8.1 Strategic D&D capabilities

Capability maturity categories	Strategic deception capabilities [see Appendix D]
People	• People to focus on detection of adversary D&D and to assess and counter foreign D&D • D&D teams operating under a standing strategic surprise/deception entity • D&D practitioners: a well-organized cadre of astute and experienced career plotters of D&D, consisting of individuals with technical virtuosity, creativity, flair, pluck, artistry, a keen interest in playing the D&D and CD game, ability to place themselves in the adversary's shoes, and a supple and narrative (or abductive, rather than analytic, or inductive-deductive) mindset • Knowledge of adversary intelligence capabilities • Knowledge to exploit preconceptions and biases of adversary intelligence • Sophisticated understanding of the adversary's intelligence-gathering processes and political/decision cycles • Knowledge of the adversary: understanding the deception target's preconceptions and perspectives well enough to know what misinformation will deceive and lead the adversary to act in the desired manner; a one-size-fits-all approach will not suffice.
Services	• Freedom and organizational capabilities to conduct wide-ranging, large-scale, long-duration, and extensive deception operations • Capabilities to exploit preconceptions and biases of adversary intelligence • Capabilities to conduct D&D sensitivity analysis of own and adversary intelligence estimates • Intelligence on adversary strategic objectives, strategy, perceptions of U.S. strengths and weaknesses, and adversary cultural norms and preferences • Capabilities to exploit the preconceptions and biases of adversary intelligence and decision-makers • Improved intelligence estimation, including multiple estimates of adversary intentions and possible plans, assumption checking, analysis of competing hypotheses, and impact estimates • Support of information operations through cyber-D&D • Creation of surprise with deception at both the operational and strategic levels; launch of sophisticated, orchestrated events that the adversary will believe, while protecting own critical information assets • Strategic coherence: a coherent strategic deception plan to achieve objectives and to determine how the deception target must act to attain its own objectives.

(continued)

Table 8.1 (continued)

Capability maturity categories	Strategic deception capabilities [see Appendix D]
Processes	• Long-standing historical, organizational, and operational traditions of using political, economic, and military strategic deception • Extensive organizational and doctrinal bases for strategic deception • National-level coordination of strategic deception across political, economic, and military objectives • Processes to inform defense strategy to include effects of own strategic D&D • Strategic counterintelligence and operations to degrade foreign intelligence capabilities • Programs to focus on detection of adversary D&D, and to assess and counter foreign D&D • D&D analysis ("red teaming") of U.S. analytic products • Situation awareness, linked to intelligence and strategy adaptive behavior adjustment and learning • Modern indications and warning process, intelligence for net assessments, and a Capability Assessment Warning and Response Office • Organizational integration of strategy, intelligence, and strategic deception, with common operational pictures and high-level coordination and control across national security elements • D&D cadre roles: including intelligence D&D action analysts engaged in spotting adversaries who seem ripe for deception and bringing them to the attention of policymakers, D&D tradecraft advisors and plotters, and D&D executive control and coordination agents • Organizational infrastructure for deception and security measures: a deception control group with the bureaucratic clout to orchestrate the deception effort, using other agencies of government as necessary • Feedback: deception control group with steadily flowing, current, and reliable information about the adversary's actions, intentions, and reactions, and intelligence on whether deception target has taken the bait, and how the target assesses and reacts to the misinformation thus acquired.
Technology and techniques	• Intelligence capabilities to gain rapid and correct knowledge of the impact of deception operations • Capabilities for perception management of adversary decision-makers, as well as D&D of adversary intelligence systems and organizations • Capabilities to deceive adversaries about own plans, intentions, and actions, with deception integral to any major operation or campaign • Channels to reach the adversary: the deception control group must have information channels to reach the adversary target, and knowledge of the target's intelligence collection, analysis, and estimation capabilities.

strategic deception capabilities in terms of the four capability categories used in the cyber-D&D CMM.

Based on this description of strategic D&D capabilities, we identify some unique features of strategic cyber-D&D capabilities and apply the CMM framework to define the specific components (people, services, processes, technologies and techniques) required for a mature capability for strategic cyber-D&D.

Table 8.2 shows an overview of the maturity levels of the cyber-D&D CMM framework. Capabilities become more standardized as they mature and move from Level 1 to Level 5. Each capability category also moves from handling tactical deceptions (at the lower levels) to strategic deceptions (at the higher levels). At the highest level, cyber-D&D influences overall doctrine for both defense and offense. At capability maturity Level 5, an organization shapes its adversaries' strategies and can optimize its own deception personnel, processes, services, and techniques.

8.2 People-CMM

Cyber-D&D personnel are the foundation for an organization's capability to deliver cyber-D&D services. The People-CMM helps planners to address the personnel issues that arise in any organization[4] and devise approaches to improving individual competencies, developing effective teams, motivating the workforce to enhance performance, and recruiting and shaping the workforce needed to fulfill the organization's business objectives.

The capability of cyber-D&D personnel has a strongly paradoxical aspect, as suggested by Amoroso[5]:

> … the success of deceptive [honeypot and honeynet] traps is assisted by the fact that intruders will almost always view designers and operators of national [cyber] assets as being sloppy in their actions, deficient in their training, and incompetent in their knowledge. This extremely negative opinion of the individuals running national infrastructure is a core belief in virtually every hacking community in the world (and is arguably justified in some environments). … this low expectation is an important element that helps make stealth deception much more feasible.

That is, when adversaries view cyber-D&D defenders as lacking basic cyber security capabilities (not to mention cyber-D&D capabilities), cyber-D&D is likely to be more successful in deflecting or defeating intruders. This paradox suggests that organizations should exercise discretion, if not outright secrecy, regarding cyber-D&D defensive capabilities, much as they currently guard offensive cyber capabilities. It also suggests that cyber-D&D defenders may consider adopting a

---

[4] See Software Engineering Institute (2001) *People Capability Maturity Model (P-CMM), Version 2.0.* Carnegie Mellon University Technical Report CMU/SEI-2001-MM-01, July 2001.

[5] Amoroso, Edward G. (2011) *Cyber attack: protecting national infrastructure.* Burlington MA: Elsevier, p. 33.

Table 8.2 Overview of the Cyber-D&D Maturity Model Framework

Maturity level	1: Initial	2: Managed	3: Defined/Standardized	4: Predictable/quantitatively managed	5: Optimizing and innovating
Generic definition of maturity levels[a]	Processes are ad hoc and chaotic. The organization usually does not provide a stable environment to support processes. Success depends on the competence and heroics of the people and not on the use of proven processes. Maturity Level 1 organizations are characterized by a tendency to overcommit and to abandon processes in crises, and are unable to repeat successes.	Work groups establish a foundation by institutionalizing selected processes for project and work management, support, and service establishment and delivery. Work groups define a strategy, create work plans, and monitor and control work as planned. Configuration management and process and product quality assurance are institutionalized; the work group measures and analyzes process performance.	The organization uses defined processes to manage work; embeds project and work management, and best practices; verifies that products meet requirements; ensures products and services meet customer needs; and ensures processes are rigorously described, tailored from organization SOPs, well characterized and understood, and described in standards, procedures, tools, and methods.	Service providers establish quantitative objectives for quality and performance, and use objective criteria in managing processes. Quantitative objectives are based on the needs of the customer, end users, organization, and process implementers. Quality and process performance is understood in statistical terms and is managed throughout the life of processes. Performance baselines and models are used to set quality and process performance objectives to achieve business objectives.	The organization evaluates its overall performance using data collected from multiple work groups. The organization continually improves its processes based on quantitative understanding of business objectives and performance needs. It uses a quantitative approach to understand variations in process and process outcomes and applies incremental and innovative process and technological improvements.

(continued)

Table 8.2 (continued)

Maturity level	1: Initial	2: Managed	3: Defined/Standardized	4: Predictable/quantitatively managed	5: Optimizing and innovating
People	• Ad hoc recruitment, training, and cyber-D&D cadre workforce practices • Staffing with personnel lacking training or experience in cyber-D&D • Difficulty retaining talented cyber-D&D plotters, planners, and controllers • No cyber-D&D personnel training or training management	• Systematic recruitment, training, and retention of cyber-D&D cadre • Multi-level skill set criteria: novice, journeyman, expert, master • Multi-level cyber-D&D training courses and curricula, from AA to BA, PhD, and post-doc • Work performance lessons learned and after-action analyses used for cyber-D&D skills enhancement programs	• Competence systems: defined skills set and performance goals • Cyber-D&D personnel competence evaluations • Career paths for cyber-D&D cadre • Best practices for hiring integrated organization-wide • Circulation of cyber-D&D cadre from training positions to planning/operational or technical positions and back	• Individual- and team-level cyber-D&D personnel assessment systems • Evidence-based quantitative personnel assessments of qualifications and on-the-job (OTJ) cyber-D&D performance • Cyber-D&D integrated with other workforce competencies • Systems to predict and manage future personnel OTJ cyber-D&D performance • Knowledge capture and transfer systems for cyber-D&D skills and techniques • Cost-benefit-impact evaluations of cyber-D&D training and personnel systems	• Continuous improvement of cyber-D&D personnel and skills: peer coaching; networked cognition; crowd-sourcing; organizational in-reach and out-reach • Grounded research and development (R&D) on cyber-D&D personnel-training-skill-performance practices and technologies: collaboration systems; training and coaching; crowd and network knowledge transfer; individual-team interactions; personnel ROI and impact analyses • Dynamic evidence-based adjustment of cyber-D&D personnel systems

Services				
• Cyber-D&D seen as esoteric, "one-off" dark art • No notion of cyber-D&D as an integrated and institutionalized cyber defensive service • Ad hoc heroic efforts • No cyber-D&D environment or support	• Defined deception delivery processes and strategy • Deception operation monitoring and management, deception process and product quality controls, and documentation for repeatability • Lessons learned and after-action assessments linked to quality control, service delivery measurement, and repeatability documentation	• Use of defined cyber-D&D TTPs and service delivery processes to service the deception target and assess impacts and results • Use of project and work management and services best practices, including deception service continuity and incident resolution and prevention • Adoption of organization-wide framework of cyber-D&D competencies, as well as for the architecture for the organization's cyber-D&D defenses	• Customer-driven quantitative objectives for quality and deception efficiency and effectiveness • Statistical analysis of cyber-D&D service efficiency and effectiveness performance • Predictable cyber-D&D service performance • Defect reduction and prevention in cyber-D&D service management	• Focus on continuous improvement in cyber-D&D services quality and delivery at the organizational level • Deception quality and service management outcomes guaranteed with high probability

(continued)

Table 8.2 (continued)

Maturity level	1: Initial	2: Managed	3: Defined/Standardized	4: Predictable/quantitatively managed	5: Optimizing and innovating
Technology and techniques	• Ad hoc development and deployment	• Systematic and cost-effective deployment of D&D technologies. • Metrics to track technology development, integration and deployment	• Catalog of D&D TTPs tailored to desired outcomes available for defensive and offensive playbook development	• High degree of predictable outcome and success • Quantitative management of development and deployment • Systemic reuse and efficiency improvements • Defect reduction • Outcome analysis of D&D techniques	• Total and continuous quality improvement • Metrics for organization-wide improvements in technology production and deployment
Processes	• No D&D support processes	• Initial organizational processes to track requirements, schedule, cost, and performance of cyber-D&D work units • Executive sponsorship of D&D process improvements	• Well-defined standardization for cyber-D&D processes: preparation, deployment, operations, and support • Standardized management of cyber-D&D operations	• Quantitative management of cyber-D&D products, services, and processes • Tracking of organization-wide metrics and performance benchmarks • D&D product and service process integration	• Continuous improvements through instrumentation and metrics, feedback, and self-correction and optimization of cyber-D&D planning, performance, and capabilities • Programs for the prevention of defects and problems • Research into new types of processes

[a]See Software Engineering Institute (2010) *CMMI for Services, Version 1.3: Improving processes for providing better services*. Carnegie Mellon University Technical Report CMU/SEI-2010-TR-034, November 2010. Software Engineering Institute (2001) *People Capability Maturity Model (P-CMM), Version 2.0*. Carnegie Mellon University Technical Report CMU/SEI-2001-MM-01, July 2001. Forrester, Eileen C., Brandon L. Buteau, and Sandy Shrum (2011) *CMMI for Services: guidelines for superior service*, 2nd ed. Boston MA: Addison-Wesley. Chrissis, Mary Beth, Mike Konrad, and Sandy Shrum (2003) *CMMI: Guidelines for Process Integration and Product Improvement*. Boston MA: Addison-Wesley

deception tactic of appearing to be Level 1 organizations with respect to cyber-D&D maturity.[6]

Level 1 People Maturity: Organizations at Level 1 (Initial) maturity may treat cyber-D&D skill as a dark art: innate, untrainable, or nonexistent. If they recognize cyber-D&D skills at all, their cyber-D&D recruiting, training, and workforce practices are ad hoc and inconsistent. Consequently, Level 1 organizations have difficulty identifying, hiring, employing, and retaining cyber-D&D skills and talent, such as cyber-D&D plotters, planners, and controllers, and respond to talent shortages with slogans and exhortations. They have no (or ill-defined) cyber-D&D workforce practices, no training and personnel management, and no trained individuals explicitly responsible for performing or managing cyber-D&D. Generally managers and supervisors in Level 1 organizations are ill prepared to perform cyber-D&D workforce responsibilities, and receive no guidance in cyber-D&D workforce management, such as evaluation, development, advancement, and knowledge management. Cyber-D&D defenders lack SOPs, rules or guidelines, and management "top cover" for their D&D activities.

Indicators of Level 2 Cyber-D&D People Maturity:
Since 2002, the PLA has been creating IW militia units, comprised of personnel from the commercial information technology sector and universities. These units represent an operational nexus between PLA CNO operations and Chinese civilian information security professionals.

In 2003… PLA media reporting indicates that IW militia units are tasked with offensive and defensive CNO and EW responsibilities, psychological warfare and deception operations, although the available sources do not explain the lines of authority, subordination or the nature of their specific tasking.

Hagestad (2012) *21st Century Chinese Cyberwarfare*

Indicators that an organization has Level 1 people maturity include:

- Nonexistent or inconsistent cyber-D&D performance
- Nonexistent or displaced responsibility for cyber-D&D
- Nonexistent or ad hoc and ritualistic cyber-D&D practices
- Workforce and management emotionally detached from defensive cyber-D&D.

---

[6] Since there also are possible benefits in some situations of appearing to be highly capable cyber-D&D defenders (e.g., for purposes of cyber deterrence), there is no one-size-fits-all tactic regarding overt or covert cyber-D&D skill presentation. Amoroso (2011) notes "the psychology of understanding and managing adversary views [of defensive cyber deception competence] is not straightforward. This soft issue must become part of the national infrastructure protection equation but will obviously require a new set of skills among security experts."

Level 2 People Maturity: Organizations at Level 2 (Managed) maturity have SOPs specifically addressing cyber-D&D staffing, training and development, performance management, compensation, personnel development and advancement, work environments, and intra-staff and staff-management communication and coordination.

Indicators that an organization has Level 2 people maturity include:

- Systematic recruitment, training, and retention of cyber-D&D cadre
- Stable cyber-D&D staff positions (e.g., plotters, planners, controllers)
- Multi-level skill set criteria (novice, journeyman, expert, master)
- Multi-level cyber-D&D training courses and curricula (differentiated degree levels, e.g., AA, BA, PhD, and post-doc)[7]
- Managers who address problems[8] that hinder cyber-D&D operations
- Management commitment to continuously improve the knowledge, skills, motivation, and performance of cyber-D&D staff
- Processes to capture cyber-D&D lessons learned and after-action analyses for cyber-D&D skills enhancement programs.

Level 3 People Maturity: Organizations at Level 3 (Defined/Standardized) maturity develop an organization-wide infrastructure across cyber-D&D personnel practices that tie the capability of the cyber-D&D personnel to achieving the organization's operational and strategic goals. The primary objective at this maturity level is to enable the organization to gain a strategic competitive advantage through various cyber-D&D competences and combinations applied to accomplish its strategic objectives, and thus make cyber-D&D personnel critical enablers of the organization's strategy. At Level 3, the organization directly connects these strategic cyber-D&D workforce competences to its strategic process, service, and technology and technique processes and capabilities.

A Level 3 organization builds an organization-wide framework of cyber-D&D competencies into the architecture for the organization's cyber-D&D defenses. Each cyber-D&D competence is an element of this architecture, and dependences among cyber-D&D competence-based processes (e.g., the engineering of specific D&D techniques for a specific deception plan and operation) describe the interactions among the

---

[7] So far as we can determine, there are no degree programs in cyber-D&D in U.S. universities at any educational level, while there are programs in *computer security*. A few institutions offers courses bearing on cyber-D&D: Neil C. Rowe and Dorothy E. Denning at the Naval Postgraduate School teach and publish extensively on cyber deception. Research on cyber deception is conducted at Dartmouth College's Institute for Security, Technology, and Society (ISTS) by (among others) Professors George Cybenko, Eugene Santos, and Paul Thompson. North Carolina State University has at least one PhD graduate in cyber-deception: James J. Yuill, author of *Defensive Computer-Security Deception Operations: Processes, Principles and Techniques.* Dissertation North Carolina State University, Raleigh NC, 2006. This dearth of U.S. training or degree programs in cyber-D&D make acquisition of trained cyber-D&D personnel problematic in the near term.

[8] Some examples of problems that would hinder performance of the cyber-D&D staff might include: work overload, environmental distractions, absent or unclear job specifications, absent or unclear performance objectives or feedback, absent or unclear authorizes, lack of relevant knowledge or skill, poor communications and coordination, low morale.

cyber-D&D defensive architectural elements. Thus, the architecture of cyber-D&D workforce and defenses must tie into the organization's strategic plan. Workforce practices become mechanisms through which this cyber-D&D defense architecture is continually realigned with changes in organization objectives. The structure of the organization's cyber-D&D workforce must evolve as strategic conditions and technologies change. The organization develops strategic workforce plans for the required capability in current or anticipated cyber-D&D competencies. These plans identify actions to acquire and develop the level of talent needed in each area of competence.

Indicators that an organization has Level 3 people maturity include:

- Cyber-D&D competence communities with common knowledge, skills, and process abilities
- Competence communities that apply collective knowledge, skills, and process abilities to cyber-D&D operations
- Measures of cyber-D&D capability (personnel, processes, services, technology and technique)
- Workforce practices and architecture that focus on motivating, training, developing, and enabling strategic cyber-D&D competences
- A cyber-D&D professional culture that emphasizes sharing responsibility for developing increasing levels of competence in the organization's strategic cyber-D&D capabilities.

Level 4 People Maturity: Organizations at Level 4 (Quantitatively Managed) maturity manage cyber-D&D defensive personnel, capability, and performance quantitatively. A Level 4 organization uses data generated by competence-based processes to establish cyber-D&D process capability baselines, and begins to predict its capability for cyber-D&D because it can quantify the capability of its cyber-D&D staff and of the competence-based processes they use. Management can make more accurate predictions about future D&D performance and better decisions about tradeoffs involving cyber-D&D service delivery, process performance, or technology and techniques issues. Personnel reuse competence-based cyber-D&D service delivery and processes of workgroups; thus, learning spreads and cyber-D&D successes increase as process reuse replaces redevelopment. Managers empower workgroups with responsibility and authority for managing day-to-day operations and turn attention to strategic organizational issues.

Indicators that an organization has Level 4 people maturity include:

- Individual- and workgroup-level personnel assessment systems for cyber-D&D professionals
- Evidence-based quantitative personnel assessments of qualifications and OTJ cyber-D&D performance (cyber-D&D successes)
- Integration of cyber-D&D is integrated with other workforce competences and processes (e.g., technologies and techniques development of cyber-D&D TTPs)
- Systems to predict and manage future personnel OTJ cyber-D&D performance
- Systems that capture and transfer knowledge of and processes for cyber-D&D skills and techniques
- Cost-benefit-impact evaluations of cyber-D&D training and personnel systems.

Level 5 People Maturity: Organizations at Level 5 (Optimizing and Innovating) focus entirely on continual improvement in cyber-D&D capabilities: to the capability of individuals and workgroups, the effectiveness of competence-based processes, and workforce cyber-D&D practices and activities. Such organizations use the quantitative management activities established at Level 4 to guide continuous improvements at Level 5.

Indicators that an organization has Level 5 people maturity include:

- Cyber-D&D personal work processes integrated into standard operating procedures for other inter-dependent workgroups
- Cyber-D&D peers, mentors, and coaches who guide improvements for individuals and workgroups
- Improvements to cyber-D&D workforce practices that come from lessons learned, suggestions, internal and external research and development, quantitative management activities.

Table 8.3 summarizes some of the key indicators of the various maturity levels of the cyber-D&D People-CMM.

8.3 Services-CMM

This CMM deals with cyber-D&D as a service on behalf of an organization, using D&D to neutralize the organization's cyber adversaries.[9] In contrast to the usual two-party relationship between service customer and service provider, in which the provider and the customer both benefit, cyber-D&D services involve relationships among three parties: the defended organization as a whole, the cadre that provides cyber-D&D services, and the adversary. Since the adversary interacts with the defending organization, delivering high-quality cyber-D&D services requires continual situation awareness, target analysis, learning, adaption, and adjustment of the cyber-D&D operations.

8.3.1 Service Processes

A process consists of set of interrelated activities that transform inputs into outputs to achieve a given purpose. The cyber-D&D effort involves general processes that apply to all work efforts, as well as processes specifically related to the delivery of

---

[9] A general capability maturity model for services, titled CMMI for Services, has been developed by the Software Engineering Institute. We apply the concepts of this model to cyber-D&D services. Software Engineering Institute (2010) *CMMI for Services, Version 1.3.* Carnegie Mellon University Technical Report CMU/SEI-2010-TR-034, November 2010. http://www.sei.cmu.edu/reports/10tr034.pdf See also Forrester, Eileen C., Brandon L. Buteau, and Sandy Shrum (2011) *CMMI for Services: Guidelines for Superior Service, 2nd ed.* Boston MA: Pearson Education, Inc.

Table 8.3 Key indicators of cyber-D&D people capability maturity

| Maturity levels | People management threads | | | |
	Developing individual capability	Building workgroups and culture	Motivating and managing performance	Shaping the workforce
5 Optimizing	Continuous improvement of cyber-D&D personnel and skill; peer coaching; networked cognition; crowd-sourcing; organizational in-reach & out-reach		Dynamic evidence-based adjustment of cyber-D&D personnel systems	R&D grounded on cyber-D&D personnel-training-skill-performance practices & technologies
4 Predictable	Evidence-based quantitative personnel assessment of qualifications & OTJ cyber-D&D performance	Systems for knowledge capture and transfer of cyber-D&D skills and techniques	Cost-benefit impact evaluations of cyber- D&D training & personnel systems; Individual & team cyber-D&D assessment systems	Cyber-D&D integrated w/other workforce competencies; systems to predict & manage future OTJ cyber-D&D performance
3 Defined	Career paths for cyber-D&D cadre	Circulation of cyber-D&D cadre from training positions to planning/ operational/ technical positions & back	Competence-based systems: skills set & performance goals; Cyber-D&D personnel competence evaluations	Best cyber-D&D personnel practices Integrated organization-wide
2 Managed	Multi-level cyber-D&D training courses & curricula: AA, BA, PhD, post-doc	Multi-level skill set criteria: novice, journeyman, expert, master	Work performance lessons learned & after-action analyses used for cyber-D&D skills enhancement programs	Systematic recruitment, training, & retention of cyber-D&D cadre

OTJ on the job

deception services.[10] Seventeen process areas affect the Service CMM: seven process areas are specific to the Services CMM, as shown in Table 8.4.[11]

8.3.2   Maturity Levels of Delivery of Cyber-D&D Services

Level 1 Service Maturity: At Level 1 (Initial), cyber-D&D services are ad hoc and chaotic. Cyber-D&D may be viewed as an esoteric "one-off" dark art, rather than as part of the organization's cyber defender services. Cyber-D&D personnel are not

[10] James R. Persse (2001) *Implementing the Capability Maturity Model.* New York NY: John Wiley & Sons, p. 47.

[11] Forrester, Eileen (2012) *CMMI for Services (CMMI-SVC): Current State.* Pittsburgh, PA: Software Engineering Institute, Carnegie Mellon University, October 2012.

Table 8.4 Service CMM process areas

Service-specific CMM process areas	Core (shared with service) CMM process areas
1. Service Delivery (SD): setting up agreements, taking care of service requests, and operating the service system;	1. Causal Analysis and Resolution (CAR): getting to the sources of selected work results and taking effective action to enable good results and prevent bad results in other work;
2. Strategic Service Management (STSM): deciding what services you should be providing, making them standard, and letting people know about them;	2. Configuration Management (CM): controlling changes to your crucial work products;
3. Capacity and Availability Management (CAM): making sure you have enough of the resources you need to deliver services and that they are available when needed—at an appropriate cost;	3. Decision Analysis and Resolution (DAR): using a formal decision-making process on the decisions that matter most in your business;
4. Service System Development (SSD): making sure you have everything you need to deliver services, including people, processes, consumables, and equipment;	4. Integrated Work Management (IWM): getting the most from defined processes and all participants when managing complex services;
5. Incident Resolution and Prevention (IRP): handling what goes wrong—and preventing it from going wrong if you can;	5. Measurement and Analysis (MA): knowing what to count and measure to manage your service;
6. Service Continuity (SCON): being ready to recover from a disaster and get back to delivering your service;	6. Organizational Performance Management (OPM): managing your improvements and innovations using a statistical understanding of your process performance;
7. Service System Transition (SST): getting new systems in place, changing existing systems, or retiring obsolete systems—all while making sure nothing goes terribly wrong with the service.	7. Organizational Process Definition (OPD): establishing standard processes and spreading them throughout your organization;
	8. Organizational Process Focus (OPF): figuring out your current process strengths and weaknesses, planning what to do to improve, and putting those improvements in place;
	9. Organizational Process Performance (OPP): making sure you understand your process performance and how it affects service quality;
	10. Organizational Training (OT): developing the skills and knowledge your people need to deliver superior service;
	11. Process and Product Quality Assurance (PPQA): checking to see that you are actually doing things the way you say you will in your policies, standards, and procedures;
	12. Quantitative Work Management (QWM): managing service to quantitative process and performance objectives;
	13. Requirements Management (REQM): keeping clear with your customers and other stakeholders about the service you provide, and adjusting when you find inconsistencies or mismatched expectations;
	14. Risk Management (RSKM): supporting the success of your service mission by anticipating problems and how you will handle them—before they occur;
	15. Supplier Agreement Management (SAM): getting what you need and what you expect from suppliers who affect your service;
	16. Work Monitoring and Control (WMC): making sure what's supposed to be happening in your service work is happening, and fixing what isn't going as planned;
	17. Work Planning (WP): estimating costs, effort, and schedules, figuring out how you'll provide the service, and involving the right people—all while watching your risks and making sure you've got the resources you need.

explicitly identified or managed. The organization provides no stable environment to support cyber-D&D services. Cyber-D&D success depends on the competence and heroic efforts of the people in the organization, rather than on the use of proven and managed cyber-D&D services or processes. Despite this, Level 1 organizations may execute effective cyber-D&D TTPs, but doing so frequently requires extraordinary efforts, and exceeds budgets and schedules. Further, the TTPs may unpredictably fail to deny or deceive or otherwise fail to meet operational needs, or pose risks to other organizational processes (e.g., OPSEC).

Level 1 service maturity organizations typically exhibit:

- Nonexistent, ad hoc, poorly defined cyber-D&D services
- Nonexistent, ad hoc, poorly defined responsibility for cyber-D&D service provision
- Nonexistent, ad hoc, ritualistic cyber-D&D service support and management
- A workforce and management emotionally detached from providing cyber-D&D defensive services.

Capability management of cyber-D&D service delivery takes place at maturity Levels 2 and 3. Other core capability management processes that support cyber-D&D service delivery occur at levels 2 through 5. The definitions of specific service delivery areas are adapted to a cyber-D&D service delivery model, and service goals (SGs) and service practices (SPs) are adapted to cyber-D&D service processes.

Level 2 Service Maturity: At maturity Level 2 (Managed), cyber-D&D work groups create the foundation for providing effective cyber-D&D services by developing service (i.e., D&D) delivery processes and linking D&D services to project and work management and to support. The work groups define a service strategy for regularly delivering cyber-D&D defense, create plans for specific cyber-D&D TTPs, and monitor and control cyber-D&D defense operations to ensure cyber-D&D is delivered as planned. They establish cyber-D&D performance (input) and impact effectiveness (output) measures and analyze cyber-D&D performance and impacts on overall organizational performance.

Indicators of Level 3 Cyber D&D Service Maturity:
… in November 2006 Chinese paper *Zhanqi Bap,* [reported] China must prepare a good plan, learn to show what is false and hide what is true, and remain flexible in order to deceive an enemy force. The intelligence an enemy gathers must be consistent with its subjective assessment. An enemy's media reporting must be controlled as well with no contradictions existing between military and civilian points of view on the situation at hand. … In particular, China's approach must be comprehensive for deception to succeed: "We must collect and analyze the characteristics of enemy commanders, enemy units, and the battlefield. We must gain a clear understanding of the main reconnaissance measures and methods the enemy uses. We must take the intelligence

collected and carefully analyze and study it, think hard about the situations our forces could encounter on the move, tie in with our actual situation and formulate countermeasures, and take truly practical measures of deception, to include the object of the deception, its content, method, security measures, and the timetable for its implementation."

Thomas, T.L (2009) *The Dragon's Quantum Leap: Transforming from a Mechanized to an Informatized Force.*

At Level 2 maturity, organizations manage cyber-D&D services, including work activities, processes, work products, and deception TTPs. Cyber-D&D work groups ensure the deception TTPs support the organization's cyber-D&D and related plans, and follow the organization's cyber deception policies. The work groups ensure the availability of adequate D&D resources, assign responsibility for performing the cyber-D&D services, and ensure those services achieve the results agreed on with the organization's planners. They monitor and control the deception services and inform the relevant stakeholders in the organization about the D&D results: successes, failures, and unknown impacts. During times of heightened attack, cyber-D&D process discipline at maturity Level 2 helps to ensure that deception TTPs and practices remain standardized, consistent with overall planning, and expressly managed.

SD, the one CMM practice area at maturity Level 2, delivers cyber-D&D services in accordance with cyber-D&D deception agreements and plans with the organization's operational and security elements, and obtains specific deception results when the deception target is serviced. SGs and SPs establish cyber-D&D service agreements; prepare for cyber-D&D service delivery; and deliver cyber-D&D services.

Level 3 Service Maturity: At maturity Level 3 (Defined) the organization's cyber-D&D becomes standardized across the organization. Cyber-D&D work groups tailor their deception services to the organization's SOPs, and defensive cyber-D&D services become organization SOPs. Cyber-D&D service processes are defined, and the purpose, inputs, entry criteria, activities, roles, measures, verification steps, outputs, and exit criteria are all specified. At Level 3, cyber-D&D services are managed more proactively, acknowledging the interrelationships with other processes.

Levels 4 and 5 Service Maturity: At maturity Level 4, the D&D service is managed quantitatively with the aid of service utilization and efficacy metrics, enabling quality improvements to be understood in statistical terms. The organization also implements processes and mechanisms to reduce and prevent cyber-D&D failures and defects. Finally, at maturity Level 5, the organization has the capability to continuously optimize and the quality and delivery of cyber-D&D services, satisfying the deception needs of the defended organization, and introduce innovations. Deception quality and service management outcomes have a high probability of success. A key distinction in the move to Level 5 is the focus on organizational service management, as opposed to individual missions and related objectives.

8.4 Processes-CMM

A process can be seen "as a set of interrelated activities, methods, and practices that use a set of inputs to develop, deliver, and support a set of products and services."[12] The Business Process Maturity Model (BPMM) defines several process areas for each maturity level except Level 1. Each process area contains goals that, if achieved, can be used as a basis to assess maturity levels. For example, maturity Level 2 (Managed) has process areas focused on the requirements management of work units, their planning, monitoring, control performance assessments, and configuration management. Maturity Level 3 (Defined) features process areas pertinent to the work and business-related management of products and services, their preparation, deployment, operations and support. Maturity Level 4 calls for quantitative process, product, and service management, as well as asset, capability, and performance management at an organizational level. Finally, maturity Level 5 calls for continuous improvement at an organizational level in planning, performance, capabilities, and the prevention of defects and problems.

Developing a cyber-D&D process maturity model entails applying the above concepts and process area notions to the domain of delivering cyber-D&D services. This raises two foundational issues. First, what exactly is a work unit for cyber-D&D—a foundational concept for maturity Level 2? Second, how should cyber-D&D products and services be integrated into the larger organization? The answers will depend to a great extent on the makeup and specialization of the organization that provides cyber-D&D, and the nature of the organization that the cyber-D&D unit(s) support. For example, in a commercial organization, cyber-D&D may be part of a larger suite of services provided by the Computer Network Operations (CNO) department. Alternatively, in an intelligence community or defense setting, there may be dedicated departments and organizations providing cyber-D&D as part of the CND operations, or specialized cyber D&D teams within CND that focus on specific adversaries or types of attacks.

> **Indicators of Level 2 Cyber D&D Process Maturity:**
> The PLA has not publicly disclosed the existence of a computer network operations [CNO] strategy distinct from other components of IW, such as electronic warfare, psychological operations, kinetic strike, and deception, but rather appears to be working toward the integration of CNO with these components in a unified framework broadly known as "information confrontation." This concept ... seeks to integrate all elements of information warfare—electronic and non-electronic—offensive and defensive under a single

---

[12] Object Management Group (2008). The Object Management Group (OMG) has developed the Business Process Maturity Model (BPMM) to help guide the maturity of processes within organizations.

command authority. …the PLA adopted a multi-layered approach to offensive information warfare that it calls Integrated Network Electronic Warfare or INEW strategy. … INEW provided the PLA with a coherent model for offensive electronic IW but did not leverage other non-electronic elements such as deception, psychological operations, or kinetic strike, nor did it attempt to link network defense to offensive operations or place them under a single command authority. Information confrontation theories currently being developed and refined within the PLA today seek to address these gaps, particularly the need for more coherent command infrastructure.

Krekel, B., P. Adams, G. Bakos (2012) *Occupying the Information High Ground: Chinese Capabilities for Computer Network Operations and Cyber Espionage*

The specifications of cyber-D&D units, services, and processes have an impact on the degree of product and service integration of cyber-D&D at the organizational level. For commercial organizations, such as e-commerce providers, cyber-D&D probably plays little role in achieving business objectives; it will remain an ancillary or supportive technique to diagnose service disruptions and improve delivery. Within an intelligence organization, however, cyber-D&D may become a central business function.

The proper granularity of a work unit as it relates to cyber-D&D again depends on the individual organization and the organization's level of specialization and capability maturity. One can envision a cyber-D&D activity as going through multiple phases: conception, implementation, deployment, engagement, and post-deployment assessment. For some organizations all these phases will comprise a single work unit; for other organizations specialized in cyber-D&D, these individual phases may constitute work units that are managed and optimized individually.

Organizations at the first (Initial) level of maturity have no specific and systematic processes centered on D&D activities. Staff with diverse expertise may be pulled in and trained on-the-fly to support cyber-D&D activities in an ad hoc and minimal fashion. At Level 2 (Managed), cyber-D&D activities are recognized and organized as work units and used as a basis for project management including tracking requirements, schedule, cost, and performance. Executive management sponsors cyber-D&D activities and takes accountability for related process improvements. Moving from maturity Level 2 to 3 (Defined) requires well-defined and organization-wide standardization processes to manage cyber-D&D products and services, their preparation, configuration, deployment, operations and support. The organization puts standards in place for building and offering specific cyber-D&D products and services, as well as organization-wide development and project management processes. Level 3 organizations also exhibit increased maturity in the business management of cyber-D&D products and services as manifested in deeper understanding of the complexity of emerging cyber threats, clear definitions of the cyber-D&D product and service offerings required to meet these threats, and highly developed and viable cyber-D&D plans.

These levels lay the foundation for the fourth maturity level, which entails quantitative management of cyber-D&D. This calls for development and tracking of organization-wide metrics and performance benchmarks for all phases of cyber-D&D activities. How much did the development of a particular D&D technique cost? What was the total life-cycle cost? Another characteristic of Level 4 is highly efficient and effective integration of D&D products and service processes covering the different functions, disciplines, and assets (including personnel) involved in supporting D&D activities.

Finally, at maturity Level 5, organizations focus on continuous improvement and optimization. Processes and infrastructure are in place for rigorous instrumentation and metrics collection, feedback, and self-correction of cyber-D&D planning, implementation, and field performance. In addition to metrics on intra-work unit execution (as present at maturity Level 4), Level 5 calls for an additional meta-metric framework to evaluate efficiency and utilization across work units and at an organizational level. Such a framework can help managers evaluate and refine the various metrics themselves. Additionally, the organization institutes processes and programs to prevent defects and problems in cyber-D&D solutions. Finally, an organization at this level of process maturity has the ability to undertake business process reengineering: that is, assess, innovate, and optimize its own cyber-D&D business processes.

8.5 Technologies and Techniques-CMM

The last component of the cyber D&D CMM is the CMM for cyber D&D technology and techniques. A symbiotic relationship exists among these components. As people, services, and processes mature, they will demand more sophisticated technology and techniques. Conversely, if an organization begins to use sophisticated technology, the associated people, services, and processes must improve to handle the additional complexity. Thus, organizations must foster the maturity of the technical aspects of cyber-D&D in tandem with more capable people, services, and processes.

8.5.1 General Characteristics of Technology Maturity Levels

Although relevant to cyber-D&D, some general maturity characteristics apply to all technology development models.[13] In addition, these maturity characteristics could pertain to various D&D technologies such as stealth, low observables, camouflage, electronic counter-measures, and other D&D technologies.

---

[13] The technology and techniques CMM appears to be an original concept that overlaps other maturity and technology assessment methods; c.f., Nazanin Azizian, Shahram Sarkani, and Thomas Mazzuchi. "A Comprehensive Review and Analysis of Maturity Assessment Approaches for Improved Decision Support to Achieve Efficient Defense Acquisition," *Proceedings of the World Congress on Engineering and Computer Science 2009* v.2, San Francisco, USA, October 20–22, 2009.

Indicators of Level 1 Cyber D&D Technology and Techniques Maturity:
In November 1999, a *Jiefanguin Bao* (*Liberation Army Daily*) article stated that
China may develop an information warfare branch of service—a "net force" …
to protect net sovereignty and engage in net warfare. Elements of net warfare
include "offensive and defensive" technologies, "scanning" technologies,
"masquerade" (deception) technology, and "recovery" technology. Masquerade
technology would assist a person who wanted to dissemble as a commander and
take over a net.
  Thomas, T. (2008) *China's Electronic Long-range Reconnaissance*

At maturity Level 1, organizations use ad hoc technology and techniques to
provide cyber-D&D services. Many of these may be home-grown and lack quality,
efficiency, or standards. At maturity Level 2, the development and deployment of
cyber-D&D techniques become more systematic and efficient, yielding noticeable
improvements in quality. The pursuit of efficiencies results in constant internal evaluations of "build vs. buy" options for technology, techniques, and skill sets. The organization develops internal metrics to track development, integration, and deployment
of cyber-D&D technology. At maturity Level 3, organization-wide standards guide
the development and deployment of D&D technologies. The organization may also
develop libraries and catalogs of technologies and techniques classified under a number
of performance and cost-related attributes.

At maturity Level 4, the development and deployment of cyber-D&D technology
are managed quantitatively. The organization establishes metrics to measure efficiency, performance, cost, etc. To improve efficiency, a greater degree of sharing and
reuse of cyber-D&D code and infrastructure will occur across various cyber-D&D
tasks. A key characteristic at this level is a high degree of predictable outcomes and
success with the cyber-D&D techniques developed and deployed. At this maturity
level, organizations put programs in place to reduce and if possible prevent defects.
Organizations routinely perform systematic post-deployment analysis of the results of
cyber-D&D techniques to assess which techniques worked under what conditions.

Lastly, at maturity Level 5, an organization has an extensive program for total
and continuous improvement and optimization. The organization systematically
reviews metrics for individual work unit efficiency, as well as organization-wide
cyber-D&D technical performance, throughout the course of the year, and develops
appropriate meta-metrics to track organization-wide cyber-D&D development and
deployment efficiency across diverse work groups.

8.5.2 Specific Technology Maturity Attributes in the Context of Cyber-D&D

Table 8.5 provides an overview of how general characteristics of technology and
techniques improve with the progression in CMM levels, and identifies specific
attributes of D&D technology that improve with increasing maturity levels, or

Table 8.5 Attributes of cyber-D&D technology and technique maturity

Technology attribute	1: Initial	2: Managed	3: Defined	4: Quantitatively managed	5: Optimizing and innovating
Expertise and technical sophistication	The functional and technical sophistication of the D&D technology produced and used is low.	Moderate degrees of technical expertise and sophistication are observed in the cyber-D&D technologies produced.	The organization has high degrees of expertise and technologies have high sophistication. Various technical attributes are specified for technology development and clear and high technical standards are used organization-wide.	The complexity and technical sophistication of cyber-D&D techniques are quantitatively defined and managed so as to provide the required tradeoffs in efficacy, precision, and efficiency.	Very high degrees of expertise and sophistication are evident (only a handful of organizations in the world will possess such characteristics).
Architectural and engineering maturity	The architectural elements for the required software and hardware and related artifacts for cyber-D&D do not reflect any cohesive or long-term planning. D&D techniques are cobbled together at the spur of the moment from existing technology and proprietary extensions. Interfaces are primarily proprietary.	Architectural planning is introduced. Initial definitions of functions and modules are created.	Architectures reflecting tunable cyber-D&D attributes are specifically planned. Cyber-D&D architecture and platform families are introduced. Initial approaches are made to modularization, extensibility and interoperability between cyber-D&D functional elements and their realization in software and hardware architectures.	Tradeoffs in cost, performance, efficiency etc., are quantitatively planned and managed in the architecture. Systematic lifecycle and life expectancy planning occurs.	Architecture families are continually optimized based on post-deployment field analytics.

(continued)

Table 8.5 (continued)

Technology attribute	1: Initial	2: Managed	3: Defined	4: Quantitatively managed	5: Optimizing and innovating
Precision	Low precision in D&D techniques as evidenced by large footprint, easy detection by adversaries, and high collateral damage. Generic cyber-D&D techniques are used and as such are not tailored to observed threat or adversary specifics.	Moderate levels of precision are evident and the ability to deceive adversaries increases. Specific information about incoming threat and adversaries etc., are factored into the crafting of the precision and accuracy of cyber-D&D techniques.	High levels of precision are defined and achieved in response to knowledge about specific threat or target types. The stealthy techniques used as well as the cover stories deployed have high levels of precision so as to evoke rapid adversary response.	Quantitative standards are defined to achieve high levels of precision. Standards can factor in specifics of attacks, adversary doctrine and tactics etc.	Technology research and innovation management procedures are established to continually increase precision and accuracy. Accumulated statistics and feedback from adversary responses to specific cyber-D&D techniques are utilized in outcome analysis to improve the precision of D&D techniques.
Efficacy	Due to limited precision and accuracy, the efficacy of cyber-D&D is low. Results are often unpredictable.	Moderate levels of efficacy are observed in the cyber-D&D techniques used. Adversary is sufficiently tempted to take the bait on some of the cyber-D&D techniques deployed.	Efficacy standards for cyber-D&D techniques are defined by the organization. This contributes to the determination of the efficacy of the overall catalogue of cyber-D&D services.	Very high efficacy of cyber-D&D techniques is achieved, as evidenced by the high rates of enticement of adversaries, low degrees of interference with legitimate internal users, minimal wastage of resources etc. The organization can manage itself to achieve specific levels of efficacy with high confidence.	The organization can continually optimize the efficacy achieved. Newer and better technology is constantly incorporated and improved.

| Efficiency | Technology is produced on an as-needed basis with ad hoc processes. No cost or efficiency targets are specified. | Technology production and deployment is managed to provide moderate levels of efficiency. Code as well as deployment techniques are shared among employees, technical departments, and D&D projects. Established toolkits and libraries are used to increase efficiency. Open source code is used when possible | Efficiency of cyber-D&D techniques and technology is now formally defined within the organization. Metrics are devised to measure technical progress and results of deception operations. As such the formulation, design, production and deployment of cyber-D&D techniques and technologies will factor in cost, time, scope, and quality. The organization may adapt its libraries and components or build them from scratch to enable high reuse across multiple D&D initiatives and efforts, thereby lowering the total cost of D&D development (current toolkits are inadequate as is). | Efficiency targets are quantitatively specified in terms of benchmarks to be met and cyber-D&D production and maintenance are managed quantitatively to meet such benchmarks. | The efficiency obtainable from cyber-D&D is continually optimized. Comprehensive metrics are gathered and utilized to guide improvements. Each phase of the development of cyber-D&D techniques may be analyzed in detail to improve efficiencies. |

(continued)

Table 8.5 (continued)

Technology attribute	1: Initial	2: Managed	3: Defined	4: Quantitatively managed	5: Optimizing and innovating
TRL Transition Success	Ad hoc/hit-and-miss success with deploying cyber-D&D techniques. Most technologies do not see "the light of day" (i.e., are not deployed in volume)	The TRL process is managed to emphasize moving technology from concept validation to field deployment	TRL transition process is defined along with expected success rates for technology maturation and field deployment. Operationally, a higher proportion of cyber D&D technology is transitioning from TRL 3 to TRL 9.	TRL transition is managed to achieve certain quantifiable thresholds of high technology readiness and to do so while lowering and managing technology risk. A systematic technology portfolio and innovation pipeline management processes are instituted.	The D&D-service provider organization has a strong track record of sophisticated technical breakthroughs and innovations that are continually optimized. The organization's products continually prove to be game changers. Innovation management and transition models are optimized.
Influence of technology on adversary doctrine and strategy	Success is viewed mostly in technical terms, such as when an adversary takes a honeytoken (bait). The staff are primarily trained to assess the technical capabilities of the adversary.	The organization has some initial recognition of the importance of specific techniques and technologies in influencing adversary strategy and doctrine.	Specific cyber D&D techniques are evaluated and categorized in terms of their potential to influence adversary doctrine and strategy. As such the linkages of technology as an enabler for higher models and doctrines of D&D are developed.	The organization can quantitatively articulate the degree of influence on strategy and doctrine that specific cyber D&D techniques used under various situations can have. Technologists, policy makers, and strategists work synergistically in multidisciplinary teams to understand how policy, doctrine, strategy, and technology interrelate.	The use of cyber D&D techniques and technologies to influence adversary doctrine, strategy, and mission success is continually reviewed, refined, and optimized. The organization uses game and decision theory to optimize defender strategy options and align tactics and operations.

technology maturity attributes (TMAs). It summarizes how TMAs for cyber-D&D can be characterized at the various maturity levels. Quantitative and qualitative metrics would be developed by an organization to assess the maturity of each TMA. Some of these metrics would also be applied at Levels 4 and 5 of the other cyber-D&D maturity components: people, services, and processes.

At this point, it becomes obvious that all four cyber-D&D maturity components—people, services, process, and technology and techniques—must work together in a holistic organizational design. These TMAs include expertise and technical sophistication, architectural and engineering maturity, precision, efficacy, efficiency (technology readiness level [TRL], transitions), and the influence of technology on adversary doctrine and strategy.

8.5.2.1   Expertise and Technical Sophistication

Organizations can assess the technical maturity of a given deception technique along multiple dimensions of expertise: engineering expertise, operational expertise, and creativity and diversity.

The first dimension is the level of engineering subject matter expertise required to construct the technique. Designing, constructing, and deploying a decoy that mimics the behavior of an embedded platform, such as a radar, a missile controller, or a centrifuge process logic controller, requires specialized expertise. Development of the Stuxnet malware, for example, required discovery of multiple vulnerabilities and weaponization of previously unknown attack methods against an extensive array of software and hardware components, and against specific models and types of hardware. Based on the open source Stuxnet accounts, the designers needed at least a Level 3 maturity in expertise and technical sophistication.

Secondly, organizations need operational expertise with regard to the opponent's likely responses to the decoy's mimicked behavior and manipulations. Stuxnet required understanding of how the Iranians typically responded to centrifuge accidents that were apparently not due to process control signals or alarms.

The third dimension of expertise encompasses the creativity and diversity of techniques used in the D&D mechanism. Multiple infection vectors and stealth techniques, as well as the ability to sense and adapt to the environmental conditions and to evade multiple detection mechanisms (in offensive situations), offer examples of creative and diverse innovation. The more original, creative, and innovative the cyber-D&D technique, the less chance there is that the adversary will recognize or characterize it.

8.5.2.2   Architectural and Engineering Maturity

A cyber-D&D technique may be technically sophisticated and yet architecturally immature. Architectural and engineering maturity is an orthogonal TMA in that higher levels of maturity reflect long-term planning for repeated and prolonged usage, increasing modularity in construction, and careful planning of architecture families to reduce development costs. At Levels 4 and 5, organizations can tune and optimize architectural features to achieve very specific performance and cost profiles as well as life expectancies.

8.5.2.3 Precision: When and Where to Aim the Cyber-D&D Technique

Precision is one of the most important attributes of any cyber-D&D technique. It is temporal-spatial in that planners must know when and where to aim the cyber-D&D techniques. Signs of low precision in cyber-D&D techniques include a large foot-print (for example, too many honeytoken files), improper placement (honeytokens spread carelessly with no strategy), easy detection by the deception target, and high levels of interference with legitimate users. Use of generic cyber-D&D techniques that are not tailored to observed threats or adversary specifics and minimal ability to collect fine-grained, target-specific information indicate low technical maturity. With increasing precision also increases the ability to deceive the target.

In the Stuxnet case study, the Duqu reconnaissance worm (and possibly Flame) apparently obtained information that allowed highly precise targeting of Iranian centrifuge systems. Increasing precision requires an understanding of network topologies and machine and file system architectures in order to calculate optimal form, number, and placement of cyber-D&D techniques. High precision lowers overhead and minimizes collateral interference and damage to legitimate users.

The following measures provide a metrics-driven assessment of precision in the cyber-D&D context:

- **The footprint of a cyber-D&D technique**. This includes such elements as code size, central processing unit (CPU) performance profile, expected active lifetime for the code, file size, number of copies of specific files. With increasing precision, the footprint should shrink.
- **Collateral interference and damage to legitimate users**. A perfectly aimed technique targets only the adversary and poses almost no interference to legitimate users of a network or system.
- **The overhead associated with a cyber-D&D technique**. The footprint, total life-cycle costs, and collateral interference and damage collectively constitute the total overhead of a D&D technique. As precision increases, the total overhead decreases.

8.5.2.4 Efficacy: How Well Did the Bait Attract a Specific Target?

Closely related to precision, but nevertheless distinct, is the TMA of efficacy. Efficacy is a composite measure of potency: that is, how quickly and how well a particular cyber-D&D technique works with respect to a specific target and objec-tive. The mark of a highly efficacious cyber-D&D technique is its ability to entice the specific target and elicit the required information in time to enable mission success. In the realm of cyber-D&D, honeytokens may be placed optimally in the network and have the potential to attract a particular malicious actor, and yet have low efficacy (potency). Efficacy may be increased by making the bait more attractive. For example, the freshness and specificity of keywords in a honeytoken file may be tuned so that the actor believes the file has recently been changed in anticipation of an imminent event.

To enhance efficacy, it is useful to recognize the two-stage process of *enticement* and *consumption*. The first brings the target to the bait, and the second gets the target to take (consume) the bait. A target may be enticed by a file, as evidenced by upload to a remote server, but may not act on it (read it) immediately.

Efficacy constituent metrics may include:

- Average time from deployment to first enticement
- Percentage of enticement opportunities missed by the adversary; the adversary came close but did not bite
- Time elapsed from enticement to consumption
- Degree of consumption—how much and how deep did the target bite?
- Time elapsed from consumption to follow-up consumption
- Time taken to evoke meaningful response from adversary
- Ability to prolong adversary presence
- Usefulness and amount of target information collected.

As maturity levels increase, the TMA in these constituent efficacy metrics improves.

8.5.2.5 Efficiency

Efficiency measures the cost and time needed to design, build (or adapt), deploy, and maintain a cyber-D&D technique. Organizations need measures that can answer questions such as "How much does cyber-D&D cost in terms of the overall percentage of mission costs?" In essence, efficiency increases when a D&D technique can be commoditized and produced in a modular and rapid manner. Using well-known and open-source toolkits and libraries to construct D&D techniques represents one way to increase efficiency, since it reduces overall custom development costs. A new and highly customized cyber-D&D technique—a cyber weapon with sophistication equivalent to that of Stuxnet—is necessarily inefficient because of the large number of resources utilized and the consequent high development costs. But over time "virtuous cycles" will begin, and increases in architectural maturity will result in modularization, extensibility, and reuse, with many variants produced more inexpensively as costs are amortized, taking advantage of increased expertise, technology learning curves, and economies of scale.

8.5.2.6 Technical Readiness Level (TRL) Transition Success

This TMA measures how well cyber-D&D technologies transition from conception to research to commercialization or operationalization, and deployment in mission operations. A higher rate of transitions from TRL 3 to TRL 9 indicates increasing

Table 8.6 Technology readiness levels (TRLs)

TRL Level	Description
1. Basic principles observed and reported	Lowest level of technology readiness. Scientific research begins to be translated into applied R&D.
2. Technology concept and/or application formulated	Invention begins. Once basic principles are observed, practical applications can be invented. Applications are speculative, and there may be no proof or detailed analysis to support the assumptions.
3. Analytical and experimental critical function and/or characteristic proof of concept	Active R&D is initiated. This includes analytical studies and laboratory studies to physically validate the analytical predictions regarding separate elements of the technology.
4. Component and/or breadboard validation in laboratory environment	Basic technological components are integrated to establish that they will work together. This is relatively "low fidelity" compared with the eventual system.
5. Component and/or breadboard validation in relevant environment	Fidelity of breadboard technology increases significantly. The basic technological components are integrated with reasonably realistic supporting elements so they can be tested in a simulated environment.
6. System/subsystem model or prototype demonstration in a relevant environment	A representative model or prototype system well beyond TRL 5 is tested in a relevant environment.
7. System prototype demonstration in an operational environment	The prototype is near or at the planned operational system. This represents a major step up from TRL 6 by requiring demonstration of an actual system prototype in an operational environment.
8. Actual system completed and qualified through test and demonstration	Technology has been proven to work in its final form and under expected conditions. In almost all cases, this TRL represents the end of true system development.
9. Actual system proven through successful mission operations	The technology is applied in its final form and under mission conditions, such as those encountered in operational test and evaluation (OT&E).

maturity in both the defender organization and the cyber-D&D services provider, as shown in Table 8.6.[14] At Levels 4 and 5, the deceiver and cyber-D&D service provider organizations can manage and optimize transition success quantitatively and in a risk-controlled manner, and institute systematic technology portfolio and innovation pipeline management processes. Sample measures for this TMA include average cost, time, and percentage of the cyber D&D technology portfolio transitioning to TRL 9, the total portfolio-wide transition cost, and the total reduction in technology risk. Improvement in these metrics will indicate increases in TRL transition maturity. Equally important, the defender and cyber-D&D service provider can collectively manage transitions to achieve certain thresholds in the metrics.

[14] The table is adapted from the DoD document "Technology Readiness Assessment (TRA) Guidance," April 2011, page 2–13. http://www.acq.osd.mil/chieftechnologist/publications/docs/TRA2011.pdf

8.5.2.7   Influence of Technology on Adversary Doctrine and Strategy

This TMA characterizes how well cyber-D&D technology and techniques, combined with people, services, and processes, succeed in influencing the target's (adversary's) doctrine and strategy. The difference between low and high TMA maturity in this area is very pronounced. Staff at low TMA levels may be trained primarily to assess the adversary's technical capabilities and thus be largely unaware of the adversary's strategic motives, behaviors, and capabilities. They view success mostly in terms of technical accomplishments; for example, a target has taken a honeytoken (bait). At the highest levels of maturity, technologists, policy makers, and strategists work synergistically in multidisciplinary teams to understand how a target's policy, doctrine, strategy, and technology interrelate and can be influenced. Changes in the target's posture from offense to defense and the time and number of defender moves to cause a change in target strategy are good bases for building appropriate metrics for this TMA element.

8.6   Implications

The CMM for cyber-D&D recognizes from the onset that maturity in cyber-D&D extends well beyond technical capabilities. A holistic view of maturity requires the development of capabilities in people, services, processes, technology and techniques as they relate to cyber-D&D.[15] As cyber-D&D maturity level increases, an organizations should be able to leverage D&D for strategic advantage and to influence the adversary's doctrines and decision making.

With the increasing complexity and frequency of cyber-attacks, organizations must devote far more energy to analyzing adversaries, especially in the APT context. Cyber-D&D can play a crucial role in establishing environments to enable such analysis, and the cyber-D&D CMM can help organizations answer questions such as: How does an organization assess its current level of cyber-D&D maturity? How does it enhance and expand its cyber-D&D services? How does it put together a blueprint for these activities? What are the costs and benefits of employing cyber-D&D at various levels of maturity?[16] A cyber-CD CMM also provides a specific basis for developing CD capabilities to detect, verify, and respond to deceptions in the cyber domain.

---

[15] If one reflects on the credits following world-class films based on imaginary content, say, *The Lord of The Rings*, one can begin to appreciate the many dimensions of capability maturity—people, services, processes, technology and techniques—needed to create and sustain such remarkable illusions. World-class cyber-D&D will also need holistic and mature organizational capabilities to produce effective deceptions in virtual cyber worlds, but probably far fewer resources than those needed to create a credible world for us of hobbits, orcs, and wizards.

[16] For cost-benefit analyses of deception, see, e.g., Whaley, B. (2007b) "The one percent solution: costs and benefits of military deception, in Arquilla, J. and D. A. Borer (2007) *Information Strategy and Warfare: A guide to theory and practice*. Routledge: New York.

Chapter 9
Cyber-D&D Lifecycle Management

Deception in computing typically involves a layer of cleverly designed trap functionality strategically embedded into the internal and external interfaces for services. Stated more simply, deception involves fake functionality embedded into real interfaces. ... Almost no reports are available on the day-to-day use of deception as a structural component of a real enterprise security program. This tendency to avoid the use of deception is unfortunate, because many cyber attacks, such as subtle break-ins by trusted insiders and Trojan horses being maliciously inserted by suppliers into delivered software, cannot be easily remedied by any other means.

Edward Amoroso (2011) *Cyber attacks: protecting national infrastructure.* Burlington MA: Elsevier.

Like any other capability to be introduced into an organization, cyber-D&D must be carefully coordinated and managed to achieve the desired results. Figure 9.1 shows the most significant facets of lifecycle management.

The most critical facets are the maturity level and the overall management model. As Chap. 7 showed, the maturity level manifests itself in the people, services, processes, and technologies within the organization, with the degree of systematization and optimization as key indicators.

The management model represents the overall approach to managing the cyber-D&D capabilities and operations from the perspectives of both capability development and operations and services. It is akin to process models in software development and as such can take on various forms. These include linear waterfall-style models, evolutionary models, as well as transform and spiral models.

The operational processes used to conduct cyber-D&D operations constitute another salient aspect of lifecycle management. In particular, cyber-D&D must function in concert with the overall defensive operations within the organization and must support cyber defense. The preparations undertaken to launch and manage the D&D capability must encompass coordination between people, services, processes, and technology.

The last two facets of lifecycle management include observables and indicators as well as related metrics. The observables and indicators vary with the lifecycle of D&D operations, but should give the cyber-D&D team insights into the progress and effectiveness of its activities. Organizations must establish a metrics framework to quantitatively and qualitatively measure and track the various observables and indicators and to run analytics over them so as to enable higher level inferences on adversary TTPs.

© Springer International Publishing Switzerland 2015
K.E. Heckman et al., *Cyber Denial, Deception and Counter Deception,*
Advances in Information Security 64, DOI 10.1007/978-3-319-25133-2_9

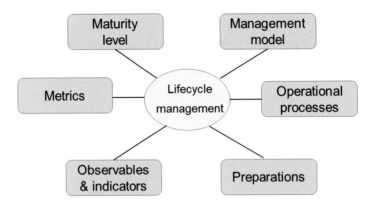

Fig. 9.1 Facets of lifecycle management

9.1 Overview of Spiral D&D Lifecycle Management

Logically, D&D could involve lifecycle phases such as planning, implementation, deployment and execution, and post-deployment analysis. However, rather than use a sequential waterfall-style model of lifecycle management, organizations would benefit from following a spiral model that iteratively drives toward increasing the overall effectiveness of the cyber-D&D capability through higher maturity and continuous process improvements. Such a model would help organizations to assess risks and effectiveness with each iteration of the spiral while promoting agile and rapid prototyping and tuning of D&D techniques and services based on outcomes observed. Figure 9.2 shows a notional view of how cyber-D&D lifecycle management can be incorporated into the well-known spiral process management model developed by Barry Boehm (1988).

9.2 Plan

Any attempt to incorporate cyber-D&D into active cyber defense must necessarily start by establishing clear and achievable goals. At a minimum, the planning phase should encompass establishing D&D goals and developing training curricula, cyber-D&D TTPs, best practices and standards, and cyber-D&D metrics. Figure 9.3 illustrates a two-dimensional goal-setting framework to aid in these tasks.

The first dimension (i.e., the rows) considers the degree of engagement and buy-in on the part of the defender organization at the tactical, operational, and strategic levels. A tactical engagement by the defender has only minimal influence on the kinetic and business operations of the organization and involves almost no engagement of upper management, stakeholders, partners, and government representatives. It can be best summarized as "We don't understand the adversary's

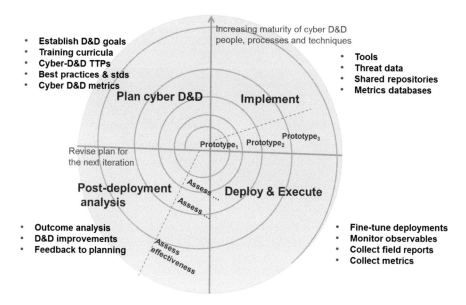

Fig. 9.2 Overview of a spiral cyber-D&D lifecycle management process

behavior or his/her intentions, but let us use cyber means to passively monitor his activities to get more clues." A tactical approach to D&D may evolve into an operational approach and thus require buy-in from those who coordinate the organization's business operations. Cyber-D&D now becomes an essential element in the protection of business operations. At the highest levels, where D&D is acknowledged as a strategic element, it requires buy-in from upper management, organizational stakeholders, and partners, which in turn demands requires cross-organizational understanding and coordination.

The second dimension, shown by the columns, represents the degree of influence that the defender's cyber-D&D activities can exert on the adversary's overall behavior, mission, and strategic objectives. Actions to exert influence can vary from passive monitoring of adversary activities in a synthetic environment such as a honeynet, to active engagements involving live interactions with the adversary, to focused attempts to influence the adversary at the tactical, operational, and strategic levels.

In planning cyber-D&D operations and campaigns, an organization must have a clear sense of the scope that it wants to address first, given the possibilities laid out by the above matrix and the limited resources available to start a cyber-D&D initiative. For example, setting up honeynets and honeypots simply to observe and perform initial reconnaissance of adversaries may offer a good starting point. Accumulated experience with adversaries will later enable the organization to examine how cyber-D&D can aid the larger cyber defense and business- and mission-related operations. As shown by the arrow, D&D operations become most effective when they can influence the adversary strategically—in other words, when the defender understands the

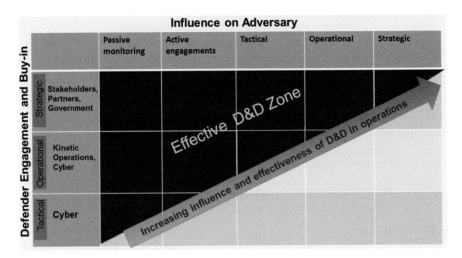

Fig. 9.3 Establishing D&D goals

adversary's overall mission. This may range from "The adversary wants to get the latest design of weapon X," to "The adversary wants to deny information so that it can influence geopolitical events in its favor."

Once the organization has clearly defined its cyber-D&D objectives, it must construct a training program. Again, the scope and the rigor of such a training program depend on the organization's D&D maturity. Technical training may entail detailed instructions on the acquisition, installation, development, and customization of various cyber-D&D tools and synthetic environments and their seamless integration into the overall network and cyber infrastructure of the organization. Cyber developers and operators may need training in order to build proficiencies in specific skill sets. D&D training should also make both cyber operators and regular users aware of the overall role of D&D in cyber defense. In addition, cyber operators and network administrators must be trained in rules of engagement specific to cyber-D&D. At the very least these rules should cover the safety, usability, efficiency, and public relations aspects of cyber-D&D for both internal users as well as adversaries.

Another crucial aspect of the planning phase consists of assembling a set of TTPs for cyber-D&D given the overall D&D goals established. Technical personnel and decision makers must understand basic D&D terminology, models, and approaches as they relate to foundational D&D tactics, as well as the risks and benefits of each tactic and the viability of each tactic relative to the available technologies (i.e., the technical means). Finally, organizations must institute clear procedures and a chain of command when it comes to managing D&D. When and how should a D&D tactic be employed? What approvals are needed? When and how should a tactic be withdrawn? Training materials must mirror increasing maturity.

The D&D planning phase also involves setting best practices and standards. This will become easier with accumulated experience and increasing maturity levels. This will establish quality and performance benchmarks, administrative, approval, reporting, contingency, and exception handling procedures to which everyone can relate.

Best practices and standards provide the basis for creating metrics. A metrics framework should serve decision makers as well as technical personnel. Higher level metrics should help decision makers assess the effectiveness of cyber-D&D operations with respect to established goals, benchmarks, and standards within the context of ongoing cyber-attacks and operations. More detailed, implementation-level technical metrics help technical personnel assess the effectiveness of the cyber-D&D techniques employed.

9.3   Implement

In the implementation phase the organization wishes to realize the plans made in the previous phase. It thus must address both the "what" (i.e., what artifacts are needed) and the "how." The "what" must include at least tools and code bases, threat data, shared repositories, and metrics databases.

Implementation must begin with assembling and developing the tools and code bases required to build the technical infrastructure for cyber-D&D. The cyber-D&D team must examine tool suites and technologies to set up honeypots, honeynets, and other deceptive environments, and make important build versus buy decisions. Next, the team must implement a system, as well as an overall data schema, to collect, organize, and index incoming threat data. This vital input signal and stimulus drives the defender's decision making. Threat data can be organized along a number of dimensions, including malware and exploit category, transaction times, and adversary characteristics. The team could create shared repositories with database storage and retrieval along with "big data" analytics to enable the secure and efficient delivery of such data to D&D operations. Lastly, the team should set up metrics databases to collect ongoing operational data on the performance and quality of D&D operations.

All the above artifacts must cohesively serve the "how"—that is, aid in the overall coordination, security, and information management of cyber-D&D. Coordination involves timeliness and clear chain of command and information flow. The artifacts could incorporate triggering and alert mechanisms and related coordination with workflow and business management functions to keep all responsible personnel informed as D&D operations progress.

The cyber-D&D team must secure all threat data, operational metrics, and related alerts and information flows so that only authorized personnel have access to them and are notified of the progress of D&D operations. Insecure cyber-D&D operations jeopardize not just D&D and defense operations but business functions as well. Thus, cyber-D&D must be careful not to accidentally expose operational details to internal legitimate users or interfere with their user experience. Thus, an overall secure information management plan needs to be put in place.

9.4 Deploy and Execute

Once implementation has been completed, the organization must deploy and execute cyber-D&D techniques, services, and supporting processes in a target environment—whether a synthetic environment such as a honeynetwork or a honeypot, the real cyber infrastructure, or a combination of both. In accordance with the spiral methodology, this approach to lifecycle management calls upon the organization implementing cyber-D&D to iterate through rapid prototypes of cyber-D&D with each spiral. At each iteration, the organization must evaluate the risks and effectiveness of the current prototype.

Among other activities, the deploy-and-execute phase should encompass fine-tuning deployments, monitoring observables, and collecting field reports and metrics. Deployments of technology by their very nature require continuous fine-tuning. This may include configuration management and other performance-related adjustments to increase the efficacy of cyber-D&D techniques and reduce operational overhead.

Researchers have attempted to explicitly characterize certain properties of the artifacts used for cyber-D&D as a step toward a systematic approach to optimizing D&D techniques. For example, in designing honeyfiles as decoys (baits), Bowen et al. (2009) mention:

1. Believability: Making the honeyfile or bait (i.e., D&D token/artifact) appear authentic to the attacker.
2. Enticingness: Making the bait attractive enough to entice the adversary.
3. Conspicuousness: Making the bait easy to locate and retrieve so as to maximize the likelihood that an attacker takes the bait.
4. Detectability: This is concerned with how detectable the defender wants to make the bait to the adversary.
5. Variability: There should be enough variability in a bait to ensure that a common invariant does not lead to easy identification.
6. Non-interference: The normal activity of legitimate users should not be interfered with.
7. Differentiability: To maximize non-interference, legitimate users should be able to easily distinguish decoy content from authentic ones.
8. Shelf-life: This is the time period during which a decoy is effective and actively in use.

As an organization's D&D maturity increases, the cyber-D&D team must define properties such as these for the various technical artifacts to be deployed, and supply guidance on fine-tuning them for deployment. Not every property can be optimized, as some will create conflicting tradeoffs. Therefore, the team must carefully choose the most appropriate subset of properties for a given threat and adversary profile.

Optimizing properties such as those listed above may require the team first to gain some experience with a particular class of threats or adversaries. The team must examine issues such as: Should variability or non-interference be increased?

Was the bait not tempting enough and the resultant shelf-life therefore very low? If so, an initial deployment and execution may be followed by additional optimizations and consequent redeployments and re-executions. This will require collection and tracking of several observables and metrics, as well as generation, filing, and dissemination of field reports. In addition to automated reports that capture low-level inferences, field reports should incorporate higher-level inferences and findings of human D&D operators and analysts.

9.5   Post-deployment Analysis

Post-deployment analysis, the last phase in the spiral, has three essential elements: outcome analysis, process improvements, and feedback to planning. Outcome analysis centers on the overall outcome of the current spiral, addressing such questions as: How effective were the cyber-D&D techniques developed and operationally deployed? What were the successes, failures, etc.? How well did the organization manage the total lifecycle costs within the spiral? To answer such questions the organization must analyze metrics data and field reports, and use the results to formulate specific D&D improvements in processes, services, and technologies. This requires careful attention to managing change for all of the D&D elements.

This phase also generates feedback to rapidly help with the next iteration of the spiral model of lifecycle management. The organization must share appropriate metrics data with relevant parties, whether those refining D&D techniques or those planning the next iteration.

Chapter 10
Looking to the Future

... the ultimate deception is misinformation. Imagine supplying the hacker with fake successes, responses, files and assets to exploit. This wastes the attackers' time and makes them feel like they have successfully hacked, unknowing that they are instead compromising a virtual world. If they don't know what they are seeing, and cannot rely on what they learn, how can they craft an attack?

Edward Roberts (2012) "Deception and the art of cyber security," scmagazine.com, February 28, 2012. www.scmagazine.com/deception-and-the-art-of-cyber-security/article/229685/

[Edward Roberts, *director of marketing at* Mykonos Software]

This book has built on the existing body of research in classical D&D and provided a theoretical framework to adapt classical D&D for cyber security, but the field of cyber-D&D has barely begun to develop. This chapter outlines promising areas for advanced research and development.

10.1 Live Defensive Operations

Further research into operational use of deception should empower cyber-D&D staff to shape the behavior of malicious actors at each phase of the cyber kill chain. Creating false targets may influence where attackers attempt an intrusion, while honeypot environments and information sharing could identify intrusion-specific tools.

Since malicious actors adapt constantly, sharing information collected in live deception operations helps other targeted organizations detect and mitigate compromise. Implementation of deception tends to be specific to each targeted organization and offensive actor, so organizations should experimentally validate plans against an operational setting to specify a functional workflow for deployment of D&D TTPs. For instance, interaction with a highly sophisticated actor may require a more realistic deception environment, or a shorter time lag between receipt of a phishing message and creation of a honeypot.

Organizations can use sandboxes to demonstrate the value of deception operations and conduct live exercises. Interaction with simulated environments is valuable when attempting to predict real-world actions and reactions of a malicious actor. The interplay between offense and defense is a practical training experience

© Springer International Publishing Switzerland 2015
K.E. Heckman et al., *Cyber Denial, Deception and Counter Deception*,
Advances in Information Security 64, DOI 10.1007/978-3-319-25133-2_10

for network defenders. Lessons learned from these environments, even if not immediately applicable in a production environment, may be valuable for future operational use as well as for identifying appropriate follow-on research. To simulate a malicious actor's behavior, the defense requires a well-founded understanding of offensive tactics and intentions.

An organization's maturity level also affects its ability to deploy deception techniques in response to intrusion attempts. Testing and measuring the correlation between cyber-D&D maturity and cyber-D&D effectiveness constitute important elements of future research.

10.2   Vulnerability Assessment

To determine vulnerability, organizations can evaluate their offensive D&D TTPs against systems configured like production environments. As actors develop new cyber-D&D exploits, these evaluations help provide context for investment in defensive security measures, including cyber-D&D. For instance, a given offensive tactic may allow pervasive compromise on unpatched systems, but patching the bug would cause an outage for business-critical software. The simulation might determine if cyber-D&D could deflect the attack during the repair period. Using a sandbox environment to examine the options offered by cyber-D&D for such issues can support decisions and actions by cyber security decision makers.

Researchers might wish to deploy security systems in an environment open to the Internet but isolated from internal systems and collect data on real attempts to compromise systems in the open environment. This would enable them to validate hypotheses about actual malicious traffic, with the downside of less reproducibility and risk of accidental compromise of internal systems if isolation mechanisms should fail.

Organizations can also use sandbox environments in conjunction with Red/Blue team exercises as safe testing grounds before deploying cyber-D&D operations in a production environment. That is, Red teams can simulate real adversarial behavior observed in the production environment and understood through campaign analysis, or observed in other organization's production environments and shared via trusted data sharing partnerships. Blue, in partnership with Blue D&D, would respond to Red's attack in the sandbox environment. This approach gives an organization the opportunity to test one or more potential active defense responses while minimizing or eliminating operational failures and unintended consequences in the production environment. Results and lessons learned can inform the organization's response and reduce the uncertainty of a chosen response.

10.3   Game Theory Models

Researchers have modeled CND and computer network attack as two-player non-cooperative incomplete information games (see, e.g., Gueye 2011; He et al. 2012; Hsu 2010; Chen 2007; Zhuang et al. 2010), including deception moves

(Carroll and Grosu 2011; Garg and Grosu 2007). Such game theory-based models provide useful insights to inform tactics (deciding what moves to make) and strategies (deciding what investments would enable possible tactical moves). For example, Carroll and Grosu (2011) investigated deception effects on interactions between the attacker and defender of a computer network using a non-cooperative two-player dynamic signaling game characterized by incomplete information. Defenders could use camouflage by either disguising a normal system as a honeypot or disguising a honeypot as a normal system.

Some strategies produce perfect Bayesian equilibria, in which neither defenders nor attackers should unilaterally deviate from their strategies. These game model equilibria allowed defenders to select the best deception strategy against the best attack strategies. Using a multiple-period game model, Zhuang et al. (2010) showed that defenders can achieve more cost-effective security through secrecy and deception (possibly lasting more than one period in a multiple-period game). Future research can adapt these game theory models to organization-specific scenarios and exercises, and new game theory models of cyber-D&D and cyber-CD may emerge as new discoveries are made in game theory (e.g., Press and Dyson 2012).

10.4   Cyber-Deception Education and Training

While training in cyber security and information assurance abounds, training in cyber-D&D is virtually nonexistent.[1] Operationally, cyber-D&D capabilities have reached only a very low level of maturity, and constitute primarily deployments of cyber-D&D TTPs such as honeynets. Very few cyber-D&D operations that match the capabilities described in this book have been documented. Because major institutions such as the DoD have not publicly assigned responsibility for cyber-D&D, it is not surprising that major components of such responsibility,[2] such as training, are undeveloped. To create and operate mature defensive cyber-D&D capabilities, as defined in this book, operators, staffs, and leaders will need training in cyber-D&D concepts, operations, and TTPs. Sandboxes, exercises, and cyber security and information assurance events such as Cyber Defense Exercises[3] and Capture the Flag competitions can help shape the elements of an effective cyber-D&D curriculum. Research is needed to identify the essential requirements for designing and developing modules of training for cyber-D&D.

From an educational standpoint in an academic setting, projects such as CyberCIEGE have successfully experimented with the use of gaming technologies

[1] Google searches show hundreds of thousands of hits for ⟨training OR courses AND "cybersecurity"⟩ but only a few dozen hits for ⟨training OR courses AND "cyber-deception"⟩, and none were actually for courses.

[2] Whitham, B. (2011) "Defining Responsibilities for Tactical Military Cyber Deception Operations," *Journal of Battlefield Technology*, v. 14, no. 3, November 2011, p. 19–24.

[3] Such as those used in the U.S. military academies and other universities.

to enable scenario-based learning about foundational cyber security concepts (Irvine et al. 2005). Set in a three-dimensional virtual world enabled by "construction and management simulation," the project directs students to achieve specific objectives and proficiencies using multi-phase scenarios. Technologies such as these create the potential to incorporate cyber-D&D steps into the scenarios. Users can choose from an array of cyber-D&D TTPs appropriately matched to the current phase of the kill chain. The scenarios can characterize each cyber-D&D TTP by a number of performance and cost tradeoffs and bring the student into a learning cycle where decisions result from "what-if analysis" and simulated renderings of the corresponding outcomes and effects on the "mission."

10.5   Chinese Cyber-Deception Research

China's information warfare, and particularly China's cyber-warfare activities, capabilities, strategies, and intentions have received extensive discussion and analysis (e.g., Hagestad 2012; Henderson 2007; Krekel et al. 2012; Lai and Rahman 2012; Mengin 2004; Mandiant 2013; Muñiz 2009; Stokes and Hsiao 2012). Some analysts have specifically focused on Chinese use of deception (Sawyer 2007) and particularly cyber-D&D and related stratagems (Hagestad 2012; Thomas 2004, 2007, 2009).

A scientometric analysis of Chinese science and technology developments in cyber-D&D would complement the widespread research on Chinese deception strategy, doctrine, and concepts. Such an examination would help to identify leading cyber-D&D researchers and research institutions; cyber-D&D research topics; networks among researchers, institutions, and topics; unique and unusual cyber-D&D keywords and terminology; and related scientific research, analyses, and developments. The survey and analysis of the scientific and technical literature would focus further analyses on the evolving roles of D&D and CD in Chinese information warfare and cyber-war.

10.6   Immune System and Biological Models

For over a decade, researchers have actively applied the model of the human immune system to cyber security. Rather than use a pure perimeter-defense approach, they view the system to be protected as an organism that must autonomously learn and adapt to survive in its harsh environment (Somayaji et al. 1997; Hespanha and Doyle 2010). For example, researchers are trying to develop an artificial immune system (AIS) called a self-adaptive computer defense immune system (CDIS) for the cyber security domain (Harmer et al. 2002). The natural resilience of biological strategies serves as an inspiration to develop systems with the innate ability to recognize threats, whether new or previously encountered, and then automatically communicate relevant threat information to other systems (Somayaji et al. 1997). In the cyber domain, new threats could consist of zero-day attacks or innovative hacking methodologies, analogous to new "strains" of disease to which a computer system or network is vulnerable (Stein et al. 2011).

A promising direction for future research would borrow inspiration from the immune system's capacity to operate autonomously, adapt to new pathogens through the use of detectors, and play the "numbers game" in defense. Thus, cyber-D&D TTPs could serve as advanced detectors in the computer system and extended network. The D&D TTPs themselves would operate autonomously to adjust to the tactics of new adversaries. Such investigations could use genetics-inspired approaches, such as genetic algorithms, to ensure that only the most efficient and efficacious cyber-D&D TTPs survive through a natural selection process that weeds out weak and ineffective TTPs.

Taking the AIS for CDIS idea one step further, future research could entail developing a biological model of D&D, perhaps leveraging existing animal deception models and metaphors. Researchers could then extrapolate this biological D&D model into a cyber security context, creating cyber-D&D TTPs able to adapt and maintain their immunity for computer defense or offense.

10.7 Cyber-Counterdeception Capability Maturity Model

A cyber-counterdeception (cyber-CD) CMM must provide a detailed and explicit framework for cyber-CD capability development. The CMM should help organizations characterize both their own and the adversary's maturity by presenting explicit observable (and possibly measurable) indicators of specific cyber-CD capabilities.

CD capabilities have been described by Bennett and Waltz (2007) and Whaley (2007a), but, notably, neither described the capabilities needed for cyber-CD. Both clearly note that counterdeception serves intelligence purposes, i.e., understanding the adversary, while D&D serve operational purposes, i.e., influencing the adversary.[4]

Simply detecting deception is insufficient for successful CD. In their book *Counterdeception: Principles and Applications for National Security* Bennett and Waltz (2007) described both CD *functions* and the components and capabilities of an *organizational CD system*. The functional capabilities are: identifying an adversary's deception operations; negate, neutralize, diminish, or mitigate the effects of, or gain advantage from, the adversary's deception operations; exploiting knowledge of the adversary's deception; penetrate through the deception to discern the adversary's real capabilities and intentions; determine what the adversary is trying to make own side believe. That is, what does the adversary want you to do?

---

[4]Other than a few references to detecting deception in social engineering situations, we found no research on cyber-counterdeception, per se.

Bennett and Waltz (2007) argue that an organization must have a variety of CD systems to perform CD functions effectively. The necessary organizational system capabilities include fundamental CD technical methods, a system architecture to support CD operations, and strategies for CD planning and collection. In addition, the organization must have information processing systems for CD analysis methodology and workflow, processing filters and knowledge bases, computational analytic support tools, and an analytic tool workflow. CD analysis, decision support, and production systems would support counterdeception analytic flow, consideration of alternative analyses, and deception warning. Finally, the organization would have to institute CD system performance and effectiveness measures.

Given these broad and general descriptions of CD capabilities, the further development of a cyber-CD CMM would require three research steps. The first would consist of translating these broad, general descriptions of CD capabilities into specific requirements for CD cyber actions. The next step would relate these specific CD actions to requirements in the cyber domain for people, services, processes, and technology and techniques capable of performing CD against cyber deceptions. The third and final step would identify the five levels of CD maturity across the dimensions of people, services, processes, technology and techniques.

10.8   Cyber-Counterdeception in Active Defense

While the fundamental principles of D&D and CD seem relatively constant, in the future, the landscapes and dynamics of their supporting tools and techniques will be constantly evolving as the "arms races" between the deceivers and the deception detectives goes on. As new tactics to conceal evolve, procedures to reveal will be developed. These pressures will be particularly acute in the cyber realm, where the virtual can evolve many times faster than the physical. Changes in technologies, policies, social interactions, even global politics will force changes in the landscapes and dynamics of the cyber-D&D versus cyber-CD contests.

Whaley offers a comforting constant in the midst of these swirling dynamics of the deception-counterdeception arms race landscapes:

> … it's fair to say that in the majority of cases, most of the overall costs of detecting deception are prepaid by already existing intelligence capabilities. …consistently effective deception analysis doesn't require more analysts or a bigger budget but simply different recruitment criteria, teaching tools, training procedures, and operational protocols.[5]

While Bennett and Waltz (2007) point to the growing influence and reach of deception in the future, cyber-D&D and cyber-CD will also become far more personal than in the past. The increasing overlap of our physical and cyber identities will continue to shift our personal landscapes and dynamics regarding deceptions and

---

[5] Whaley, B. (2007f) "The one percent solution: Costs and benefits of military deception," in Arquilla, J. & D. A. Borer, eds. (2007) *Information Strategy and Warfare: A guide to theory and practice*. New York: Routledge.

their detection. The opportunities and the challenges for cyber deception and for counterdeception cyber forensics keep changing, as Bloom (2013) summarized:

> Knowledge will continue to explode about what people buy and have bought, where they are and where they have been, with whom we communicate, and so on. Such knowledge will facilitate data mining both for individuals, groups of people, and all people. Greater predictive validity may well occur … especially if there's massive cross-referencing of an individual's data with that of presumed friends, families, and associates. But there also will be greater deception and counterdeception possibilities for the more ingenious of good and bad actors.[6]

Unlike traditional counterintelligence, "Almost every action in the cyber realm can be recorded, detected, identified, analyzed, replayed, tracked, and identified" (Bodmer et al. 2012). This provides an abundance of potential intelligence for counterdeception analysts, which can then be used against adversaries in counterdeception operations.

In the "arms race" between deceivers and detectors, deceivers may eventually become cognizant of the detector's intelligence gathering means and methods, and simply work around them. That is, deceivers will show cyber-CD analysts, via their own intelligence collection capabilities, exactly what they expect to see and help them to deceive themselves. Given that all deception is inherently psychological, it is key that deception detectors are trained in self-deception and cognitive biases.[7] The detection organization's best defense against a capable adversary is a capable cadre of D&D, CD, and C-D professionals.

Adversaries are likely to bring more, and more effective, cyber-D&D to future cyber warfare,[8] cyber crimes, and cyber terrorism. The dynamics of the cyber and technology innovation landscapes offer tremendous opportunities in the future to the cyber deceiver. But they also offer potential opportunities to the cyber deception detectives. Until nations adopt cyber-D&D defenses, however, and leverage those experiences into cyber-CD defensive capabilities, it may well be that these future opportunities and advantages will go solely to the cyber attackers.

---

[6] Bloom, R. (2013) *Foundations of Psychological Profiling: Terrorism, Espionage, and Deception.* Boca Raton FL: Taylor & Francis Group.

[7] See, for example, Caverni, Fabre & Michel Gonzalez, eds. (1990) *Cognitive Biases.* New York: Elsevier, and Yetiv, S. (2013) *National Security Through a Cockeyed Lens: How Cognitive Bias Impacts U.S. Foreign Policy.* Baltimore: Johns Hopkins University Press.

[8] One 2009 report suggested the Chinese will employ integrated network electronic warfare which includes "using techniques such as electronic jamming, electronic deception and suppression to disrupt information acquisition and information transfer, launching a virus attack or hacking to sabotage information processing and information utilization, and using anti-radiation and other weapons based on new mechanisms to destroy enemy information platforms and information facilities." Krekel, Bryan (2009) *Capability of the People's Republic of China to Conduct Cyber Warfare and Computer Network Exploitation.* McLean VA: Northrop Grumman Corporation.

10.9   Moving Forward

Regardless of the application, cyber-D&D can serve as a force multiplier for cyber security, tipping the scales in favor of the defense. The synthesis of technical network defense methods with proven D&D techniques will strengthen organizations' ability to recognize and thwart malicious intrusions. Improved cyber defenses can force malicious actors to move more slowly, expend more resources, and take bigger risks, while enabling the defender to possibly avoid cyber attacks, or at least to maintain essential operations despite cyber degradation.

ERRATUM

Cyber Denial, Deception and Counter Deception

Kristin E. Heckman, Frank J. Stech, Roshan K. Thomas,
Ben Schmoker, and Alexander W. Tsow

© Springer International Publishing Switzerland 2015
K.E. Heckman et al., *Cyber Denial, Deception and Counter Deception*,
Advances in Information Security 64, DOI 10.1007/978-3-319-25133-2

DOI 10.1007/978-3-319-25133-2_11

The volume number of the book was incorrect. It should read as 64. This has been updated in this volume.

The online version of the original book can be found at
http://dx.doi.org/10.1007/978-3-319-25133-2

© Springer International Publishing Switzerland 2016
K.E. Heckman et al., *Cyber Denial, Deception and Counter Deception*,
Advances in Information Security 64, DOI 10.1007/978-3-319-25133-2_11

E1

Appendix A: Cyber-D&D Taxonomy

This taxonomy presents an orderly classification of cyber-D&D TTPs according to their relationship to classical D&D TTPs. This work draws on publications by authoritative sources as well as the body of knowledge in the security community. Grateful recognition is given to the National Institute of Standards and Technology, Sandia's Information Design Assurance Red Team (IDART) framework, and MITRE's Common Attack Pattern Enumeration and Classification (CAPEC) project.

Malicious actors use offensive TTPs to gain access to a target resource, while security personnel use defensive TTPs to protect their resources from compromise. This appendix is therefore divided into two high-level sections: use of cyber-D&D TTPs by malicious actors, and use of cyber-D&D TTPs by defenders against malicious actors.

Usage by Malicious Actors

Figure A.1 shows the offensive TTPs deployed by malicious actors to gain control of a target machine or network, implemented by abusing technical vulnerabilities in software or cognitive loopholes in people.

To help correlate these offensive cyber-D&D TTPs with the concepts of revealing and concealing facts and fictions, Fig. A.2 presents a Venn diagram based on the D&D methods matrix in Chap. 2. The diagram characterizes each of the offensive TTPs according to how it relates to the traditional model of revealing or concealing truths and fictions.

This Venn diagram leads to several observations. First, it has only one intersection denoting TTPs that both simulate and dissimulate. This suggests some opportunity space in crafting new offensive D&D TTPs at the non-existent intersections. Second, most of the TTPs fall along the simulation-dissimulation axis, which suggests potential opportunity space in crafting new TTPs that reveal facts and conceal fictions. Third, there are no identifiable TTPs in which adversaries conceal fictions.

© Springer International Publishing Switzerland 2015
K.E. Heckman et al., *Cyber Denial, Deception and Counter Deception*,
Advances in Information Security 64, DOI 10.1007/978-3-319-25133-2

Fig. A.1 Offensive Cyber-D&D TTPs

Fourth, the largest category is conceal facts, which lends support to the notion presented in Sect. 6.3 that adversaries need to avoid detection to achieve their objectives. Fifth, there are few TTPs in which adversaries reveal facts voluntarily, given the disincentives in overtly showing their presence. Given the notion presented in Sect. 6.3 that defenders must detect to achieve their objective, the adversary has very few TTPs that readily alert defenders of the adversary's actions/ presence.

Below we outline each of these offensive tactics and techniques in more detail, using the categories of the D&D methods matrix as the organizing framework.

Reveal Facts

Denial of Service

Definition: Attempts to exhaust the resources of a machine preventing normal operation of a system. Multiple machines could participate in a distributed denial of service (DDoS) attack or users may 'opt-in' as part of a coordinated protest.

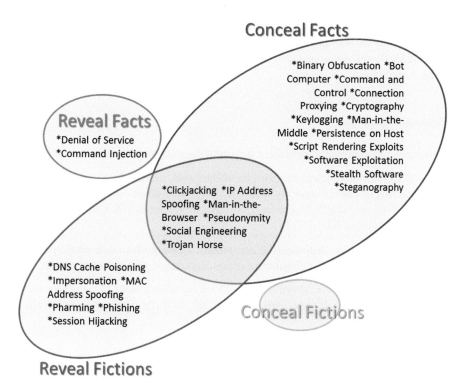

Fig. A.2 Offensive Cyber-D&D Tactics

Method: Either transmit an overwhelming amount of data to the target or exploit software resource allocation limits. Vulnerabilities in network-facing software can be triggered by incoming packets to cause a denial of service condition, for instance a memory exhaustion bug caused by half-open TCP connections. Application logic that requires nontrivial processing is generally vulnerable to requests that take more time to process than generate.

Usage by Financially Motivated Actors: Coordinated networks of infected machines can be used to take competitors offline, prevent access to sites to cover fraudulent activity, or extract ransoms from targeted organizations.

Usage by Targeted Actors: Motivated actors could suppress political opponents and activists, make systems unavailable in conjunction with a physical attack, and prevent defenders from reacting to ongoing intrusions.

References

Handley, Rescorla. *RFC 4732: Internet Denial of Service*. The IETF Trust, 2006. https://tools.ietf.org/html/rfc4732
CWE-770: Allocation of Resources Without Limits or Throttling. The MITRE Corporation. http://cwe.mitre.org/data/definitions/770.html

CAPEC-119: Resource Depletion. The MITRE Corporation. http://capec.mitre.org/
  data/definitions/119.html
CERT/CC. *Denial of Service Attacks.* 2001. https://www.cert.org/tech_tips/denial_
  of_service.html

Command Injection

Definition: Execution of user-entered data as system commands.

Method: Exploit insufficient sanitization of user data, allowing valid system commands as part of normal input, typically to server-side scripts. For instance, a vulnerable service might allow incoming user input formatted as SQL queries to extract from a backend database.

Usage by Financially Motivated Actors: Actors might wish to enumerate public-facing systems in order to compromise email accounts or personal information.

Usage by Targeted Actors: Intrusions are aided by compromise of public servers, allowing their use as intermediary proxies and to further compromise website visitors.

References

OWASP—Command   Injection.   https://www.owasp.org/index.php/Command_
  Injection

Conceal Facts

Binary Obfuscation

Definition: The structure of software can be manipulated to conceal its functionality and increase the effort and cost involved in analyzing it.

Method: Adding malicious functionality to legitimate applications, adding large sections of useless "junk" code, and encryption techniques to conceal malicious code.

Usage by Financially Motivated Actors: A financially motivated actor's goal is to avoid detection by security companies and antivirus, and increase reverse-engineering efforts by competitors and security analysts.

Usage by Targeted Actors: Customized implants might be heavily obfuscated to prevent detection and analysis. If an unpatched vulnerability is being exploited, obfuscation of the exploit code prevents other attackers from mimicking the same methods.

References

David Kennedy. *Metasploit: The Penetration Tester's Guide*, 2011. pp 103
NIST Special Publication 800-83: Guide to Malware Incident Prevention and
   Handling

Bot Computer

Definition: An infected computer capable of following instructions from an unauthorized actor. A bot network comprises multiple machines under a unified control
method—typically responses from remote servers.

Method: Machines are often infected through widely targeted malware leveraging
client-side exploits, persisting by evading detection from antivirus software. Infected
machines are typically home users or small businesses that lack the resources for
detection and cleanup.

Usage by Financially Motivated Actors: Credentials harvested from bots enable
identity theft, money laundering, and further spread of infection. Infected machines
can be used to launch denial of service attacks and spam campaigns, or can be re-sold
for general purpose on the black market.

Usage by Targeted Actors: Infected machines act as proxies for launching intrusions
and provide a resilient infrastructure for control of Trojan horses. Stolen information can be re-used in future phishing campaigns and for better targeting of specific
victims.

References

Botnets. Honeynet Project. http://www.honeynet.org/papers/bots
Tracking Botnets. **Roman Hüssy**. https://www.abuse.ch/

Command and Control

Definition: Communication between malware on a victim machine and a remote
server. Traffic is often obfuscated to prevent detection by security controls.

Method: Implants typically report a machine's network address, user credentials,
and screen captures to its control server and wait for further instructions. File listings
and credentials can be uploaded, and additional software can be downloaded to the
compromised machine.

Usage by Financially Motivated Actors: Actors use a set of domain or IP addresses
for control, or generate them on the fly in the client. Peer to Peer mechanisms are
sometimes used to ensure resilient communication between server and clients.
HTTP and IRC communications are common, including non-traditional communi-

cation methods like HTML comments and social media. Custom-developed command and control network protocols are also common, including those deliberately designed to mimic another benign protocol.

Usage by Targeted Actors: Implants connect to multiple domains, including backup domains that become active after a delay. Dynamic DNS may be used to provide flexibility and additional concealment of attacker identity. Legitimate sites are often compromised and used as part of a controller infrastructure. Encrypted and covert communication methods are commonly used to conceal traffic.

References

Michael Sikorski, Andrew Honig. *Practical Malware Analysis*. No Starch Press, 2012.
Mandiant. *M-Trends 2011*. 2011. http://www.mandiant.com/resources/m-trends/

Connection Proxying

Definition: Routing traffic through intermediate machines that provide a level of concealment for the source machine. An anonymizing proxy allows users to hide web browser activity. An anonymizing proxy can be used to bypass web security filters to access blocked sites (e.g., enterprise blacklisted sites) which could contain infected webpages.

Method: Software running on hosts provide forwarding of IP packets on the behalf of the source machine. Proxy software can be legitimately installed on a machine or planted on compromised machines by a malicious actor. Tor is an example of a global network that uses blind proxies for enhanced anonymity.

Usage by Financially Motivated Actors: These actors are motivated to conceal their location to avoid law enforcement intervention or disruption. Legitimate sites and other infected machines might act as proxy nodes to make attribution difficult, and impede cleanup efforts.

Usage by Targeted Actors: Actors may compromise trusted subsidiaries to communicate with compromised hosts within another network, with the goal of preventing attribution of an intrusion's origin.

References

Michael Ligh, Steven Adair, Blake Harstein, Matt Richard. *Malware Analyst's Cookbook*. Wiley, 2010.
Tor Project. torproject.org, 2012

Cryptography

Definition: Generation of cipher text indistinguishable from randomly chosen data.

Method: Transform data such that a secret key is required to decipher the message. Symmetric encryption assumes both parties have the same key, while asymmetric encryption derives a public and private key for each correspondent.

Usage by Financially Motivated Actors: Encryption is used to deny access to command and control traffic, obscure files for ransom purposes, and obscure data in-memory to evade detection.

Usage by Targeted Actors: End-to-end communication encryption methods can be used to effectively prevent access to communication, sometimes using customized algorithms. Stolen data can be encrypted on disk to prevent detection while being sent to an external server.

References

Bruce Schneier. *Applied Cryptography*. Wiley, 1996.
Michael Hale Ligh. *Abstract Memory Analysis: Zeus Encryption Keys*. http://mnin. blogspot.com/2011/09/abstract-memory-analysis-zeus.html. 2011.
M. Bennett and E. Waltz. *Counterdeception Principles and Applications for National Security*. Artech House: Boston, MA, 2007.
I. C. Paar and J. Pelzl. *Understanding Cryptography: A Textbook for Students and Practitioners*. Springer-Verlag: New York, NY, 2010.

Keylogging

Definition: Unauthorized keystroke capture.

Method: Recording of keystrokes on an infected machine by intercepting keystrokes events, reading host memory or reading signals from hardware devices.

Usage by Financially Motivated Actors: Keylogging can enable theft of credit card information and financial credentials.

Usage by Targeted Actors: Compromise of enterprise credentials can allow access to sensitive information associated with the user.

References

Kenneth May. (2013). *Threatasaurus: The A-Z of computer and data security threats*.

Man-in-the-Middle

Definition: Active attack in which the attacker modifies traffic between a client and server, allowing attempts to break confidentiality and integrity of transferred data.

Method: Intercept traffic between a client and server by exploiting issues in local network or Internet routing. ARP Spoofing, DNS poisoning, and modified BGP routes can be used for this purpose.

Usage by Financially Motivated Actors: Traffic from a victim can be intercepted and leveraged for financial gain. Interception of broadcast traffic on an unsecured wireless network using ARP spoofing, and capturing unencrypted FTP credentials are examples of man-in-the-middle attacks.

Usage by Targeted Actors: Assuming access to communication collection abilities, authentication credentials for remote users, or allowing unauthorized use of victim credentials. For broad collection efforts, actors might abuse trust in certificate authorities to issue fraudulent certificates and allow decryption of Internet traffic.

References

CWE-300: Channel Accessible by Non-Endpoint ('Man-in-the-Middle'). The MITRE Corporation. http://cwe.mitre.org/data/definitions/300.html
CAPEC-94: Man in the Middle Attack. The MITRE Corporation. http://capec.mitre.org/data/definitions/94.html
M. Bennett and E. Waltz. *Counterdeception Principles and Applications for National Security*. Artech House: Boston, MA, 2007.
I. C. Paar and J. Pelzl. *Understanding Cryptography: A Textbook for Students and Practitioners*. Springer-Verlag: New York, NY, 2010.

Persistence on Host

D&D Method: Conceal Facts

Definition: Installation of code to maintain control over a computer system across reboots and process terminations. This enables malware to survive initial cleanup efforts and continue executing.

Method: Write a binary to disk that is executed periodically on the system, then execute on startup or login. A malicious process might create their own service that is automatically executed on boot or user login.

Usage by Financially Motivated Actors: Credentials are captured from infected machines over time, with the goal of staying resident for long periods of time. The client is often actively hostile to analysis or detection tools, and uses multiple processes to prevent removal.

Usage by Targeted Actors: Actors may install multiple clients with orthogonal persistence mechanisms in order to regain control of target systems in the event of remediation.

References

Michael Sikorski, Andrew Honig. Practical Malware Analysis. No Starch Press, 2012.
Michael Ligh, Steven Adair, Blake Harstein, Matt Richard. *Malware Analyst's Cookbook*. Wiley, 2010.
Mark Russinovich. *Malware Hunting with the Sysinternals Tools*. Microsoft TechEd Conference. 2012. https://blogs.msdn.com/b/deva/archive/2012/06/16/teched-2012-mark-russinovich-s-malware-hunting-with-the-sysinternals-tools.aspx

Script Rendering Exploits

Definition: A server-side vulnerability enabling execution of untrusted scripts by trusted websites.

Method: Causing a user to load a malicious script in the context of a website, by exploiting bugs in server-side handling of active code. In the worst-case, this allows a malicious actor to effectively take actions on behalf of the user.

Usage by Financially Motivated Actors: A malicious site may compromise the user's session authentication information, allowing access to financial accounts by the actor. Transfers or purchases can then be made on behalf of the user.

Usage by Targeted Actors: Vulnerabilities in web services could be used to infect users, by loading scripts to trigger client-side exploitation. For instance, a bug in web-based email might load a malicious script that triggers a browser exploit to install a Trojan horse.

References

Cross-site Scripting (XSS). Open Web Application Security Project. https://www.owasp.org/index.php/Cross-site_Scripting_(XSS)
Cross-Site Request Forgery (CSRF). Open Web Application Security Project. https://www.owasp.org/index.php/Cross-Site_Request_Forgery_(CSRF)

Software Exploitation

Definition: Vulnerabilities in client-side software such as web browsers or document viewers that cause malicious code to execute on a user's system without the user's knowledge.

Method: Delivery of malicious content via websites, email, or mobile devices to trigger the execution of code that compromises information. Often a buffer overflow or memory access violation is used to trigger the initial exploit by leveraging issues in how operating systems manage memory access protections.

Usage by Financially Motivated Actors: Actors might compromise popular sites and attempt to exploit browser vulnerabilities to infect a large number of users. For instance, a popular news site hosting a Java exploit which installs a Trojan horse to steal financial information.

Usage by Targeted Actors: A legitimate website might be compromised by the actors to deliver specifically tailored exploits to a small group of people. To precisely target victims, they might leverage cookies to identify local system information and selectively embed malicious code to infect specific types of browsers coming from certain IP address ranges.

References

CWE 120: Classic Buffer Overflow. The MITRE Corporation. http://cwe.mitre.org/data/definitions/120.html

Fraser Howard. A closer look at the Redkit exploit kit. http://nakedsecurity.sophos.com/2013/05/09/redkit-exploit-kit-part-2/

Kindlund, Darien. CFR Watering Attack Details. http://www.fireeye.com/blog/technical/targeted-attack/2012/12/council-foreign-relations-water-hole-attack-details.html

Baumgartner, Kurt. Central Tibetan Administration Website Strategically Compromised as Part of Watering Hole Attack. https://www.securelist.com/en/blog/9144/Central_Tibetan_Administration_Website_Strategically_Compromised_as_Part_of_Watering_Hole_Attack

Stealth Software

Definition: Conceal the presence of malicious software on a system by subverting the operating system or underlying hardware. Processes, network connections, and files are hidden from normal users of the system in order to persist longer. A rootkit is a piece of software that hides executing programs or processes.

Method: Filter results of certain system commands via modification of system memory or modifying operating system structures. Technical methods include inline hooking, IAT hooking, SSDT hooking, MSR alteration, DKOM manipulation, MBR modification, and firmware reflashing. These methods often conceal activity of other malicious tools, and allow malicious users to use the system without the victim's knowledge.

Usage by Financially Motivated Actors: Actors desire a resilient network of infected machines and want to avoid detection by antivirus products. Stealth software often requires high investment to remove from a system, potentially causing disruption.

Usage by Targeted Actors: Targeted actors may conceal their presence using similar naming schemes as legitimate system services (e.g., installing as a Windows Audio Driver service). Sophisticated technical means can allow for passive monitoring of incoming network traffic for commands using additional network drivers.

References

"Rootkits: Attacking Personal Firewalls," Alexander Tereshkin, Codedgers, Inc. (Blackhat 2006)

"Rootkits: Subverting the Windows Kernel," Greg Hoglund, James Butler. Addison-Wesley, 2006

"Hardware Backdooring is Practical," Jonathan Brossard. Toucan System. Blackhat 2012

"Stealth Malware," Xeno Kovah. MITRE Corporation, 2012

Steganography

Definition: Concealing the presence of covert communications.

Method: Secretly hide the covert communication within open material protected by a secret hiding process and private key. Steganography can be implemented using open software such as *steghide* for digital photographs and video.

Usage by Financially Motivated Actors: Configuration settings and commands might be sent by covert inclusion in image files.

Usage by Targeted Actors: Implants might generate valid HTTP traffic and use a covert channel built into the server's presented content, such as using command and control via HTML tags.

References

M. Bennett and E. Waltz. *Counterdeception Principles and Applications for National Security*. Artech House: Boston, MA, 2007.

A. Desoky. *Noiseless Steganography: The Key to Covert Communications*. CRC Press: Boca Raton, FL, 2012.

"Hide and Seek: An Introduction to Steganography." Niels Provos, Peter Honeyman. http://www.citi.umich.edu/u/provos/papers/practical.pdf

"Alureon and Steganography." Microsoft Malware Protection Center. https://blogs. technet.com/b/mmpc/archive/2011/09/25/a-tale-of-grannies-chinese-herbs-tom-cruise-alureon-and-steganography.aspx

Reveal Fictions

DNS Cache Poisoning

Definition: Modification of entries in the Domain Name System to resolve domain names to IP addresses other than intended.

Method: Sending unsolicited DNS responses for a particular domain to cache a different IP address for other requestors. Also possible by modifying a local host's file to preclude a DNS server request.

Usage by Financially Motivated Actors: Infected machines can be redirected to malicious sites, unwanted advertising, or ransom attempts.

Usage by Targeted Actors: Traffic can be routed to other destination servers, allowing for exploitation of specific victims.

References

Dan Kaminsky. *Black Ops 2008*. Blackhat US. 2008. http://www.slideshare.net/dakami/dmk-bo2-k8
CAPEC-142: DNS Cache Poisoning. The MITRE Corporation. http://capec.mitre.org/data/definitions/142.html

Impersonation

Definition: Unauthorized use of another person's credentials for fraudulent purposes. Social security and credit card numbers are highly targeted, as well as account credentials for social media.

Method: Opening new accounts using a person's vital information, creating credit cards using their information, and using stolen credentials to transfer money.

Usage by Financially Motivated Actors: Fraud often involves online purchases and transfers using compromised user credentials. Money mules are used to funnel money out of compromised accounts via irreversible transactions to destinations in other areas.

Usage by Targeted Actors: Compromised personal email accounts and social media profiles are used to gather information about current targets. Compromised user credentials are often used to improve efficacy of social engineering campaigns.

References

Symantec. *Symantec Threat Report*. 2011. http://www.symantec.com/content/en/us/enterprise/other_resources/b-istr_main_report_2011_21239364.en-us.pdf
CAPEC-151: Identity Spoofing (Impersonation). The MITRE Corporation. http://capec.mitre.org/data/definitions/151.html

MAC Address Spoofing

Definition: Creating a different IP address to MAC address mapping than was intended by the user.

Method: The actor sends unsolicited ARP replies to a local gateway and associates their machine's MAC address with the IP address of another host on the network. A poorly configured switch may then send traffic destined for other machines to the actor instead.

Usage by Financially Motivated Actors: If a commercial entity provides wireless access to their network without controls to divide production systems, an actor may be able to re-route traffic destined for internal systems to their own machine. For instance, if payment terminals send credit card information to a pre-configured IP address without authenticating the destination machine, actors on the same network could transparently intercept those requests.

Usage by Targeted Actors: An actor can intercept data or prevent traffic from reaching its intended destination. This method can be leveraged for man-in-the-middle, denial of service, or session hijacking, which would allow a targeted actor access to internal user names, passwords, or other sensitive information.

References

Ramachandran, Vivek and Nandi, Sukumar. (2005). Detecting ARP Spoofing: An Active Technique. In Information Systems Security: First International Conference ICISS 2005. Jajodia, Sushil and Mazumdar, Chandan (Eds). Springer. http://books. google.com/books?id=4LmERFxBzSUC&pg=PA239#v=onepage&q&f=false
Cardenas, Edgar D. (2003). MAC spoofing: An introduction. Global Information Assurance Certification Paper, SANS Institute. August 23. http://www.giac.org/ paper/gsec/3199/mac-spoofing-an-introduction/105315.

Pharming

Definition: Creating a malicious replica of another website.

Method: "Cloning" tools can be used to copy a site and capture authentication attempts. Server-side scripts can enumerate visitors and deliver exploits as well.

Usage by Financially Motivated Actors: Domains may be registered with minor typos to capture visitors attempting to browse the legitimate site. Malicious scripts may be hosted on compromised sites, while DNS poisoning often re-directs visitors to these sites.

Usage by Targeted Actors: A targeted actor might leverage pharming to harvest sensitive credentials by sending a phishing message containing links to the site, and collecting login information.

References

Social Engineer Toolkit, "cloner.py" http://www.social-engineer.org/framework/
    Computer_Based_Social_Engineering_Tools:_Social_Engineer_
    Toolkit_%28SET%29
CAPEC-89: Pharming. The MITRE Corporation. http://capec.mitre.org/data/defini-
    tions/89.html

Phishing

Definition: Masquerading as a trustworthy entity via communications in order to elicit sensitive information. A variant of phishing is spearphishing, which is targeted phishing to a limited number of users to collect sensitive information or enterprise credentials.

Method: Crafting fraudulent communications from a plausible sender with an impetus to open an attached file or click an included link. In contrast, spearphishing involves sending a limited number of messages with a specific theme to the recipient. Included URLs are frequently camouflaged as legitimate sites and redirect the user to a malicious website to capture credentials and install Trojan horse software.

Usage by Financially Motivated Actors: Actors send emails themed with urgent financial advice containing malicious links or files. May also include guidance to send money or information to for simple fraud.

Usage by Targeted Actors: A limited number of recipients might receive emails containing malicious payloads which masquerade as expected communications from a trusted sender.

References

"Social Engineering: The Art of Human Hacking," Hadnagy, 2011 p. 284
CAPEC-163: Spear Phishing. The MITRE Corporation. http://capec.mitre.org/data/
    definitions/163.html
NIST Special Publication 800-83: Guide to Malware Incident Prevention and
    Handling

Session Hijacking

D&D Method: Reveal Fictions

Definition: Impersonating a user by replaying captured session information during an established connection.

Method: Intercept a session identifier for a user and provide it to a web site on their behalf. Often implemented by capturing a user's locally stored authentication cookie.

Usage by Financially Motivated Actors: Actors may intercept financial credentials when a victim authenticates to a bank web site in order to transfer money without the victim's knowledge.

Usage by Targeted Actors: Well-resourced actors may be able to intercept requests across the Internet and replay them, allowing access to protected resources.

References

"PHP Security Guide: Sessions." PHP Security Consortium. http://phpsec.org/projects/guide/4.html

CAPEC-102: Session Sidejacking. The MITRE Corporation. http://capec.mitre.org/data/definitions/102.html

M. Bennett and E. Waltz. *Counterdeception Principles and Applications for National Security*. Artech House: Boston, MA, 2007.

C. Paar and J. Pelzl. *Understanding Cryptography: A Textbook for Students and Practitioners*. Springer-Verlag: New York, NY, 2010.

Reveal Fictions; Conceal Facts

Clickjacking

Definition: Tricking a user into clicking on an interactive element that performs an unintended operation. This type of UI Redressing is used to install malware implants, monetize ad campaigns, and spread malware via social media.

Method: Crafted postings that take advantage of a website's layout to hide a "Share" button behind the "Close" button.

Usage by Financially Motivated Actors: Clickjacking can trick site visitors into taking unintended actions, such as making a purchase instead of interacting normally with the webpage.

Usage by Targeted Actors: In conjunction with a pharming site, actors may deceive victims to download a malicious binary instead of interacting with the site as intended.

References

Gustav Rydstedt, Elie Bursztein, Dan Boneh, Collin Jackson. *Frame Busting: a Study of Clickjacking Vulnerabilities.* Stanford University, 2010. http://seclab.stanford.edu/websec/framebusting/framebust.pdf

CAPEC-103: Clickjacking. The MITRE Corporation. http://capec.mitre.org/data/definitions/103.html

IP Address Spoofing

Definition: Creation of packets with a forged source IP address.

Method: Modify the header for an IP packet to include a different source address, which also involves changing the packet's checksum. Well-behaved routers will often drop packets that appear to emanate from bogus source addresses.

Usage by Financially Motivated Actors: This method can augment DoS attacks to conceal the source of incoming traffic. Actors might evade IP-based blacklists by changing their source address frequently.

Usage by Targeted Actors: Initial exploitation activity is highly sensitive to detection, so concealing the source of a network connection is advantageous to an attacker. Vulnerabilities in lower-level networking protocols typically don't require an authenticated sender, making this method feasible in such cases.

References

Tanase, Matthew. (2003). IP Spoofing: An Introduction. *The Security Blog*. http://www.symantec.com/connect/articles/ip-spoofing-introduction.

Man-in-the-Browser

Definition: Modification of web pages to add or change page content without a user's intent.

Method: A malicious program might inject client-side script languages such as JavaScript into the local copy of a page, by exploiting the fact that web pages are loaded on an untrusted client machine.

Usage by Financially Motivated Actors: A banking customer might have their payment request modified, allowing an actor to change the destination account amount. This method is particularly effective when combined with the ability to hide past transaction history.

Usage by Targeted Actors: A user might have their browser session compromised by malicious software, allowing access to sensitive internal resources. Such an attack is feasible even while using second-factor authentication, since the content must be rendered on the client-side for the user.

References

RSA. (2010). Making Sense of Man-in-the-browser Attacks: Threat Analysis and Mitigation for Financial Institutions. White Paper, http://viewer.media.bitpipe.com/1039183786_34/1295277188_16/MITB_WP_0510-RSA.pdf.

Pseudonymity

Definition: The act of creating an alternate identity that is weakly tied to a person's physical identity. One person may use different pseudonyms on various services, and one pseudonym could be used by a collection of individuals (such as Anonymous).

Method: Creation of a name that has little or no relation to vital information.

Usage by Financially Motivated Actors: Accounts whose creation does not require validation are often abused by actors to generate spam and effect fraud. Actors also are highly incentivized to use multiple separate names to avoid identification by law enforcement.

Usage by Targeted Actors: Email accounts and domains are often registered through false personas for use in phishing attacks.

References

Andreas Pfitzmann. *Anonymity, Unlinkability, Unobservability, Pseudonymity.* Anonymity, 2000. http://dud.inf.tu-dresden.de/literatur/Anon_Terminology_ v0.23.pdf

Social Engineering

Definition: Manipulation of people with the purpose of gaining information or an advantage.

Method: Exploit a trust relationship to deceive someone, often by mimicking a known good interaction. For instance, a user is more likely to open an incoming message that is supposedly sent from an acquaintance than from a stranger.

Usage by Financially Motivated Actors: Users might receive an email that purports to be from their financial institution, but is in actuality a phishing attack. Establishing a pretext for the purpose of the communication makes this attack more effective, for example, an email that refers to the victim by name and includes a correct phone number.

Usage by Targeted Actors: Malicious actors who have access to human intelligence and effective social engineering may be able to gain physical access to sensitive facilities, or deliver sophisticated exploits to systems which are otherwise not accessible via network communications.

References

Kenneth May. (2013). *Threatasaurus: The A-Z of computer and data security threats.*
"Social Engineering: The Art of Human Hacking," Hadnagy, 2011

Trojan Horse

Definition: Malicious software crafted to appear benign to the target user.

Method: Infect a user computer by exploiting vulnerabilities in client-side software or the underlying operating system to collect sensitive information or prevent normal operations of the machine. Typically includes the ability to communicate with operators for instructions and acquire additional modules.

Usage by Financially Motivated Actors: Actors deliver malware used to harvest financial information and join botnets for purposes of spamming and DoS attacks. Software is meant to hide from the typical home computer user and security researchers and is generated using publicly available exploit frameworks such as Metasploit, or ZeuS variants.

Usage by Targeted Actors: These actors typically gather sensitive information from government, military, and defense industrial base targets, with the intent of persisting and avoiding detection by host antivirus and network detection. Implants are often created by dedicated developers and leverage openly available tools when possible.

References

"The Dark Visitor." Scott J. Henderson. 2007
"Rise of the Blackhole Exploit Kit." Tim Rains. https://blogs.technet.com/b/security/archive/2012/07/19/the-rise-of-the-black-hole-exploit-kit-the-importance-of-keeping-all-software-up-to-date.aspx
"Overview of Exploit Packs." Mila Parkour. http://contagiodump.blogspot.com/2010/06/overview-of-exploit-packs-update.html

Usage by Defenders

The TTPs deployed by defenders against malicious actors can be categorized from a cyber security perspective as shown in Fig. A.3. That is, defensive cyber-D&D TTPs can be generally categorized as enabling their visibility into user actions/behavior, disabling the actor's visibility into user actions/behavior, or honeypot-type TTPs.

To correlate these defensive cyber-D&D TTPs with the concepts of revealing and concealing facts and fictions, Fig. A.4 is a Venn diagram based on the structure of the D&D methods matrix presented in Chap. 2. Each of the defensive TTPs is categorized in the Venn diagram based on whether it generally reveals or conceals facts or fictions, or some combination thereof.

This Venn diagram leads to several observations. First, there are two intersections: one denoting TTPs that both simulate and dissimulate, and one denoting TTPs that

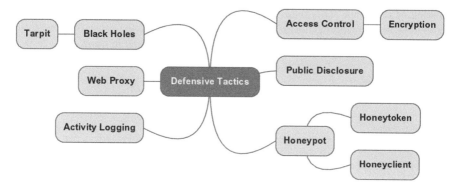

Fig. A.3 Defensive Cyber-D&D TTPs

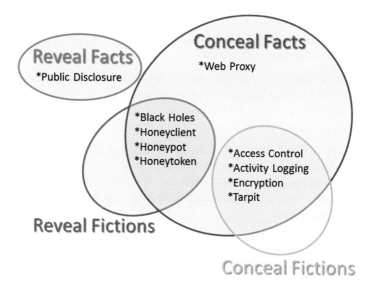

Fig. A.4 Defensive Cyber-D&D Tactics

can be used to conceal either facts or fictions. This suggests some opportunity space for crafting new defensive D&D TTPs in the non-existent intersections. Second, no identifiable TTPs only reveal fictions or only conceal fictions. This suggests potential opportunity space in crafting new TTPs for these sets. Third, there is a set of concealment TTPs which can be used to conceal either facts or fictions. Fourth, all but one of the TTPs are associated with concealment or denial. Perhaps this indicates the "defensive" posture practiced by most organizations, in which the primary means of protection is to deny access to critical information and infrastructure. This also suggests potential opportunity space for developing defensive TTPs that use simulation to mislead, confuse, or influence the adversary. Fifth, there is a large intersection for concealing facts and fictions. Several of these techniques are related to detection. This lends support to the notion presented in Sect. 6.3 that defenders must detect the adversary to achieve their objectives.

Each of these defensive tactics and techniques is explained in more detail in the next several sections, which are organized according to the categories of the D&D methods matrix.

Reveal Facts

Public Disclosure

D&D Method: Reveal Facts

Definition: Any authoritative information released by an organization to the public.

Method: Whitepapers, briefs, press releases, etc. that are publicly distributed through news media, corporate websites, etc.

Usage against Financially Motivated Actors: Performing responsible disclosure of a successful intrusion can influence related businesses to appropriately adapt their security posture. For instance, releasing details of ATM skimmer installations may raise awareness of the problem for reticent banking institutions.

Usage against Targeted Actors: Release of information about the actor and their methods can cause a commensurate "re-tooling" period as the actors replace their infrastructure and refactor intrusion methods. This will likely have a short-term effect of disrupting current operations with little long-term impact on their ability to conduct new operations.

References

Fung, Brian. (2014). The mysterious disappearance of China's elite hacking unit. *The Washington Post*, April 10, http://www.washingtonpost.com/blogs/the-switch/wp/2014/04/10/the-mysterious-disappearance-of-chinas-elite-hacking-unit/.

Conceal Facts

Web Proxy

D&D Method: Conceal Facts

Definition: A method for masking the source of web requests.

Method: A proxy makes a request on behalf of a third party for a resource, filtering both outgoing and incoming information. This is usually implemented via HTTP header modification. This effectively prevents the owner of an external site from viewing the requestor's identifying information.

Usage against Financially Motivated Actors: Web proxies can be used by an organization to filter outgoing traffic to web sites, stripping HTTP headers such as the User-Agent. A proxy can be set to only load content from particular sites, thereby filtering malicious content that otherwise would be executed by the requestor.

Usage against Espionage Motivated Actors: A proxy can be used to prevent actors from enumerating system-specific information which could then be used to develop a customized exploit.

References

Chow, Peter. (2012). Surfing the Web Anonymously—The Good and Evil of the Anonymizer. SANS Institute, InfoSec Reading Room, http://www.sans.org/reading-room/whitepapers/detection/surfing-web-anonymously-good-evil-anonymizer-33995.

Squid Proxy. (2014). Removing the X-FORWARDED-FOR header. http://wiki.squid-cache.org/SquidFaq/ConfiguringSquid

Conceal Facts; Conceal Fictions

Access Control

Definition: Selective restriction of access to information systems and data content.

Method: Access control can be implemented in a number of ways, utilizing both physical/tangible (e.g., smartcard, biometric reader, key-fob) and informational/intangible means (e.g., password, pin, security challenge question responses).

Usage against Financially Motivated Actors: Defenders conceal facts by determining how much control and access over data content is shared with others (i.e., who is authorized). Defenders can conceal fictions by using access control in conjunction with fictional assets.

Usage against Targeted Actors: Permission controls provide access to those authorized or deny access to those not authorized to system resources when concealing factors. Defenders can conceal fictions by using access control in conjunction with fictional assets.

References

Purohit, Vinay (2007). Authentication and Access Control—The Cornerstone of Information Security. TRIANZ White Paper, http://www.tutorialspoint.com/white-papers/40.pdf.

Activity Logging

Definition: A record of the events occurring within an organization's systems and networks.

Method: Systems can be configured to capture data about events occurring on the system and network, and transfer those logs to network defenders. These logs are typically stored and transferred over a secure channel to prevent modification by unauthorized parties.

Usage against Financially Motivated Actors: Suspicious transactions can be logged for later inspection by analysts—including the ability to correlate related events. For instance, a money transfer may be accompanied by a legitimate user logon, but the recipient is international and acting as a money mule.

Usage against Targeted Actors: Certain system files might act as alerting mechanisms, triggering a warning to network defenders if modified in any way. This method allows detection of persistence tools that an actor might install on a compromised system, commonly used to maintain access over long periods of time.

References

Kent, Karen and Souppaya Murugiah. Guide to Computer Security Log Management NIST 800-92. http://csrc.nist.gov/publications/nistpubs/800-92/SP800-92.pdf
Spafford, Eugene. Kim, Gene. Purdue University. 1994. Experiences with Tripwire. https://www.cerias.purdue.edu/assets/pdf/bibtex_archive/94-03.pdf

Encryption

Definition: Translating data into a secret code, referred to as cipher text, which can be decrypted into plain text by using a secret key or password.

Method: Encryption can be used to secure desktops, laptops, removable media, CDs, email, network files, cloud storage, and other devices. Encryption can be configured such that data is automatically decrypted for authorized users. That is, authorized users would not be required to enter an encryption key or password for access.

Usage against Financially Motivated Actors: Applying provably strong encryption to transactions prevents an actor from modifying or reading sensitive data in transit. Message authentication can also be used to verify the integrity of data sent and received.

Usage against Targeted Actors: Encryption can be used to conceal facts and secure sensitive information so that if it is stolen, it cannot be accessed by the targeted actor. Weak encryption might be used to encrypt fake information which is enticing to the targeted actor, thereby wasting their time and resources.

References

Singh, Simon. (2000). *The Code Book: The Science of Secrecy from Ancient Egypt to Quantum Cryptography*. Random House: New York.

Tarpit

Definition: A service that purposely delays incoming connections.

Method: After responding to a request, the machine running the tarpit does not open a socket or prepare a connection. The remote site sends its ACK and believes the three-way handshake is complete. It begins to send data which never reaches a destination. The connection will eventually time out, but since the system believes the connection is live, it will attempt to retransmit, back-off, retransmit, etc. for a period of time.

Usage against Financially Motivated Actors: Tarpits can be used with TCP traffic to group email senders into different traffic classes with bandwidth limitations, thereby reducing the amount of abusive email traffic. Honeypots might also leverage tarpits to slow the progress of automated or manual attacks.

Usage against Targeted Actors: In conjunction with other deception methods, a tarpit might allow defenders to appear stronger than other targets, creating an incentive for the actor to target someone else.

References

Labrea Tarpits http://labrea.sourceforge.net/

Reveal Fictions; Conceal Facts

Black Holes

Definition: Network addresses where incoming traffic is silently discarded without informing the source that the data did not reach its intended recipient.

Method: Designate an IP address in routing tables without a target machine, to which all incoming packets are dropped. A DNS-based Black hole List (DNSBL) or Real-time Black hole List (RBL) is a list of IP addresses published through the Internet Domain Name System (DNS) for computers or networks linked to spamming. Most mail server software can be configured to reject or flag messages sent from a site on such lists.

Usage against Financially Motivated Actors: Defenders might configure internal DNS servers to resolve domains against a blacklist, which silently drops incoming spam messages. Incoming HTTP connections from blacklisted sources might also be dropped to protect against distributed denial of service attacks.

Usage against Espionage Motivated Actors: An internal black hole might act as a tripwire to detect incoming requests for internal domain enumeration (i.e., detecting a ping scan which originates from inside the enterprise network).

References

Cisco Systems. (2005). Remotely Triggered Black Hole Filtering—Destination Based and Source Based. White Paper. http://www.cisco.com/web/about/security/intelligence/blackhole.pdf.

Honeyclient

D&D Method: Reveal Fictions; Conceal Facts

Definition: Software that simulates the behavior of a vulnerable client application to gather information on malicious servers.

Method: Emulate a web browser by generating web requests with a specific browser or referring site. Vulnerabilities and undocumented behavior can be implemented to enhance realism. For example, a web crawler may present itself as a vulnerable version of a popular browser in order to capture the attack technique that an attacker is using. The web crawler can be implemented as a program which mimics the behavior of a human user navigating the Internet.

Usage against Financially Motivated Actors: A vulnerable application can be simulated and deployed against a wide number of Internet sites, useful for finding web pages compromised by exploit kits.

Usage against Espionage Motivated Actors: A subset of sites can be crawled for malicious content, to detect waterhole attacks and proactively block access to malicious scripts.

References

Harstein, Blake. Jsunpack-n: Client-side JavaScript emulation. https://code.google.com/p/jsunpack-n/

Dell'Aera, Angelo. Thug: Low Interaction Browser Honeyclient. http://www.honeynet.org/node/827

Wang, Yi-Min, Beck, Doug, Jiang, Xuxian, Roussev, Roussi, Verbowski, Chad, Chen, Shuo, and King, Sam. Automated Web Patrol with Srtider HoneyMonkeys: Finding Web Sites that Exploit Browser Vulnerabilities, unpublished paper, http://research.microsoft.com/en-us/um/redmond/projects/strider/honeymonkey/NDSS_2006_HoneyMonkey_Wang_Y_camera-ready.pdf, last accessed 28 February, 2014.

Honeypot

D&D Method: Reveal Fictions; Conceal Facts

Definition: A deliberately vulnerable environment constructed to gather information about malicious actors who attempt to misuse it. Honeypots designed to detect and study attacks on network services are called server-side. Honeypots designed to detect attacks on client applications are called client-side honeypots, or honeyclients. Honeypots can be low-interaction (i.e., an emulated resource), high-interaction (i.e., a real or virtual resource), or hybrid (i.e., a combination of both low- and high-interaction functionalities).

Method: A honeypot is used to denote a single machine that collects malware, while honeynets consist of a network of honeypots.

Usage against Financially Motivated Actors: Honeypots are often deployed by security researchers to gather information on infected machines. These can be used to delay the course of an ongoing intrusion, or capture information about the behavior of a bot network.

Usage against Espionage Motivated Actors: A well-crafted honeypot may be effective in collecting information about targeted intrusions, with the caveat that sophisticated actors will likely detect the fiction relatively quickly.

References

Provos, Niels. "A Virtual Honeypot Framework." USENIX Security Symposium. Vol. 173. 2004.

Honeytoken

D&D Method: Reveal Fictions; Conceal Facts

Definition: An entity with no practical use, but which serves as a tripwire to detect unauthorized use. Deployed by security research, vendors and enterprise security teams to gather information about malicious insiders or attackers that are targeting the organization.

Method: Providing a fake credit card number, fake user account, document, or presentation that would never be used legitimately and monitoring for its usage to gather intelligence. Spam detection can be aided by publicly posted email accounts to which any incoming messages are added to a black list filter.

Usage against Financially Motivated Actors: An organization could include a subset of honeytoken credit card accounts whose use indicates compromise of the database.

Usage against Espionage Motivated Actors: An organization could develop a set of fake documents which appear to contain sensitive, but plausible content. Access to the documents would be an indicator of pervasive network compromise or potentially a malicious insider.

References

Spitzner, Lance. Honeytokens: The Other Honeypot. http://www.symantec.com/connect/articles/honeytokens-other-honeypot

Appendix B: False Virtual Persona Checklists

Some deceptions that are possible in the virtual world (e.g., compromising credentials) are more difficult in the physical world. Identity management, manipulation, and social engineering are far more readily accomplished in the virtual world because of the limited sensation and perception allowed by digital media. This limitation is perhaps best captured by the *New Yorker* cartoon shown in Fig. B.1 with the caption, "On the Internet nobody knows you're a dog."[1] People can easily preserve anonymity on the Internet, as the Internet protocols make trusted attribution and traceback very difficult.

Figure B.2 describes a successful generic approach to creating highly persistent, self-replicating, and self-distributing cyber personae.

Setting up a false persona that does not merely behave plausibly, but that can withstand open source scrutiny, presents a challenge. A persona's history cannot suddenly appear; it should be visible via a variety of way-back snapshots. This suggests that planners must craft some false personae, with continuous care and feeding, for years before deployment. This long-term planning and preparation will surely deplete resources. Not all personae must withstand a high degree of scrutiny; a convincing backstory can potentially suffice in such cases.

Techniques for Creating a Deceptive Virtual Persona

Some guidelines on creating a credible virtual identity include:

- Scan the suggestions, try some, and rely on the most productive items. Let others on your team try the least productive (for you) suggestions—they probably have different creative and crafting styles.
- Compare and share the team results on details of the persona on your team's "legend wall." Highlight potential inconsistencies, disconfirmations, and uncertainties; develop story lines to deal with legend and persona problems.
- Revisit some suggestions as the legend wall fills up to address gaps and uncertainties.

---

[1] Peter Steiner, *The New Yorker*, July 5, 1993, © Condé Nast; http://en.wikipedia.org/wiki/On_the_Internet,_nobody_knows_you're_a_dog

© Springer International Publishing Switzerland 2015
K.E. Heckman et al., *Cyber Denial, Deception and Counter Deception*,
Advances in Information Security 64, DOI 10.1007/978-3-319-25133-2

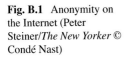

Fig. B.1 Anonymity on
the Internet (Peter
Steiner/*The New Yorker* ©
Condé Nast)

"On the Internet, nobody knows you're a dog."

- Appoint a devil's advocate to challenge the details of the persona and legend.
  Post the challenges and responses on the team legend wall.
- Assume your counter-deception opposite numbers are using similar (or better)
  checklists against your personae and legends.

Screenwriting the Legend

Develop the legend: the history and life story of the persona. Know the deceptive
purpose of the persona. Know and understand the persona's demographics (e.g., age,
gender, ethnicity) to create an appropriate geographical, socio-economic, cultural,
and psychological profile. If you can use an actual identity as the basis of the persona, the legend will be far more credible, but the actual person must be controlled
to avoid leakage: either deceased (and the online death records concealed or obfuscated) or fully controlled by the deceiver (all online contacts under deception control). Plant credible online records about fictional personae planted in appropriate
domains, or in deception-controlled domains, that are consistent with typical real
online personae for individuals with comparable legends. Likewise, the timestamps
of these records must be realistic; that is, they should not all suddenly appear over a
short period of time. The persona's online activity should reflect a pattern of life
(e.g., social media early mornings and evenings on weekdays; business cell phone
and email access in the midday on weekdays).

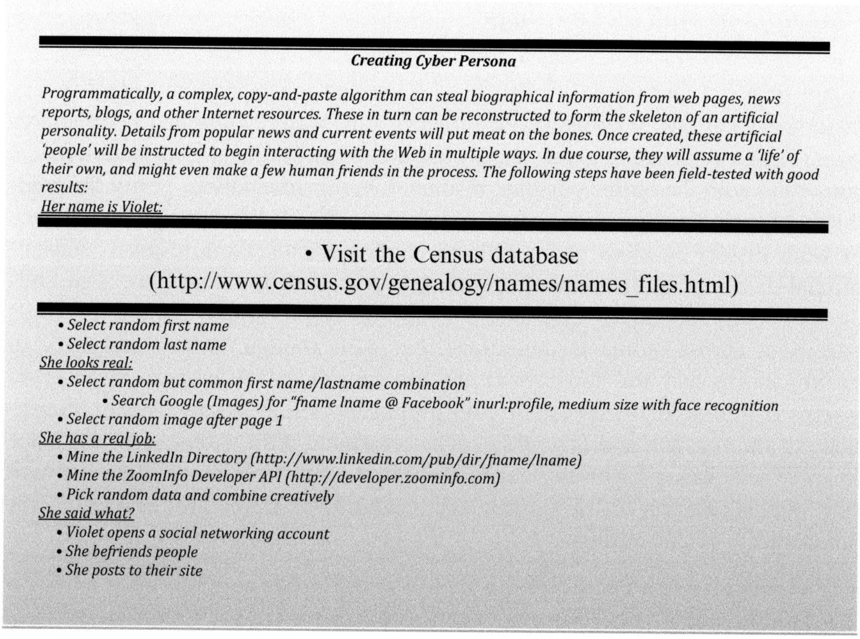

Creating Cyber Persona

Programmatically, a complex, copy-and-paste algorithm can steal biographical information from web pages, news reports, blogs, and other Internet resources. These in turn can be reconstructed to form the skeleton of an artificial personality. Details from popular news and current events will put meat on the bones. Once created, these artificial 'people' will be instructed to begin interacting with the Web in multiple ways. In due course, they will assume a 'life' of their own, and might even make a few human friends in the process. The following steps have been field-tested with good results:

<u>*Her name is Violet:*</u>

- Visit the Census database
(http://www.census.gov/genealogy/names/names_files.html)

- *Select random first name*
- *Select random last name*

<u>*She looks real:*</u>
- *Select random but common first name/lastname combination*
    - *Search Google (Images) for "fname lname @ Facebook" inurl:profile, medium size with face recognition*
- *Select random image after page 1*

<u>*She has a real job:*</u>
- *Mine the LinkedIn Directory (http://www.linkedin.com/pub/dir/fname/lname)*
- *Mine the ZoomInfo Developer API (http://developer.zoominfo.com)*
- *Pick random data and combine creatively*

<u>*She said what?*</u>
- *Violet opens a social networking account*
- *She befriends people*
- *She posts to their site*

Fig. B.2 Guidelines for Creating a Cyber Persona

"John Mitchell's Principle"

"Watch what we do, instead of what we say." Screenwrite the behavior in the legend, then itemize the details needed for the online persona. Instantiate the persona across multiple online domains by creating user profiles in social network services (e.g., Facebook, Asiantown.net, LinkedIn) on online networking or dating services. Use blogs and express legend-consistent opinions, and express parts of the cover story and legend identity across multiple venues. Vary accuracy and consistency to correspond to psychological realities: accounts of childhood memories should not demonstrate photographic recall. Accounts of brief encounters should be brief. Natural reticence, embarrassment, and personal identity management should be reflected in online persona materials.

Confirm the Fine Print on the Resume

Compare online legend documentation, online "pocket litter" (e.g., e-mail folders), and other personal ephemera to Googled elements, present and past press releases, public records, mandatory disclosures (e.g., licenses, census addresses), published personnel data, publication citations, reference works, etc. Plant direct or indirect confirmation information where you would expect such information to be. For example, support claims of foreign travel with consistent photos and photo tags. Avoid obvious deceptions such as "Photoshop-ped" photos.

"Takeoffs as Well as Landings"

Avoid physical and virtual "collisions." Timeline the legend and identify key historical locations, schools, service history, etc. Manufacture and plant appropriate online evidence of existences, roles, and other pertinent information that is consistent with the online persona: resume, CV, documentation. Verify the credibility of birth location address and timeframe. Manufacture and plant evidence of work history as close as possible to employer data. Exploit quasi- and unofficial data repositories. Create online persona sequences (e.g., births of children, schools attended) that make temporal sense. Make temporal details consistent across online instantiations, but with enough "noise" and error to avoid patterns that are "too correct and too consistent." Attempt to make timestamps of online data consistent with purported online history. Make descriptions in the persona and legend history correspond with independent evidence (e.g., "There was a highway next to my house…"). Use Google street view to "see" actual locations in the persona and legend. Use Google images for contemporaneous views of settings.

Create Multiple Sources

Plant online the supporting elements of your subject's online persona. Build online evidence of the other persons described in the subject persona's biography: spouses, ex-spouses, family members, neighbors, classmates, teachers, co-workers, and mailing lists from associations (e.g., church, school, clubs, forums, etc.). Make sure current and former details are consistent with facts (e.g., online e-mail addresses, telephone numbers, etc.) and verify consistency (e.g., residence in Washington, DC, associated with 2xxxx zip codes and 202- phone numbers, and dates when area codes and zip codes were created). Build and plant peripheral facts reflected in the persona, across various online sources. Make sure online personae of relatives generally correspond to the data in the subject persona.

Keeping Book

Appoint a team legend and persona continuity editor/supervisor to check the consistency and continuity of photos, documents, and artifacts associated with the persona, especially across multiple online venues. For example, "the new car" can only be "the new car" at a given time, and in a few places. Reflect age, wear and tear, maturity. Persona details from (supposedly) different times and places should reflect some variability, not contain identical (e.g., copy, cut, and paste) information. Reuse of older legend material in new legend material is okay; use of newer material in supposedly older materials suggests impossible time traveling.

Fake Independence of Sources

Attempt to plant confirming assertions and details for the persona, including apparently irrelevant and immaterial details, in presumably independent online venues and sources. Conceal connections among online sources and any control by the persona. Plant believable explanations and accountings across various online locations and seemingly independent sources for any unavoidable persona loose ends, inconsistencies, and blocks of "missing time" (i.e., time periods where no online subject persona data seem to exist).

Smell Test

Check how you and others on your team feel about your creation, focusing on the subject, the persona, the subject's cover story, and the subject's legend. Too fishy? Too perfumed? Just right? Why? Probe your feelings and reactions to identify possible clues and leads that can be investigated by your counterdeception adversaries.

Set the Scene

Use online resources to physically examine the locations identified in the persona or legend (e.g., birthplace, first home, current home), and examine locational evidence, artifacts, remains, etc., to determine pocket litter information, confirming details, and special knowledge that add verisimilitude to the legend and persona. Identify and use elements of what was really present and what was absent during time periods corresponding to the online persona and legend.

Explore and Exploit Online Resources

Identify the local information resources that must have or could have details on your persona: phone books, records, family albums, or genealogy sites. Build and plant appropriate records or create and plant alternative plausible explanations. Use online photos, videos, and audio records only if they are ambiguous or reflect consistency and verification of textual aspects of legend and persona; avoid self-incrimination via careless use of multimedia legend materials. Check the properties of any multi-media used to ensure the metadata are consistent with the legend.

Use Test Audiences

Run the details of the persona and the legend though an independent test audience, preferably authoritative, and "outside" the chain of command. Attend to audience questions, concerns, likes, and dislikes for clues or leads to deception. Repair problems noted by audiences.

Use the Spin Cycle Judiciously

Use knowledge of how people commonly defend their personal identity to craft specific contingency responses and defenses for your persona. For major pitfalls and problems in the legend and persona, prepare "shocking" self-revelations that serve as deceptive distractions or feints, leading away from the real problems in the deception. Confessing to small deceptions to preserve the persona's self-identity may lead the deception target away from detecting larger deceptions. Prepare and plant evidence to "confirm" these pre-generated "spontaneous" shocking confessions.

Do the Math

If possible, avoid using many numbers, and manufacture realistic evidence to verify any numbers used in the legend or the persona (e.g., bank accounts, salary history, number of children, length of marriage, athletic records, and accomplishments). Check numbers claimed and numbers published for continuity, compatibility, and consistency. Craft claimed numbers to be consistent with prior data, comparable figures, and common sense benchmarks. If necessary, extrapolate trends and compare to related trend data. Check numbers with references and outside experts. Make sure the numbers seem to make common sense.

"The View from the Other Side"

Should your persona have rivals, competitors, or enemies? If so, build and plant multiple, alternative persona descriptions crafted to indirectly and "independently" reinforce the legend and persona. Make these contrarian accounts explainable given the persona and legend you are creating. Exploit stereotypes, folk psychology, and avoid too much complexity.

Step Back from the Dots

Determine how fresh eyes view the "big picture" created by the details of your persona and legend. What alternative premise or posit ("counter-person") is also consistent with the dots you created? Can you use these alternative pictures to reinforce your persona or legend? What evidence to challenge or disprove your persona or legend does the total configuration of dots suggest? Stepping back, let fresh eyes describe your persona and the activities suggested by the legend: what does your "persona" do; how is it important; why is it important? Are the big picture and alternative views of persona and legend consistent with your deception goals and objectives?

Sources: Based on Anthony Marro, "When the government tells lies," *Columbia Journalism Review*, March/April 1985; Tom Rosenstiel "Yakety-yak: The lost art of interviewing," *Columbia Journalism Review*, Jan/Feb 1995; Sherry Ricciardi, "Smoke screen," *American Journalism Review*, Dec 2000; M. L. Stein, "Good questions emerge out of good information," *Nieman Reports*, Summer 2002; Ellen Goodman, "Important questions happen before reporting begins," *Nieman Reports*, Summer 2002; Antonio J. Mendez with Malcolm McConnell, *The Master of Disguise: My Secret Life in the CIA.* New York: HarperCollins Publishers, 1999; Antonio J. Mendez and Matt Baglio, *Argo: how the CIA and Hollywood pulled off the most audacious rescue in history.* New York: Penguin Group, 2012; Christopher Andrew and Vasili Mitrohkin, *The Sword and the Shield: The Mitrohkin Archive and the Secret History of the KGB.* New York: Basic Books, 1999; Oleg Kalugin, *Spymaster: My Thirty-two Years in Intelligence and Espionage Against the West.* New York: Basic Books, 2009.

Counterdeception Techniques for Detecting a Deceptive Virtual Persona

Some suggestions on how to check the validity of a virtual identity include:

- Scan the suggestions, try some, and rely on the most productive items. Let others on your team try the least productive (for you) suggestions—they probably have different search and investigative styles.
- Compare and share the team results regarding key details of the persona on your team's "evidence wall." Highlight consistencies, inconsistencies, confirmation, disconfirmations, and uncertainties; track and manage leads to be followed up.
- Revisit some suggestions as the evidence wall fills up, but still shows gaps and uncertainties.
- Assume your deception opposite numbers are using similar (or better) checklists to build credible online persona and legend.

"John Mitchell's Principle"

In July 1969, after meeting with a group of African American civil rights workers who protested the Administrations action on the Voting Rights Act of 1965, U.S. attorney general, John Mitchell advised, "You will be better advised to watch what we do, instead of what we say." This principle can be applied to cyber-D&D by exploring several questions. Does the person's online behavior seem to conform to characteristics of the online persona and the "legend" that person seems to be trying to create? Does the persona deviate from the perceived demographic (e.g., age, gender, ethnicity)? If so, is the deviation significant or slight (i.e., within reasonable statistical error bars based on measures of central tendency for the demographic)? For example, does a scholar frequent scholarly groups? … attend scholarly conferences? …publish scholarly papers? … review scholarly books? Can scholarly credentials (e.g., degrees) be verified from online (e.g., alumni) records? What is the persona's pattern of life? Is it routine and predictable? How detectable is anomalous behavior? Does the pattern of life conform to the persona's "legend?"

Check the Fine Print on the Resume

Compare online personal documentation (e.g., resumes and CVs, Facebook /social site data) to other online open sources: press releases, public records, mandatory disclosures (e.g., licenses, census addresses), publication citations, reference works, etc. Does confirmation exist where you would expect to find it? For example, do photos and photo tags tend to support claims of foreign travel—or the opposite, disprove denials of foreign travel?

"Takeoffs as Well as Landings"

Identify any historical locations, schools, service history, etc., in the online persona and search for physical existences, roles, and other pertinent information that is consistent or inconsistent with online persona materials: resume, CV, and other documentation. Does the birth location address exist? Did it exist at time of birth? Verify elements of work history with online employer data. Do online persona sequences (e.g., births of children, schools attended) make sense? Are they consistent across online instantiations? Are timestamps of online data consistent with purported online history? Do descriptions by the persona history correspond with independent evidence (e.g., "There was a highway next to my house…")? Use Google street view to "see" locations in the persona and legend. Use Google images for contemporaneous views of settings.

Develop Multiple Sources

Examine in detail all online representation of the subject persona. Seek out online evidence of others described in the persona: spouses, ex-spouses, family members, neighbors, classmates and alumni, teachers, co-workers, and mailing lists from associations (e.g., church, school, clubs, forums, etc.). Examine current and former online e-mail addresses, telephone numbers, etc., and verify consistency (e.g., residence in Washington, DC, associated with 2xxxx zip-codes and 202- phone numbers; dates when area and zip codes were used consistent with dates they were introduced). Use other online resources to discover and confirm peripheral facts reflected in the persona. Do online personae of relatives correspond to data in the subject persona?

Keeping Book

Check consistency and credibility of photos, documents, and artifacts associated with the persona, especially across multiple online venues. Persona details from (supposedly) different times and places should reflect some variability, and not identical (i.e., copy, cut, and paste) information. Reuse of older legend material in new legend material is okay; use of newer material in supposedly older materials suggests impossible time traveling.

Confirm All Sources

Attempt to independently confirm assertions and details of the persona, including apparently irrelevant and immaterial details. Use online sources to follow up on loose ends, inconsistencies, and large blocks of "missing time" (i.e., time periods when no online subject persona data seem to exist).

Smell Test

How do you and others on your team feel about the subject, the persona, the subject's cover story, and the subject's legend? Why? Probe feelings and reactions to surface possible deception clues and leads that can be investigated.

Go to the Scene

Use online resources to physically examine locations identified in the persona or legend (e.g., birthplace, first home, current home); examine locational evidence, artifacts, etc., to determine inaccuracies, inconsistencies, and missing elements. Attempt to establish what was really present *and* what was absent during time periods corresponding to the online persona and legend.

Explore and Exploit Online Resources

Search any local information resources: phone books, records, family albums, and genealogy sites. Examine online photos, videos, and audio records for consistency and verification of textual aspects of the legend and persona. Do the multi-media elements of the legend look, sound, and feel natural or artificial? Check the properties for the multi-media; are the metadata consistent with the legend?

Use Independent Experts and Fact-Checkers

Run details of persona investigation and conclusions through an independent credibility filter, preferably authoritative, and "outside" the chain of command. How does your persona and legend "evidence board" look to the outsiders?

Anticipate the Spin Cycle If You Confront the Subject

Know how people commonly defend their personal identity. Be prepared for "shocking" self-revelations that may be distractions or feints. Have proof that computer activity was generated by the persona and not by a third party with access to the persona's files. Criminals may "hide in prison," confessing to small crimes to avoid investigation of larger crimes; be prepared to follow up on spontaneous confessions.

Check the Math

If possible, independently verify numbers asserted in the persona (e.g., bank accounts, salary history, number of children, length of marriage, athletic records, and accomplishments). Are numbers claimed and numbers published comparable? Examine claimed numbers and compare to prior data, comparable figures, and common sense benchmarks. Extrapolate trends and compare to related trend data. Check numbers with references and outside experts. Do the numbers seem to make sense?

"The View from the Other Side"

Seek out minority, opposition, or contrarian views on the persona from online rivals, competitors, and enemies. Build multiple, alternative persona descriptions and legends and compare them to the gathered information. Were contrarian accounts explainable?

Connect the Dots

What "big picture" do the persona and legend details describe? What alternative premise or posit ("counter-person") is also consistent with the dots? What is the evidence to challenge or disprove the persona or legend? What does the "persona" mean? How is it important? Why is it important? Could the "persona" be even more significant and deceptive than it appears?

Sources: Based on Anthony Marro, "When the government tells lies," *Columbia Journalism Review*, March/April 1985; Tom Rosenstiel "Yakety-yak: The lost art of interviewing," *Columbia Journalism Review*, Jan/Feb 1995; Sherry Ricciardi, "Smoke screen," *American Journalism Review*, Dec 2000; M. L. Stein, "Good questions emerge out of good information," *Nieman Reports*, Summer 2002; Ellen Goodman, "Important questions happen before reporting begins," *Nieman Reports*, Summer 2002; Antonio J. Mendez with Malcolm McConnell, *The Master of Disguise: My Secret Life in the CIA*. New York: HarperCollins Publishers, 1999; Antonio J. Mendez and Matt Baglio, *Argo: how the CIA and Hollywood pulled off the most audacious rescue in history*. New York: Penguin Group, 2012; Christopher Andrew and Vasili Mitrohkin, *The Sword and the Shield: The Mitrohkin Archive and the Secret History of the KGB*. New York: Basic Books, 1999; Oleg Kalugin, *Spymaster: My Thirty-two Years in Intelligence and Espionage Against the West*. New York: Basic Books, 2009.

Appendix C: Deception Maxims Applied to Defensive Cyber-D&D

Deception maxims developed for offensive operations can be adapted to defensive cyber-denial and deception (D&D) operations for computer network defense (CND). The right-hand column shows deception maxims and their explanations adapted to defensive cyber-D&D needs and cyber-D&D examples.

Deception Maxim[a]	Maxim Explanation[b]	Cyber-D&D Examples for CND (adapted from Rowe, 2008; Cohen, 2007; and Rowe, 2004[c])
1. Magruder's Principle	It is generally easier to induce an opponent to maintain a preexisting belief than to present notional evidence to change that belief. Thus, it may be more fruitful to examine how an opponent's existing beliefs can be turned to advantage than to attempt to alter these views.	*Attackers will assume they are undetected and that computer responses will be accepted as veridical:* • Give false excuses for being unable to do something requested by attackers • Falsify file-creation timestamps as would be expected for an active user (i.e., backdate files to the past) • Build honeypot environment with similarities to actual environment (e.g., server types, usernames, etc.)

(continued)

© Springer International Publishing Switzerland 2015
K.E. Heckman et al., *Cyber Denial, Deception and Counter Deception*,
Advances in Information Security 64, DOI 10.1007/978-3-319-25133-2

(continued)

Deception Maxim[a]	Maxim Explanation[b]	Cyber-D&D Examples for CND (adapted from Rowe, 2008; Cohen, 2007; and Rowe, 2004[c])
2. Limitations to human information processing	There are several limitations to human information processing that are exploitable in the design of deception schemes: *Acclimatization*: small changes over time in observables; *Conditioning*: repeated presentation of stimuli; *Law of small numbers*: generalize from very small samples; *Availability*: conclusions from memorable examples; *Representativeness*: conclusions based on superficial resemblances; *Negative evidence*: drawing inferences from absence of evidence, assuming absence of evidence is evidence of absence; *Fallacious evidence*: drawing inferences from evidence known or suspected to be false; *Unimaginativeness*: dismissing the unlikely as impossible	*Develop deception ploys that tend to overwhelm human processing or exploit human limits:* • Delay in processing commands • Tamper with attacker communications to corrupt command results • Swamp attacker with messages (e.g., denial of service)
3. Multiple forms of surprise	Surprise can be achieved using novel locations, strength, actors, intention, style, and timing.	*Select a few key deception areas for maximal surprise, and support with veridical information:* • Use protocol-level deception to present false services to an attacker • Transfer attacker to a deception environment (e.g., high interaction honeypot) • Repurpose attacker's malware and target their system • Set up vulnerable systems or users to attract attackers (e.g., low interaction honeypot)
4. Jones's Lemma	Deception becomes more difficult as the number of channels available to the target increases. Nevertheless, within limits, the greater the number of channels that are controlled by the deceiver, the greater the likelihood that the deception will be believed.	*As much as possible know and control channels used by attackers:* • Monitor attacker activities using hidden network and host-based means • Disallow attacker commands that would reveal additional information about deception environment • Disallow attacker commands in ways that require additional attacker information • Filter outgoing web traffic from compromised machines • Disallow access to internal resources from a suspected compromised machine • Exploit channels that are clearly uncontrolled (e.g., open sources) for information that reinforces deception information via controlled channels

(continued)

(continued)

Deception Maxim[a]	Maxim Explanation[b]	Cyber-D&D Examples for CND (adapted from Rowe, 2008; Cohen, 2007; and Rowe, 2004[c])
5. A choice among types of deception	The deception planner can *reduce* the ambiguity in the mind of the target in order to make the target more certain of a particular falsehood rather than less certain of the truth. That is, the target should be quite certain, but wrong. Alternatively, the deception planner can *increase* the ambiguity in order to conceal the critical elements of the truth by increasing the range of incorrect alternatives and/or the supporting evidence. That is, increasing the noise may enhance the ambiguity. Increasing the ambiguity may be beneficial when the target already has several elements of truth in his possession.	*Conceal critical information:* • Make valuable data or servers appear unimportant • Hide security software in plain sight by using process renaming • Rename high vulnerability files *Mislead with false but critical and compelling information:* • Present files with deceptive contents
6. Axelrod's Contribution: The husbanding of assets	There are circumstances where deception assets should be husbanded, despite the costs of maintaining them and the risk of exposure, until they can be put to more fruitful use.	*Conserve high value deceptions and time their use to gain high value effects:* • Transfer Trojan horses back to attacker • Software with a Trojan horse that is sent to attacker • Transfer attacker from a low interaction honeypot to a high interaction honeypot
7. Sequencing rule	Deception activities should occur in a sequence that prolongs the target's false perceptions of the situation for as long as possible.	*Sequence deception ploys to increasingly deceive, mislead, and conceal:* • Give false system data • Expose false vulnerabilities in software • Systematically misunderstand attacker commands • Introduce delay in command processing • Plant disinformation to cover leaks and compromises (e.g., via user file contents)

(continued)

(continued)

Deception Maxim[a]	Maxim Explanation[b]	Cyber-D&D Examples for CND (adapted from Rowe, 2008; Cohen, 2007; and Rowe, 2004[c])
8. The importance of feedback	Accurate feedback from the target increases the deception's likelihood of success. Observable "comeback" responses, designed into the deception-triggered actions intended for the target, can be used to assess the success or failure of the deception operations. Overt and covert back-channel access to the target can be similarly exploited.	*Use ploys that lead attacker to reveal additional information, or behave in revealing ways:* • Systematically misunderstand attacker commands • Tamper attacker communications to corrupt command results • Encourage repeated attacks with enticements to reveal attacker's pattern of life and enable digital forensics (e.g., to geo-locate attacker) • Embed tell-tails in data attackers will exfiltrate
9. The Monkey's Paw	The deception may produce subtle and unwanted side effects. Deception planners should be sensitive to this possibility and attempt to minimize unwanted side effects.	*Ploys may have unintended consequences or side-effects; prepare "blow-offs" and "cool-outs" to minimize "blow-back" effects:* • Frighten attacker with false messages from incident responders or authorities • Present attacker with myriad honeypot systems
10. Care in the design of planned placement of deceptive material	Great care must be taken when designing schemes to leak notional plans. Apparent windfalls are subject to close scrutiny and are often disbelieved. Genuine leaks often occur under circumstances generally thought to be improbable. Deceptive information is more likely to be accepted by the target if the target has to work for it; the target must 'discover' the evidence, and should have to work hard for it, to be more convinced of its authenticity and value. Information that is easily obtained seems to be less credible and of doubtful value.	*Assume attackers will question authenticity:* • Transfer Trojan horses back to attacker—works better if attacker sees this as yield from a nefarious exploit • Software with a Trojan horse that is sent to attacker—make the attacker want to get it and work hard to get it • Using library functions for defensive deceptions offers great opportunity but there is great complexity in producing just the right effects without providing obvious evidence that something is not right; i.e., making it too easy for attacker to get to the "good stuff" *Assume attackers will accept authenticity:* • Seed deception environment with crafted information that the attacker expects to steal (i.e., relevant files, internal memos) • Make heightened security posture claims public

[a.] *Deception Maxims: Fact and Folklore*, Washington DC: Central Intelligence Agency; and Princeton, NJ: Everest Consulting Associates and Mathtech, Inc., October 1980
[b.] Adapted from *Deception Maxims*, Ibid. and from Michael Bennett and Edward Waltz (2007) *Counterdeception Principles and Applications for National Security*. Boston MA; Artech House
[c.] Rowe, N. C. (2008). Deception in Defense of Computer Systems from Cyber Attack. *Cyber Warfare and Cyber Terrorism*; Cohen, F. (2007). A Framework for Deception. *National Security Issues in Science, Law, and Technology: Confronting Weapons of Terrorism,* 13, 123. Rowe, Neil C. (2004) "A model of deception during cyber-attacks on information systems." In *IEEE First Symposium on Multi-Agent Security and Survivability,* pp. 21-30. IEEE, 2004

Appendix D: Strategic Denial & Deception Capabilities

This appendix summarizes historical and contemporary research on the components of a mature strategic denial and deception (D&D) capability. The descriptions include analyses of Soviet and U.S. strategic D&D capabilities, analyses and recommendations of the Defense Science Board, and recommendations by scholars and analysts regarding strategic D&D capabilities in the Information Age. Chapter 8 of this book used these descriptions of mature strategic D&D capabilities to define the basic elements of a capability maturity model (CMM) for strategic cyber-D&D capabilities.

The head of the U.S. Intelligence National Indications Center[1] concluded in 1972 that "the U.S. Government…is vulnerable to deception:"

> The average U.S. intelligence analyst today [circa 1972] is almost totally unprepared to cope with an enemy deception effort—and this will likely be true also of his supervisor and the policy planner. Our experience of recent years justifies a conclusion that the U.S. Government, at both its intelligence and policy levels, is vulnerable to deception.

This concern—that the United States is unprepared to deal with adversary strategic D&D—reappears repeatedly up to the present. An appraisal of strategic D&D[2] in 2000 noted:

> A concern about the threat of high-level denial and deception has waxed and waned among Americans since the end of World War II. … how much of a threat does denial and deception pose to American interests today? Do globalization, proliferating communication technologies, and the dissemination of vast amounts of information make effective foreign denial and deception more or less likely? Will more information and data sources make policymakers better informed or will the proliferation of information simply create confusion?

---

[1] Davis, Euan G. and Cynthia M. Grabo (1972) "Strategic Warning and Deception." Joint Chiefs of Staff Strategic Planning Seminar, April 1972. https://www.cia.gov/library/center-for-the-study-of-intelligence/kent-csi/vol16no4/html/v17i1a05p_0001.htm

[2] Roy Godson and James J. Wirtz (2000) "Strategic Denial and Deception," *International Journal of Intelligence and Counter-Intelligence*, v. 13, pp. 424–437.

© Springer International Publishing Switzerland 2015
K.E. Heckman et al., *Cyber Denial, Deception and Counter Deception*,
Advances in Information Security 64, DOI 10.1007/978-3-319-25133-2

Organizers of a recent (2012) CACI International symposium[3] again noted U.S. vulnerabilities to strategic D&D:

> ... strong, confident nations lack the natural incentive to employ surprise, denial and deception–indeed, these are often dismissed as "weapons of the weak." This is why surprise, denial and deception are the ultimate asymmetric threats: they exploit our natural proclivities and inherent vulnerabilities, capitalizing on vanity, complacency and self-delusion. Unable to take their opponents head on, these actors rely on shock and psychological dislocation as force multipliers.

Kass and London[4] also warned in a 2013 paper:

> Given the United States' global interests and alliance commitments, adversaries have a major incentive to use denial and deception against U.S. intelligence collection and analysis. ... Terrorist and criminal networks are especially reliant on—and adept at—denial and deception at all levels. Proliferators of WMDs and advanced weapons systems, as well as illicit narcotics and people traffickers, are also highly incentivized to avoid detection by modern intelligence, surveillance and reconnaissance ...There is limited understanding [in the United States] of the unique ways in which nations and non-state actors view denial and deception as force-multipliers.

Some intriguing empirical evidence suggests that historically the United States and its allies were less willing than their adversaries to use strategic D&D operations during the Cold War and less effective when they did use it. Charters and Tugwell[5] compared cases of "Eastern" (i.e., Soviet Bloc) and "Western" (i.e., U.S. and allies) strategic deception operations during the Cold War (i.e., through 1990); their analyses are summarized in Tables D.1 and D.2.

Charters and Tugwell's analyses show 50 % more cases of "Eastern" strategic deception operations than "Western" (12 versus 8 cases). The "Eastern" operations were more often successful or partially successful (91 % versus 63 %), and "Eastern" deception operations were much more likely to have positive impacts on the deception sponsor's wider policy (73 % versus 25 %). These data, and the assessments of analysts, scholars, and the Intelligence Community during and after the Cold War consistently suggest the need for better "Western" understanding of the capabilities and impacts of strategic D&D.

U.S. intelligence organizations have long been concerned with adversary capabilities for strategic D&D, especially those of the Soviet Bloc countries. The Central Intelligence Agency's 1957 Special National Intelligence Estimate highlighted the following strategic deception capabilities in Communist governments:

- Control over the information respecting their countries available to the outside world;

---

[3] London, J. P. and Lani Kass (2012) "Surprise, Deception, Denial, Warning and Decision: Learning the Lessons of History," CACI International Inc.

[4] Kass, Lani and J. Phillip "Jack" London (2013) "Surprise, Deception, Denial and Warning: Strategic Imperatives," *Orbis*, v. 57, n. 1, Winter 2013, pp. 59–82. http://www.sciencedirect.com/science/article/pii/S0030438712000786

[5] David A. Charters & Maurice A. Tugwell, eds. (1990) *Deception Operations: Studies in the East-West Context*. London: Brassey's.

Table D.1 Cold war deception operations: Eastern

Charters & Tugwell chapter	Case study	Deception purpose	Type of target	Results of deception	Impact on sponsor's wider policy
1	Reichstag Fire	Anti-fascist Mobilization	Adversary Publics	Successful	Positive
2	Klugmann	Anti-Mihailovich Pro-Tito Mobilization	Adversary Leaders and Publics	Successful	Positive
3	Orthodox Church	Mobilization of Christians	Adversary Publics	Partly Successful	Generally Positive
4A	Khrushchev's Inflated Claims	Concealment of Strategic Inferiority	Adversary Leaders and Publics	Successful	Negative
4B	Soviet Missiles for Cuba	Concealment of Deployment	Adversary Leaders	Failure of dissimulation exposed operation	Negative
5 A	Four Soviet Interventions	Concealment and Surprise	Adversary Leaders	Successful	Positive
5 B	Four Soviet Interventions	Legitimacy	Domestic and Adversary Publics	Partly Successful	Positive but Created Problems
6	Six-Day War	Anti-Israel Mobilization	Client Leaders	Successful but ran out of control	Negative
7	Vietnamese Deceptions	Anti-U.S., Pro-Hanoi Mobilization	Adversary Publics	Successful	Positive
8	Aldo Moro	Anti-US Mobilization	Adversary Publics	Partly Successful	Positive but Very Weak
9	KAL 007	Legitimacy	Domestic and Adversary Publics	Partly Successful	Positive
10	Peace Offensive	Anti-Defense Mobilization	Adversary Publics	Partly Successful	Positive
12 Cases				91 % Successful or Partly Successful	73 % Positive Impact

- Ability to systematically falsify national information, and masses of internally consistent but actually deceptive data;
- Control over outside observation of national life;
- Unconstrained by concerns for public involvement or reaction;
- Knowledge of U.S. intelligence capabilities;

Table D.2 Cold war deception operations: Western

Charters & Tugwell chapter	Case study	Deception purpose	Type of target	Results of deception	Impact on sponsor's wider policy
11	Protocol M	Anti-Soviet Mobilization	Domestic Publics	Successful Until Exposed	Positive
12A	CIA in West Europe	Anti-Communist Mobilization	Allied Publics	Successful Until Exposed	Positive
12B	CIA and the Munich Radios	Anti-Soviet Mobilization	Allied and Domestic Leaders and Publics	Successful Until Exposed	Initially Positive; Negative when Exposed
13	Suez, 1956	Legitimacy	Domestic and Allied Leaders and Publics	Partly Successful	Negative; Distorted Policy & Undermined Trust
14 A	U-2 Operations	Concealment	Adversary Leaders	Failure of Dissimulation Exposed Operation	Negative
14 B	Post U-2 Cover-up	Legitimacy	Domestic Leaders and Publics	Failed: Simulations not credible	Negative; Undermined Trust
15	Bay of Pigs	Legitimacy	Domestic Leaders and Publics	Failure of Dissimulation Exposed Truth	Negative
16	Enemy Strength in Vietnam	Mobilize U.S. Confidence in War Effort	Domestic Publics	Successful until Tet Offensive Exposed True Enemy Strength	Negative
8 Cases				63 % Successful or Partly Successful	25 % Positive Impact

- Freedom and organizational capabilities to conduct wide-ranging, large scale, long continuance, and extensive deception operations;
- Intelligence capabilities to gain rapid and correct knowledge of the impact of deception operations;
- Knowledge and capabilities to exploit preconceptions and biases of U.S. and allied intelligence.[6]

---

[6]Central Intelligence Agency (1957) *Special National Intelligence Estimate Number 100-2-57: Soviet Capabilities for Deception,* 28 May 1957. CIA Historical Review Program Release as Sanitized. www.foia.cia.gov/docs/DOC_0000269470/DOC_0000269470.pdf

Analysts of the Soviet Union in the early 1990s warned of Soviet strategic deception[7] as having:

- Long-standing historical, organizational, and operational traditions of using political, economic, and military strategic deception;
- Extensive organizational and doctrinal bases for strategic deception;
- National-level coordination of strategic deception across political, economic, and military objectives;
- Capabilities for perception management of adversary decision-makers, as well as denial and deception of adversary intelligence systems and organizations.

More recently, military commentators and advisors have called for greater U.S. strategic deception capabilities, and have described the specific capabilities required. For example, in 2009 the Defense Science Board[8] recommended the following strategic deception capabilities:

- Processes to inform defense strategy to include effects of own strategic denial and deception;
- Capabilities for denial and deception sensitivity analysis of own and adversary intelligence estimates;
- Intelligence on adversary strategic objectives, strategy, perceptions of U.S. strengths and weaknesses, and adversary cultural norms and preferences;
- Sophisticated understanding of the adversary's intelligence-gathering processes and political/decision cycles, and capabilities to exploit the preconceptions and biases of adversary intelligence and decision-makers;
- Strategic counterintelligence and operations to degrade foreign intelligence capabilities;
- Programs and people to focus on detection of adversary denial and deception, and to assess and counter foreign denial and deception;
- Denial and deception analysis ("red teaming") of U.S. analytic products;

---

[7] See Glantz, David (1989) *Soviet Military Deception in the Second World War*. London: Frank Cass. Dailey, Brian D. and Patrick J. Parker, eds. (1987) *Soviet Strategic Deception*. Lexington, MA: Lexington Books. Charters, David A. and Maurice A. J. Tugwell, eds. (1990) *Deception Operations: Studies in the East-West Context*. London: Brassey's.

[8] See Defense Science Board (2009) *Summer Study on Capability Surprise. Volume I: Main Report, September* 2009, Office of the Under Secretary of Defense for Acquisition, Technology, and Logistics, Washington, D.C. 20301-3140. Weaver, Warren S. (2010) *Organizing for Operational Deception*. School of Advanced Military Studies United States Army Command and General Staff College, Fort Leavenworth, KS. Weaver's is one of several dozen theses and papers by military personnel at various military schools and war colleges calling for greater use of and capabilities for military deception. See also Glenney, William (2009) "Military Deception in the Information Age: Scale Matters," in Brooke Harrington ed. (2009) *Deception: From Ancient Empires to Internet Dating*. Stanford: Stanford University Press. Daniel, Donald C. F. (2005) "Denial and Deception," in Jennifer E. Sims & Burton Gerber eds. (2005) *Transforming U.S. Intelligence*. Washington DC: Georgetown University Press. Shulsky, Abram (2002) "Elements of Strategic Denial and Deception," in Roy Godson & James J. Wirtz (2002) *Strategic Denial and Deception: The Twenty-First Century Challenge*. New Brunswick NJ: Transaction Publishers.

- Improved intelligence estimation, including multiple estimates of adversary intentions and possible plans; assumptions checking, and analysis of competing hypotheses, impact estimates;
- Situation awareness, linked to intelligence and strategy adaptive behavior adjustment and learning;
- Denial and deception teams, under a standing strategic surprise/deception entity;
- Modern indications and warning process, intelligence for net assessments, and a Capability Assessment Warning and Response Office;
- Capabilities to deceive adversaries about own plans, intentions, and actions, with deception integral to any major operation or campaign;
- Supporting information operations through cyber deception;
- Creating surprise with deception both at the operational and strategic levels, undertaking sophisticated, orchestrated events, which the adversary will believe, while protecting own critical information assets;
- Organizational integration of strategy, intelligence, and strategic deception, with common operational pictures and high-level coordination and control across national security elements.

In summary, strategic deception capabilities[9] seem to require:

- *Strategic Coherence:* a coherent strategic deception plan in mind to achieve own objectives, and to determine how deception target must act to attain own objectives;
- *Understanding the Adversary:* understand the deception target's preconceptions and perspectives well enough to know what misinformation will deceive and lead the adversary to act in the desired manner, a one-size-fits-all approach will not suffice;
- *Cadre of D&D Practitioners:* a well-organized cadre of astute and experienced career *plotters* of denial and deception, individuals with technical virtuosity, creativity, flair, pluck, artistry, a keen interest in playing the D&D and counterdeception game, ability to place themselves in the adversary's shoes, with a supple and narrative (or abductive, rather than analytic, or inductive-deductive) frame of mind;
- *D&D Cadre Roles:* including intelligence *D&D action analysts* engaged in spotting adversaries who seem ripe for deception and bringing them to the attention of policymakers, D&D tradecraft advisors and plotters, and D&D executive control and coordination agents;
- *Organizational Infrastructure for Deception and Security Measures*: a deception control group with the bureaucratic clout to orchestrate the deception effort, using other agencies of government as necessary;

[9] Shulsky, Abram (2002) "Elements of Strategic Denial and Deception," in Roy Godson & James J. Wirtz (2002) *Strategic Denial and Deception: The Twenty-First Century Challenge.* New Brunswick NJ: Transaction Publishers. Daniel, Donald C. F. (2005) "Denial and Deception," in Jennifer E. Sims & Burton Gerber eds. (2005) *Transforming U.S. Intelligence.* Washington DC: Georgetown University Press.

- *Channels to Reach the Adversary:* the deception control group must have information channels to reach the adversary target, and knowledge of target's intelligence collection, analysis, and estimation capabilities;
- *Feedback:* deception control group must have steadily flowing, current, and reliable information about the adversary's actions, intentions, and reactions, and intelligence on whether deception target has taken the bait, and how the target assesses and reacts to the misinformation thus acquired.

Military officers seem to concur with these recommendations for Information Age capabilities for strategic D&D. Webb[10] sees the Information Age as a boon to strategic deceivers, with manageable costs:

> ...the Information Age has dramatically increased the ability of a deceiver to plan and execute strategic deception. The abundance of information facilitates the deceiver's ability to have a more in-depth understanding of the target's perception of the environment and how he collects information. This knowledge in conjunction with the expansive channels available to transfer information increases the effectiveness of deception. Finally, the Information Age affords the deceiver with greater capability to receive feedback that ultimately enhances the ruse. The benefits also come with a cost. The Information Age introduces new challenges to modern deceivers. Information overload and keeping disinformation above the noise level is more difficult amidst the vast quantities of information available. Multiple channels and an abundance of information challenge the deceiver to develop a deception plan that remains coherent through several mediums and sources all occurring in a shorter amount of time.

To perform *information age strategic deception* Glenney[11] described additional necessary capabilities that apply to *strategic cyber-D&D*:

- Part of a compelling competition of ideas;
- Significant intellectual capital, resources, and time;
- Part of all military planning at the strategic and operational levels of war;
- Enhanced by modern technology;
- Assumed to be part of the strategy of all adversaries;
- Conducted by the united states in full compliance with international law and the norms of warfare, recognizing that the adversary may not be comparably constrained;
- Conducted in a dynamic, complex multi-target, multi-organizational environment;

---

[10] Webb, Michael D. (2006) *Creating a New Reality: Information Age Effects on the Deception Process.* Thesis to School of Advanced Air and Space Studies, Air University, Maxwell Air Force Base, Alabama, June 2006. Other commentators endorse information age deception capabilities at the tactical and operational levels: "Proper utilization of deception at the tactical and operational level is essential, especially in this era of insurgency and "three block" warfare. In short, to achieve U.S. objectives … smaller U.S. forces are going to have to outwit, not just out gun, the enemy." Martin, Charmaine L. (2008) *Military Deception Reconsidered.* Thesis Naval Postgraduate School, Monterey, California, June 2008, p. 37.

[11] Glenney, William (2009) "Military Deception in the Information Age: Scale Matters," in Brooke Harrington ed. (2009) *Deception: From Ancient Empires to Internet Dating.* Stanford: Stanford University Press.

- Targeted at both adversary decision makers, relevant organizations, and more diffuse targets (including national populations).

As noted, Chap. 8 drew on these historical and contemporary descriptions of mature strategic D&D capabilities to define the basic elements of a capability maturity model (CMM) for strategic cyber-D&D capabilities.

Appendix E: Definitions

Acronyms

A-Type Deception	Ambiguity-Type Deception
APT	Advanced Persistent Threat
CCD	Camouflage, Cover, and Deception
D&D	Denial and Deception
DNS	Domain Name System
EEDI	Essential Elements of Deception Information
EEFI	Essential Elements of Friendly Information
IO	Information Operations
M-Type Deception	Mislead-Type Deception
MILDEC	Military Deception
NDDI	Non-Discloseable Elements of Deception Information (NDDI)
NEFI	Non-Essential Elements of Friendly Information
OPSEC	Operations Security
RATs	Remote Access Trojans

Glossary of Terms

This section is a glossary of generic terms that are likely to be encountered when reading about D&D. Some, but not all, of these terms are used in this book.

© Springer International Publishing Switzerland 2015
K.E. Heckman et al., *Cyber Denial, Deception and Counter Deception*,
Advances in Information Security 64, DOI 10.1007/978-3-319-25133-2

Term	Definition
A-Type (Ambiguity-Type) Deception	The purposeful intent to increase ambiguity by surrounding a target with irrelevant information, or to cause confusion based on a lack of certainty. The aim is to keep the target unsure of one's true intentions. A number of alternatives are developed for the target's consumption, built on misinformation that is both plausible and sufficiently significant to cause the target to expend resources to cover it. See also M-Type Deception; Active Deception.
Access Control	Access control is the selective restriction of access to systems and data. Controls can include physical or knowledge-based authentication, from a smartcard to passwords or challenge questions.
Active Deception	The deceiver reveals deceptive facts and fictions to mislead the opponent, while concealing critical facts and fictions to prevent the opponent from forming the correct estimates or taking appropriate actions. Active deception normally involves a calculated policy of disclosing half-truths supported by appropriate "proof" signals or other material evidence.
Advanced Persistent Threat (APT)	APT refers to malicious actors that are organized, technically capable, and persistently attempt to gain access to their targets. These actors are typically motivated by either large financial gain or intelligence gathering. Coordination of intrusion attempts and exploitation of previously unknown vulnerabilities are hallmarks of APT actors, as are encrypted communication, stealth techniques, and development of custom exploitation tools. Persistent intrusion attempts and the ability to reliably access victim networks is another key differentiator between sophisticated and opportunistic actors.
Adaptive Camouflage	In biology, camouflage that an animal actively adapts, often rapidly, to its surroundings. For example, the coleoid cephalopods (i.e., octopus, squid, cuttlefish) possess soft bodies, diverse behavior, elaborate skin patterning capabilities, and a sophisticated visual system that controls body patterning camouflage. Cephalopods use keen vision and sophisticated skin—with direct neural control for rapid change and fine-tuned optical diversity—to rapidly adapt their body pattern for appropriate camouflage against an array of visual backgrounds: colorful coral reefs, temperate rock reefs, kelp forests, sand or mud plains, seagrass beds and others.
Agent of Influence (agent po vliyaniyu/agent vliyaniye)	This is a form of Soviet Active Measures (aktivnye meropriatia). A controlled agent whose loyalties and sources of influence are disguised or covert, typically operating in an opinion or media leadership role.
Aggressive Mimicry	In biology, aggressive mimicry occurs when a predator or parasite mimics a harmless species, thus avoiding detection and improving its foraging success.
Anonymizing Proxy	An anonymizing proxy is software to relay connections on behalf of a client, with the intent of concealing client information such as point of origin.

(continued)

(continued)

Term	Definition
Aposematism	In biology, aposematic warning signals are sent by prey to convey clear warning signals to their attackers, such as strong odors, bright colors and warning sounds. Mimics may imitate such signals to dissuade predators (e.g., a sheep in wolf's clothing). Conversely, a deadly species (e.g., Texas coral snake) may mimic an aposematic harmless one (e.g., Mexican milk snake); the deadly species then profits when prey species mistake the predator mimic for the less dangerous aposematic organism.
Attack surface	The term attack surface refers to points in software where vulnerabilities could cause access by an unauthorized process or user. While difficult to enumerate, issues often includes user input processing, protocol and file format parsing, and executing code in memory.
Automimicry	In biology, automimicry, or intraspecific mimicry, is a form of Batesian mimicry within a single species. Automimicry occurs, for example, when there is a palatability spectrum within a population of harmful prey. For example, monarch butterflies (Danaus plexippus) feed on milkweed species of varying toxicity. Some larvae feed on more toxic plants and store these toxins within themselves, while others do not. The less palatable caterpillars thus profit from those that ingest high levels of toxic substances, just as other butterfly species benefit from mimicry of Monarchs. Other examples include snakes, in which the tail resembles the head, and show behavior such as moving backwards to confuse predators such as insects and fishes with eyespots on their hind ends to resemble the head. When males mimic females or vice versa this may be referred to as sexual mimicry.
Backdoor Trojan	A backdoor Trojan is a covert channel through which an attacker can access and control system resources. A system user may be fooled into running a backdoor Trojan that poses as legitimate software, or users may infect their machine by visiting a malicious webpage. Upon execution, a backdoor Trojan can add itself to the system's startup routine, where it can then monitor the system until a network connection is established. The network connection allows the attacker to take control of the user's system. See also Trojan Horse.
Background Matching	In biology, a form of crypsis where the appearance of the prey generally matches the color, lightness, and pattern of one (specialist) or several (compromise) background types to reduce detection by predators.
Boot Sector Malware	Boot sector malware is a modified version of a machine's onboard startup code that includes malicious code. This allows malware to persist across operating system re-installation, and load in the context of a privileged execution mode.
Bot/Zombie, Botnet	A bot or a zombie is a machine able to be accessed by an unauthorized user. A botnet is a network of compromised machines accessible by the same actor(s). Often infections occur through web exploits and phishing emails.

(continued)

(continued)

Term	Definition
Buffer Overflow	A buffer overflow refers to the copying of a data buffer into memory without first checking its length. This may cause a program to crash or execute data in the context of code. Such vulnerabilities can be exploited by writing a function's return address on the stack to point to an attacker-controlled location, in order to execute arbitrary code.
Caches (military subsistence)	A source of subsistence and supplies, typically containing items such as food, water, medical items, and/or communications equipment, packaged to prevent damage from exposure and hidden in isolated locations by such methods as burial, concealment, and/or submersion, to support isolated personnel.
Camouflage	The use of natural or artificial material on personnel, objects, or tactical positions with the aim of confusing, misleading, or evading the enemy.
Clickjack, Clickjacking	Clickjacking is a means for tricking a system user into unknowingly clicking a disguised interactive element that performs an unintended operation. For example, crafted postings may take advantage of a website's layout to hide a "Share" button behind the "Close" button.
Combination (kombinatsiya)	This is a form of Soviet Active Measures (aktivnye meropriatia). Combination (kombinatsiya) is the relating, linking, and combining of active measures and operational undertakings in different times and places to enhance overall military, operational, and political results.
Counterdeception	Counterdeception involves detecting, characterizing, and penetrating adversarial deception operations. This includes the process of discerning the adversary's real capabilities and intentions to assess what is real, and to determine what the adversary is trying to make you believe in order to understand what the adversary wants you to do. Counterdeception is characterized by three dimensions of action: (1) awareness; (2) detection and exposure; and (3) discovery and penetration.
Concealment	Concealment is protection from observation or surveillance.
Controlled Information	(1) Controlled information is information conveyed to an adversary in a deception operation to evoke desired appreciations. (2) Controlled information is information and indicators deliberately conveyed or denied to foreign targets to evoke invalid official estimates that result in foreign official actions advantageous to U.S. interests and objectives.
Conduits	Within military deception, conduits are information or intelligence gateways to the deception target. Examples of conduits include: foreign intelligence and security services, intelligence collection platforms, open-source intelligence, and news media—foreign and domestic.
Cookies	Cookies are small text files sent to visiting clients from a web server to maintain state across sessions. Depending on browser configuration, cookies may be stored on the user's system without their knowledge or consent. Though the same-origin policy limits access of a cookie to the site that set it, sensitive information is still accessible to a program on the client.

(continued)

(continued)

Term	Definition
Counter-reconnaissance	Counter-reconnaissance includes all measures taken to prevent hostile observation of a force, area, or place.
Counter-surveillance	Counter-surveillance includes the passive and active measures taken to prevent observation by the enemy.
Cross Site Request Forgery	Cross site request forgery is an attack that forces an end user to execute unwanted actions on a web application in which he/she is currently authenticated. An attacker might exploit a cross-site scripting flaw to inject code that is then executed in another user's context.
Cross Site Scripting	Cross site scripting is the exploitation of a flaw that enables attackers to inject malicious scripts into websites. A malicious script executing on the client might access cookies, load other scripts, or display ads.
Crypsis	In biology, crypsis is a broad concept that encompasses all forms of avoiding detection, such as mimicry, camouflage, hiding, etc., primarily through the mechanisms of background matching. Crypsis is the ability of an organism to avoid observation or detection by other organisms. It may be either a predation strategy or an anti-predator adaptation. Methods include camouflage, nocturnality, subterranean lifestyle, transparency, and mimicry. Crypsis can involve visual, olfactory or auditory camouflage. To distinguish crypsis from simple hiding (e.g., behind an object in the environment), the features of a crypsis animal reduce the risk of detection when the animal is in plain sight.
Dazzle Camouflage, Dazzle Painting, Dazzle Patterning	This is a form of disruptive coloration camouflage, concealing real edges and contours, while creating false edges and contours, to thwart perception of an object's real shape, orientation, and velocity. Dazzle painting (or parti-coloring) may, or may not, be combined with counter-shading to enhance background matching. Credited to artist Norman Wilkinson and zoologist John Graham Kerr, dazzle painting consisted of complex patterns of geometric shapes in contrasting colors, interrupting and intersecting each other. It is best known for application to naval vessels in World Wars I and II.
Deception	Deception is the deliberate misrepresentation of reality to gain a competitive advantage. Actions executed to mislead foreign decision-makers, causing them to derive and accept desired appreciation of political, military, or other capabilities, intentions, operations, or other activities that evoke foreign actions that contribute to the deception originator's objectives. Those measures designed to mislead the enemy by manipulation, distortion, or falsification of evidence to induce him to react in a manner prejudicial to his interests.
Deception Administrative Means	Deception administrative means are the resources, methods, and techniques to convey or deny oral, pictorial, documentary, or other physical evidence to a deception target.
Deception Chain	The deception chain is a theoretical model that can be used by cyber defenders to develop adaptive and resilient defensive responses. The model is divided into phases for planning, preparing, and executing a deception operation: Purpose, Collect Intelligence, Design Cover Story, Plan, Prepare, Execute, Monitor, and Reinforce.

(continued)

(continued)

Term	Definition
Deception Means	Deception means are the methods, resources, and techniques that can be used to convey information to a foreign power. There are three categories of deception means: physical means, technical means, and administrative means.
Deception Measures	Deception measures are the channels of information used to provide false "indicators" to an opponent in support of deception tasks. Information passes back and forth between opposing forces on a battlefield by what is seen, heard, smelled, picked up by communications-electronics (CE), and otherwise sensed or measured. Types of deception measures are, therefore, classed as visual, sonic, olfactory, and electronic.
Deception Physical Means	Deception physical means are the activities and resources used to convey or deny selected information to a foreign power. Physical means include operational activities and resources such as: movement of forces; exercises and training activities; dummy and decoy equipment and devices; tactical actions, logistics actions, and location of stockpiles and repair facilities; test and evaluation activities; and reconnaissance and surveillance activities.
Deception Technical Means	Deception technical means are the military material resources and their associated operating techniques used to convey or deny selected information to a foreign power. Technical means include: deliberate radiation, alteration, absorption, or reflection of energy; emission or suppression of chemical or biological odors; emission or suppression of nuclear particles; and multi-media (e.g., radio, television, sound broadcasting, or computers).
Deception Objective	The desired result of a deception operation expressed in terms of what the adversary is to do or not to do at the critical time and/or location.
Deception Story	A scenario that outlines the friendly actions that will be conveyed to cause the deception target to adopt the desired perception.
Deception Target	The deception target is the adversary decision maker with the authority to make the decision that will achieve the deception objective. To be successful, deception must achieve a desired impact on the thinking and actions of the deception target audience: a national or military decision maker, and the intelligence analyst working for the decision maker. See also Target Audience.
Decoy	A decoy is an imitation in any sense of a person, object, or phenomenon that is intended to deceive enemy surveillance devices or mislead enemy evaluation.
Demonstration	A demonstration is a show of force where a decision is not sought and no contact with the adversary is intended. A demonstration's intent is to cause the adversary to select an unfavorable course of action (COA). It is similar to a feint but no actual contact with the adversary is intended. See also Diversion.
Denial	Denial is the ability and effort to prevent or impair the collection of intelligence by the enemy. Denial most often involves security and concealment to prevent collection (e.g., by foreign agents, photographic surveillance, electronic monitoring, or even the media) from detecting and collecting information on secretive diplomatic or military matters.

(continued)

(continued)

Term	Definition
Denial of Service	A denial of service is an attempt to exhaust the resources of a machine, preventing normal usage by transmitting an overwhelming amount of data or exploiting poor enforcement of resource allocation limits in software. If actors creating a Denial of Service condition are located in multiple locations, it is known as a Distributed Denial of Service (DDoS) attack. Actors may be unwilling participants in a botnet or even 'opt-in' as part of a coordinated protest.
Desired Perception	In military deception, desired perception is what the deception target must believe for it to make the decision that will achieve the deception objective.
Disguise	A disguise is an altered object made to look like something else; a form of Display.
Disinformation (dezinformatsiya)	In espionage or military intelligence, disinformation is the deliberate spreading of false information to mislead an enemy as to one's position or course of action. Disinformation also includes the distortion of true information in such a way as to render it useless. Disinformation may include distribution of forged documents, manuscripts, and photographs, or spreading malicious rumors and fabricated intelligence. Form of Soviet Active Measures (aktivnye meropriatia). Disinformation (dezinformatsiya) is overt and covert propaganda, psychological operations (i.e., white, gray, black), controlled press operations, and political warfare operations.
Dispersal Mimicry	In biology, dispersal mimicry occurs when a mimic benefits from an encounter with another species (i.e., the dupe) by imitating characteristics of a third species. For instance, some fungi, smelling like carrion, have their spores dispersed by insects feeding on carrion.
Display	In military deception, a display is a static portrayal of an activity, force, or equipment intended to deceive the adversary's visual observation. Displays have an opposite objective from concealment in that they are to draw the enemy's attention in order to mislead him. Displays may be conducted to project the deception story. Displays are the simulation, disguising, and/or portrayal of friendly objects, units, or capabilities in the projection of the military deception story. Such capabilities may not exist, but are made to appear so. Displays may include: simulations or projections of objects or systems that do not actually exist; disguises and altered objects made to look like something else; or portrayals or presentations of units or activities to represent nonexistent units or activities. Although considered acts in themselves, portrayals usually include disguises and simulations.
Disruptive Coloration	In biology, an organism's body will present characteristic shapes to a potential detector (e.g., attacker, predator) due to the shapes of different body parts and their organization within the organism. Disruptive coloration makes the detection of edges and boundaries of the prey organism more difficult for the predator to perceive. False boundaries can be created by abutting contrasting colors in places where no real boundary occurs. By differential blending, real boundaries can be made more difficult to detect by being broken up so that there is not a constant coloration, or constant contrast, along the boundary. Dazzle painting of military buildings and vehicles is an example of disruptive coloration.

(continued)

(continued)

Term	Definition
Distractive Markings	In biology, distractive markings direct the 'attention' or gaze of the receiver (i.e., the predator) from traits that would give away the prey animal, such as its outline.
Dissimulation	Dissimulation is the process of concealing facts, that is, concealing the essential elements of friendly information (i.e., the EEFI).
Diversion	In military deception a diversion is the act of drawing the attention and forces of an enemy from the point of the principal operation; an attack, alarm, or feint that diverts enemy attention. See also Demonstration. Form of Soviet Active Measures (aktivnye meropriatia); Diversion (diversiya) influencing or encouraging, under false pretenses, opponent or neutral organizations into activities less threatening or more favorable to the Soviet Union (e.g., encouraging leftist peace movements to focus on Western rather than Soviet military capabilities).
DNS Cache Poisoning	DNS cache poisoning is a modification of Domain Name System (DNS) entries to map a different IP address to a given domain name. Usually attempted to route traffic to an attacker-controlled computer to violate confidentiality or integrity of the data.
Drive-by Download	A drive-by download occurs when a user visits a malicious website and active scripts attempt to exploit client-side vulnerabilities. These may include loading Flash, Java, or scripting languages to trigger memory overflows.
Dummy	A dummy is an imitation of something on the battlefield. When a dummy is used to draw the enemy's attention away from some other area, it is termed a decoy. It is not necessary to have specially manufactured equipment for use as dummies. If not extensively damaged, unserviceable or combat-loss items can be used, Also, dummies may be available from supply stocks, or they may be constructed locally using salvage. The distance from which the enemy observes friendly items or actions dictates what degree of realism is required for a dummy.
Dupe	In biology, any species or organism that is exploited by the deceptions of another species or organism. The target of a deception.
Essential Elements of Deception Information (EEDI)	EEDI are revealed fictions that are an essential basis for creating false perceptions.
Essential Elements of Friendly Information (EEFI)	EEFI are the critical aspects of a friendly operation that, if known by the enemy would subsequently compromise, lead to failure, or limit success of the operation, and therefore, must be protected from enemy detection.
Fabrication (fabrikatsiya)	This is a form of Soviet Active Measures (aktivnye meropriatia). Fabrication (fabrikatsiya) includes forgeries; manufacturing false but realistic artifacts, ranging from false papers for agent legends, to generating streams of false evidence and documents to bolster disinformation stories in the media, to manufacturing entire Potemkin villages.

(continued)

(continued)

Term	Definition
Feedback	Feedback is information collected on the friendly and enemy situation that reveals how well the deception cover story is being portrayed by the friendly side and other channels of cover story information, if the deception target is responding to the deception cover story information and portrayals, and if the deception plan is working to get the adversary to act as desired by the friendly side, thus accomplishing the deception objective.
Feint	A feint is an offensive action involving contact with the adversary conducted for the purpose of deceiving the adversary as to the location and/or time of the actual main offensive action.
Flicker-fusion Camouflage	In biology, flicker-fusion camouflage occurs when markings, such as stripes or spots, blur during motion to match the color/lightness of the general background, preventing detection of the prey animal when in motion.
Honeyclient	A honeyclient is software that simulates the behavior of a vulnerable client application by generating web requests with pre-configured headers and options.
Honeypot	A honeypot is a deliberately vulnerable environment constructed to gather information about unauthorized users. Any access to a honeypot is assumed to be suspicious, giving defenders the ability to pre-emptively detect intrusion attempts.
Honeytoken	A honeytoken is any false information whose attempted use should be regarded as suspicious. A honeytoken may be included on a honeypot, to detect re-use of compromised information.
Identification Deception	Identification deception includes false identities, documentation, and other signatures.
Impersonation	Impersonation is the unauthorized use of another person's credentials for fraudulent purposes. Social security and credit card numbers are highly targeted, as well as account credentials for social media. Methods include opening new accounts using a person's vital information, cloning credit cards, and using stolen credentials to transfer money.
Information Operations (IO)	Information operations are the integrated employment, during military operations, of information-related capabilities in concert with other lines of operation to influence, disrupt, corrupt, or usurp the decision-making of adversaries and potential adversaries while protecting our own. See also Military Deception; Operations Security.
Jamming	Jamming involves interfering with communications, surveillance, or operations. See Denial of Service.
Keylogging	Keylogging is keystroke capture using software or hardware to gather credentials for unauthorized use.
Kill Chain (Intrusion Kill Chain; Cyber Kill Chain)	The kill chain is a way of visualizing intrusions including phases employed by malicious actors. The phases include Reconnaissance, Weaponize, Deliver, Exploit, Control, Execute, and Maintain.
M-Type (Mislead-Type) Deception	M-Type, or misleading, deception involves achieving a reduction of ambiguity, as perceived by the intended target, by building up attractiveness of a wrong alternative. This may be more difficult than A-type deception because it requires time and carefully orchestrated resources to build a series of misleading false signals. See A-Type Deception; Active Deception.

(continued)

(continued)

Term	Definition
Man-in-the-middle	Man-in-the-middle is an active attack in which the attacker modifies traffic between a client and server, allowing attackers to intercept traffic from the client by acting as a gateway (ARP spoofing), or by abusing a trust relationship (self-signed SSL certificates), thus gaining control of the user's interactions with the system.
Manipulation	Manipulation is a deceptive practice of quoting factual information out of context or reporting only part of a given situation, to support a deception cover story.
Masking	Masking is a technique, such as camouflage or electronic measures, which conceals characteristics to make an operation invisible.
Masquerade	In biology, masquerade is a general form of mimicry, or deceptive resemblance, in which one organism resembles another, in both characteristics and behaviors. Masquerade prevents predator recognition of the prey, which resembles an uninteresting object, such as a leaf or a stick.
Military Deception, MILDEC (maskirovka)	MILDEC is actions executed to deliberately mislead adversary military, paramilitary, or violent extremist organization decision makers, thereby causing the adversary to take specific actions or inactions that will contribute to the accomplishment of the friendly mission. Also called MILDEC. Form of Soviet Active Measures (aktivnye meropriatia). Military deception (maskirovka) includes camouflage, concealment, deception, imitation, disinformation, secrecy, security, feints, diversions, and simulations in aid of attaining military surprise.
Military Deception Tactics	MILDEC tactics may include: mask an increase in or redeployment of forces or weapons systems spotted by the adversary; shape the adversary's perception and/or identification of new forces or weapons being introduced into combat; reinforce the adversary's preconceived beliefs; distract the adversary's attention from other activities; overload adversary ISR collection and analytical capabilities; create the illusion of strength where weakness exists; desensitize the adversary to particular patterns of friendly behavior to induce adversary perceptions that are exploitable at the time of friendly choosing; confuse adversary expectations about friendly size, activity, location, unit, time, equipment, intent, and/or style of mission execution, to effect surprise in these areas; or reduce the adversary's ability to clearly perceive and manage the battle.
Military Deception Techniques	MILDEC techniques are four basic deception techniques underlying MILDEC operations: feints, demonstrations, ruses, and displays.
Mimicry	In biology, mimicry is the similarity of one species to another that protects one or both. This similarity can be in appearance, behavior, sound, scent and location, with the mimics found in similar places to their models. Mimicry occurs when a group of organisms, the mimics, evolve to share common perceived characteristics with another group, the models. Mimicry is a primary defense that operates before a predator initiates any prey-catching behavior, with the function of preventing pursuit by the predator. In Müllerian mimicry, two or more species with effective defenses share a similar appearance. In Batesian mimicry, members of a palatable species resemble an unpalatable or otherwise defended species.

(continued)

(continued)

Term	Definition
Mimesis	In biology, mimesis falls between camouflage and mimicry. In mimesis, the mimic takes on the properties of a specific object or organism, to which the predator is indifferent. The term "mimesis" applies to animals that resemble twigs, bark, leaves or flowers, and may be classified as camouflaged (e.g., resembling an inedible object like a rock) but are also classified as mimics. The order of stick and leaf insects, Phasmida (i.e., from the Latin 'phasma,' meaning phantom, apparition, spectre or ghost), are mimesis mimics and are camouflaged as sticks or leaves.
Mobile Phone Malware	Mobile phone malware is malicious code executing on a mobile platform, typically Android, iOS, or Blackberry. Due to the concentration of personal information on such devices, compromise is often valuable to both criminal and targeted actors. Pirated copies of software and over-the-air exploits are a common vector for distribution of this malware.
Motion Camouflage	In biology, motion camouflage is movement by the prey animal in a fashion that decreases the probability of movement detection by the predator.
Motion Dazzle	In biology, motion dazzle occurs when a prey animal's markings make estimates of speed and trajectory difficult by the predator. See Dazzle.
Non-Discloseable Elements of Deception Information (NDDI)	NDDI is fictions, such as information, physical entities, events, or processes, which are hidden from the target.
Non-Essential Elements of Friendly Information (NEFI)	NEFI is the factual information, physical entities, events, and processes that the deceiver reveals. These should be believed and accepted by the target, but the NEFI must be carefully engineered to lead the target away from perceiving and understanding the whole truth.
Notional	The adjective "notional" is combined with other military terms—for example, notional plans, notional weapons, and notional order of battle (OB)—to indicate false objects or plans the friendly force wishes the opponent to accept as real. Notional describes a false activity conducted to project the deception story to the opponent analysts and targets.
Notional Order of Battle	The notional order of battle consists of deception operations that are used to create and sustain the portrayal of notional units and their activities to inflate the enemy's order of battle of friendly units. The notional units in the enemy order of battle (OB). Thus, tasking a company to perform as a "notional battalion" directs it to organize, or geographically deploy, and using deception measures, display the characteristic signature of a battalion to the opponent's surveillance. The purpose is to place a friendly battalion in the opponent's estimate of the friendly forces' OB at the time and place called for in the deception story.
Notional Unit	A notional unit is a false portrayal of a unit; an economy of force measure to support a deception, causing the opponent to obtain a false appreciation of friendly strength, composition, and intentions. To be credible, notional units must: occupy the right amount of terrain; conduct the appropriate activities; have the right indicators: visual, sonic, olfactory, and electronic; and follow accepted operational patterns.

(continued)

(continued)

Term	Definition
Operational Deception	In the military, operational deception refers to deception operations in support of the operational level of war. Operational deception is within the purview of theater Army component, Army group, field Army, and in some cases, corps commanders. The objective of deception operations at the operational level of war is to influence the decisions of opponent commanders before battle occurs.
Operations Security (OPSEC)	OPSEC is a process of identifying critical information and subsequently analyzing friendly actions attendant to military operations and other activities. Operations security is a process of identifying essential elements of friendly information (EEFI) and subsequently analyzing friendly actions attendant to military operations and other activities to identify those actions that can be observed by adversary intelligence systems; determine indicators that hostile intelligence systems might obtain that could be interpreted or pieced together to derive critical information in time to be useful to adversaries; and select and execute measures that eliminate or reduce to an acceptable level the vulnerabilities of friendly actions to adversary exploitation.
Operations Security (OPSEC) Indicators	OPSEC indicators are actions or information, classified or unclassified, obtainable by an adversary that would result in adversary appreciations, plans, and actions harmful to achieving friendly intentions and preserving friendly military capabilities. See: Essential Elements of Friendly Information (EEFI).
Operations Security (OPSEC) Measures	OPSEC measures are methods and means to gain and maintain essential secrecy about critical information.
Operations Security (OPSEC) Vulnerability	An OPSEC vulnerability is a condition in which friendly actions provide operations security indicators that may be obtained and accurately evaluated by an adversary in time to provide a basis for effective adversary decision-making.
Palter, Paltering	Paltering is acting insincerely or misleadingly, or deceiving by manipulation of the truth. Deceptive practices of fudging, twisting, shading, bending, stretching, slanting, exaggerating, distorting, whitewashing, and selective reporting of the truth to serve a deceptive purpose. The palter falls short of being an outright lie in two important dimensions. First, the palter may not be literally false. Second, the typical palter may seem less harmful or deceitful than the typical lie, while creating the same effect as an outright lie.
Parasitic Virus (aka File Virus)	A parasitic virus is a program that attaches itself to an executable program. When a program infected with a parasitic virus is launched, the virus code is executed. The virus then passes control back to the original program to hide itself. The operating system registers the virus as part of the program and gives it the same privileges. The virus uses these privileges to copy and install itself in memory, or make changes on the user's computer.
Passive Deception	A passive deception allows a misleading interpretation of facts and fictions to go uncorrected. Passive deception misleads the opponent, preventing (e.g., through Operations Security) any actions that might reveal critical facts and fictions, and thus preventing the opponent from forming correct estimates or taking appropriate actions. Passive deception is primarily based on secrecy and camouflage, on hiding and concealing one's intentions and/or capabilities from the adversary.

(continued)

(continued)

Term	Definition
Penetration (proniknovenniye)	This is a form of Soviet Active Measures (aktivnye meropriatia). Penetration (proniknovenniye) operations involve inserting controlled agents into sensitive positions, as contrasted to agent recruitment.
Perception Management	Perception management includes actions to convey and/or deny selected information and indicators to foreign audiences to influence their emotions, motives, and objective reasoning as well as to intelligence systems and leaders at all levels to influence official estimates, ultimately resulting in foreign behaviors and official actions favorable to the originator's objectives. In various ways, perception management combines truth projection, operations security, cover and deception, and psychological operations.
Persistence on Host	Persistence on host included the installation of code to maintain control over a computer system across reboots and process terminations. This enables malware to survive initial cleanup efforts and continue executing.
Pharming	Pharming is the cloning of a legitimate site in order to create a plausible malicious replica. Drive-by scripts can be hosted on the replica, and victim user credentials captured on attempted logins. Typically generated using exploit packs and tools that scrape a site's linked pages. Attackers harvest credentials to sensitive sites by sending phishing messages containing links to the malicious replica of the sensitive site requiring credentials.
Phishing	Phishing is a method of masquerading as a trusted person in digital communications. Often used to entice victims to execute attached malware or visit malicious websites. See also Spearphishing.
Portrayal	A portrayal is a presentation of units or activities to represent nonexistent units or activities. Although considered acts in themselves, portrayals usually include disguises and simulations. A form of Display.
Preconception	A preconception is an opinion or conception formed in advance of actual knowledge.
Pretexting	Pretexting is a manipulation of a target using an invented scenario with the purpose of performing some advantageous action. Attackers exploit processes of the target organization by contacting employees and posing as someone who should have access to sensitive information. Pretending to be an IT administrator is a common tactic for penetration testers who use pretexting. Convince employees to reveal sensitive information that can be leveraged to the attacker's advantage (e.g., gain access to the target's computer resources to inform further software exploitation; elicit sensitive information in conversation by assuming a trusted or innocuous role).
Provocation (provokatsiya)	This is a form of Soviet Active Measures (aktivnye meropriatia). Provocation (provokatsiya) operations are intended to incite actions by the opponent that are detrimental to the opponent and favorable to the deceiver.

(continued)

(continued)

Term	Definition
Proxying	Proxying is routing traffic through intermediate machines that provide a level of concealment for the source machine. For instance, IP packets may be forwarded for a client through another server to its eventual destination. Tor is an example of a global network that uses blind proxies for enhanced anonymity.
Pseudonymity	Pseudonymity is the act of creating an alternate identity that is weakly tied to a person's physical identity. One person may use different pseudonyms on various services, and one pseudonym could be used by a collection of individuals (e.g., such as Anonymous). Creation of a name that has little or no relation to vital information. Financially motivated attackers may register 'shill' accounts for auction fraud, create accounts whose only purpose is to leave spam comments on forums, and rotate between multiple names to evade identification by law enforcement. Attackers may create accounts for spear phishing and victim targeting, register domain names using shell accounts, and participate in forums with lower chance of discovery.
Remote Access Trojans (RATs)	RATs are programs used to control a system from a remote location. This software typically includes the ability to transfer files, capture screenshots, track keyboard inputs, and control system processes. See Backdoor Trojan.
Rootkit	A rootkit is software that hides system information on a machine. Often used to hide malware activity on an infected host, including network connections and process execution.
Ruse	A ruse is a trick of war designed to deceive the adversary, usually involving the deliberate exposure of false information to the adversary's intelligence collection system. A cunning trick designed to deceive the adversary to obtain friendly advantage. It is characterized by deliberately exposing false or confusing information for collection and interpretation by the adversary.
Sandbox, Sandboxing	Sandboxing is a method for confining untrusted code or programs to an untrusted helper application; executing untrusted files in a virtual environment to monitor for unexpected activity. Defenders might open email attachments and downloaded files in a sandboxed version of a real system to ensure that the files are not malicious.
Security Countermeasures	Security countermeasures are those protective activities required to prevent espionage, sabotage, theft, or unauthorized use of classified or controlled information, systems, or material. See Operations Security.
Session Hijacking	Session hijacking involves impersonating a user by replaying captured session information during an HTTP connection. Attackers intercept a session identifier for a user and provide it to a web site on behalf of the attacker rather than the legitimate user.
Signature Control	Signature control is the manipulation of a platform's emission and physical characteristics, such as radar cross section, infrared modulation, radar pulse repetition rate, etc. in order to reduce an adversary's ability to detect, track, and engage friendly units during combat operations.

(continued)

(continued)

Term	Definition
Simulation	Simulation is the process of revealing fictions, or the essential elements of deception information (EEDI). Projections of objects or systems that do not actually exist. Portrayals are presentations of units or activities to represent nonexistent units or activities. Although considered acts in themselves, portrayals usually include disguises and simulations. A form of Display. See Essential Elements of Deception Information (EEDI).
Smoke Screen	A smoke screen is a smoke cloud produced by chemical agents or smoke generators.
Smoke Generators	Smoke generators are devices that provide visible obscuration by producing smoke for screening or signaling.
Social Engineering	Social engineering refers to methods used to influence users into performing insecure actions advantageous to the cyber attacker. Social engineers may influence users to open a malicious webpage, execute an unwanted file attachment, or share usernames and passwords that can be used for additional malicious activity (e.g., sending email, that represents the social engineer as an authorized user, with access or information requests).
Software Obfuscation	Software obfuscation consists of technical methods to conceal software functionality and increase the cost of reverse engineering. These methods can be used legitimately to prevent software piracy, or for malicious purposes to evade security software. Methods include adding malicious functionality to legitimate applications, adding large sections of useless "junk" code, and encryption techniques to conceal malicious code.
Spearphishing	Spearphishing is the process of crafting communications so an unsuspecting recipient will open a maliciously crafted attachment, or click a malicious link. These messages deliver targeted malware used to gain a foothold on the victim's targeted network.
Spyware	Spyware is software that allows advertisers or malicious actors to gather sensitive information without user permission. Websites will display pop-up messages prompting the user to download a software utility that the site claims is needed, or the spyware may be downloaded automatically without the user's knowledge. Spyware can track user activity, such as website browsing, and report it to unauthorized third parties, without revealing its purpose.
SQL Injection	A SQL injection is an exploit that takes advantage of database query software that does not adequately validate queries. SQL injections and cross-site scripting might be combined to compromise a website's source code or backend databases.
Startle displays	In biology, startle displays may disrupt the attack of a predator. Startle displays may involve the sudden appearance of distinctive markings, such as spots and bright colors, by the prey animal.
Stealth Software	Stealth software includes methods for concealing the presence of malicious software on a system by subverting the operating system or underlying hardware. Processes, network connections, and files are hidden from normal users of the system in order for the stealth software to persist longer. Technical methods include inline hooking, IAT hooking, SSDT hooking, MSR alteration, DKOM manipulation, MBR modification, and firmware reflashing. See Rootkits.

(continued)

(continued)

Term	Definition
Steganography	Steganography involves concealing the presence of covert communications, stolen information, or malicious code. Attackers secretly hide the covert communication, information, or malware within open material (e.g., audio, video, image files) protecting the illicit material by a secret hiding process and private key. Steganography can be implemented using open software such as *steghide* for digital photographs and video.
Strategic Deception	Strategic deception refers to deception operations at the strategic level of war and peace. Strategic deception occurs during war or peace when countries attempt to mask their diplomatic and military strategy either by confusing or misleading their opponents. This level of deception involves a nation's highest decision makers using diplomacy, economics, intelligence, and virtually every conceivable dimension of modern conflict to mislead or confuse opponents. Strategic deception may extend political deception by using military activities. It may also be large-scale, long-term projections of false intelligence to aid theater objectives. Although the objectives may be military, strategic deception supports national policies and plans and may be supported by nonmilitary agencies.
Tactical Deception	Tactical deception is deception operations at the tactical level of war. Tactical deception is deliberate action to achieve surprise on the battlefield. This type of deception is done so that the tactical outcome of battles and engagements is favorable and, subsequently, operationally exploitable. The goal is to maintain operational fluidity. Tactical deception actions may support a strategic or operational effort. Tactical deception refers to the short term actions of corps or lower units within the battle area.
Target Audience	The target audience of the deception effort is the opponent or participant with the authority to make the decision that will achieve the deception objective. To be successful, deception must achieve a desired impact on the thinking and actions of the deception target audience: a national or military decision maker, or the intelligence analyst working for the decision maker. See Deception Target.
Transparency	In biology, transparency is a method of hiding from attackers and predators by making the prey animal body transparent to visual wavelengths and thus appearing to the predator to be the background. Many invertebrate taxa, including crustaceans, squid, and octopuses have highly transparent members.
Trojan Horse	A Trojan horse is a classic deception method of hiding a malicious "package" or weapon inside a desirable "gift" (e.g., Beware of Greeks bearing gifts). Malicious software crafted to appear benign to the target user. Trojan horses infect a target victim computer by exploiting vulnerabilities in document viewing software and/or the underlying operating system. Designed to hide from host antivirus and network detection. Typically generated using a mix of public and custom exploit packs.

(continued)

(continued)

Term	Definition
Virus	A virus is a software program that can spread by self-duplication. Viruses spread across computers and networks by hiding and making copies of themselves, usually without the knowledge of the infected system owners. Viruses can attach themselves to other programs or hide in code that automatically executes when the user opens certain types of files. Viruses can also exploit operating system security flaws to execute and spread automatically.
Visual Deception	Much of an opponent's intelligence is based on what is observed. Hence, effective visual deception is critical to the projection of the deception story. Two items commonly used in visual deception are Dummies and Decoys. Camouflage is an important element in deception actions to prevent the opponent from observing evidence of the true operation.
Watering Hole Attack	A watering hole attack involves targeting a group of victims by adding malicious code to legitimate websites commonly frequented by a target. Attackers can then filter incoming users and selectively exploit client-side vulnerabilities to install malware.
Worm	Worms are viruses that create copies of themselves across networks, both local and the Internet. Unlike computer viruses, worms can propagate themselves, instead of using a host program or file, by making an exact copy and using a network to spread. Some worms can open a back door on a system allowing a malicious actor to gain control.

References

Alberts, D. S., Huber, R. K., and Moffat, J. (2010). NATO NEC C2 Maturity Model, Washington, DC: DoD Command and Control Research Program.

Albright, D., P. Brannan and C. Walrond (2010). "Did Stuxnet Take Out 1000 Centrifuges At the Natanz Enrichment Plant?" Institute for Science and International Security, 22 December 2010. http://isis-online.org/uploads/isis-reports/documents/stuxnet_FEP_22Dec2010.pdf

Aldridge, J. (2012). *Targeted Intrusion Remediation: Lessons from the Front Lines.* Paper presented at the Blackhat USA, 2012, Las Vegas, NV. www.blackhat.com/usa/bh-us-12-briefings. html#Aldridge

Amoroso, E. G. (2011). *Cyber attacks : protecting national infrastructure.* Burlington, MA: Butterworth-Heinemann.

Andress, J., Winterfeld, S., & Rogers, R. (2011). *Cyber warfare : techniques, tactics and tools for security practitioners.* Amsterdam; Boston: Syngress/Elsevier.

Arquilla, J. and D. A. Borer (2007). *Information Strategy and Warfare: A guide to theory and practice.* Routledge: New York.

Azizian, N., Sarkani, S., & Mazzuchi, T. (2009). *A Comprehensive Review and Analysis of Maturity Assessment Approaches for Improved Decision Support to Achieve Efficient Defense Acquisition.* Paper presented at the World Congress on Engineering and Computer Science 2009, 20-22 Oct. 2009, San Francisco, CA.

Barbier, M. (2007). *D-day deception: Operation Fortitude and the Normandy invasion.* Praeger Security International, Westport, CT.

Barnum, S. (2014). Standardizing Cyber Threat Intelligence Information with the Structured Threat Information eXpression (STIX). MITRE White Paper.

Bennett, M., & Waltz, E. (2007). *Counterdeception principles and applications for national security.* Norwood, MA: Artech House.

Bloom, R. (2013). *Foundations of Psychological Profiling: Terrorism, Espionage, and Deception.* Boca Raton, FL: Taylor & Francis Group.

Bodmer, S., M. Kilger, G. Carpenter, and J. Jones (2012). *Reverse Deception: Organized Cyber Threat Counter-Exploitation.* McGraw-Hill: New York.

Boehm, B. W. (1988, May). A Spiral Model of Software Development and Enhancement. Computer 21, 5, 61-72. DOI= 10.1109/2.59. http://dx.doi.org/ 10.1109/2.59

Bowen, B. M., Hershkop, S., Keromytis, A. D., and Stolfo, S. J. (2009). Baiting inside attackers using decoy documents. In SecureComm'09: Proceedings of the 5th International ICST Conference on Security and Privacy in Communication Networks.

Bruce, J. B. & M. Bennett (2008). "Foreign Denial and Deception: Analytical Imperatives," in George, R. Z. & J. B. Bruce (2008). Analyzing intelligence: origins, obstacles, and innovations. Washington DC: Georgetown University Press.

© Springer International Publishing Switzerland 2015
K.E. Heckman et al., *Cyber Denial, Deception and Counter Deception*,
Advances in Information Security 64, DOI 10.1007/978-3-319-25133-2

Carr, J. (2012). *Inside Cyber Warfare*, 2nd Ed. O'Reilly Media: Sebastopol, CA, .

Carroll, T. E., & Grosu, D. (2011). A game theoretic investigation of deception in network security. *Security and Communication Networks, 4*(10), 1162-1172.

Caverni, F. & M. Gonzalez, eds. (1990) Cognitive Biases. New York: Elsevier.

Chen, Z. (2007). Modeling and Defending Against Internet Worm Attacks. PhD thesis, Georgia Institute of Technology, May 2007. http://citeseerx.ist.psu.edu/viewdoc/download?doi=10.1.1.83.6082&rep=rep1&type=pdf

Chen, H. (2012). *Dark web exploring and data mining the dark side of the web*. New York, NY: Springer.

Chrissis, M. B. K. M. S. S. (2003). *CMMI : guidelines for process integration and product improvement*. Boston: Addison-Wesley.

Cialdini, Robert. (2006). *Influence: The Psychology of Persuasion*. City: HarperBusiness.

CERN (Conseil Européen pour la Recherche Nucléaire). (2008). Birth of the Web Retrieved 2012, from http://public.web.cern.ch/public/en/about/webstory-en.html

Cohen, A. and Hamilton, R. E. (2011). The Russian Military and the Georgia War: Lessons and Implications. ERAP Monograph, June 2011. Carlisle Barracks PA: Strategic Studies Institute, U.S. Army War College.

Cohen, F., Lambert, D., Preston, C., Berry, N., Stewart, C. & Thomas, E. (2007). *A Framework for Deception*. Retrieved from http://all.net/journal/deception/Framework/Framework.html

Crowdy, T. (2008). *Deceiving Hitler: Double Cross and Deception in World War II*. Osprey Publishing, New York.

Czosseck, C. G. K. (2009). *The virtual battlefield perspectives on cyber warfare*. Amsterdam; Washington, DC: Ios Press.

Dacier, Marc, Corrado Leita, Olivier Thonnard, Van-Hau Pham, and Engin Kirda (2010). "Assessing Cybercrime Through the Eyes of the WOMBAT," in Sushil Jajodia, Peng Liu, Vipin Swarup, Cliff Wang, eds. (2010). *Cyber Situational Awareness: Issues and Research.* New York: Springer.

Davis, E. G. & Grabo, C.M. (1972). "Strategic Warning and Deception." Joint Chiefs of Staff Strategic Planning Seminar, April 1972. https://www.cia.gov/library/center-for-the-study-of-intelligence/kent-csi/vol16no4/html/v17i1a05p_0001.htm

Dawes, R.M. (2001). Everyday Irrationality: How Pseudo Scientists, Lunatics, and the Rest of Us Systematically Fail to Think Rationally. Boulder CO: Westview Press.

Donald, C. & Daniel F.(2005). "Denial and Deception," in Jennifer E. Sims & Burton Gerber eds. *Transforming U.S. Intelligence.* Washington DC: Georgetown University Press.

Defense Science Board. (2009). *Summer Study on Capability Surprise. Volume I: Main Report, September 2009*, Office of the Under Secretary of Defense for Acquisition, Technology, and Logistics: Washington, D.C.

Department of Defense. (2012). *Annual Report to Congress: Military and Security Developments Involving the People's Republic of China 2012*. Washington DC: Office of the Secretary of Defense.

Department of Defense. (2012). JP 3-13.4 *Military Deception*.

Department of Defense. (2014). JP 3-13 Information Operations.

Dierks, T., & Allen, C. (1999). The TLS Protocol, Version 1.0. Retrieved from https://tools.ietf.org/html/rfc2246

Economist (2014). "Banks and fraud: Hacking back--Bankers go undercover to catch bad guys," The Economist, April 5th 2014. http://www.economist.com/news/finance-and-economics/21600148-bankers-go-undercover-catch-bad-guys-hacking-back

Edinger, H. (2013). "Stuxnet and the Treatment of Cyber Attacks under International Law." JHU SAIS Bologna Center, January 2013.

Elsäesser, C. & F. J. Stech (2007). "Detecting Deception," in Kott, A. & W. M. McEneaney eds (2007) Adversarial reasoning: computational approaches to reading the opponent's mind. Boca Raton FL: Taylor & Francis Group.

Endsley, M. R. & Robertson, M. M. (1996). *Team situation awareness in aircraft maintenance*. Lubbock, TX: Texas Tech University.

Epstein, E. J. (1991). Deception: The Invisible War between the KGB and the CIA. New York: Random House.

Fall, K. (2003). *A Delay-Tolerant Network Architecture for Challenged Internets*. Paper presented at the Proceedings of ACM SIGCOMM 2003: Conference on Computer Communications, August 25, 2003—August 29, 2003, Karlsruhe, Germany. Retrieved from http://conferences.sigcomm.org/sigcomm/2003/papers/p27-fall.pdf

Falliere, N., L. O. Murchu, and E. Chien (2011). W32. Stuxnet Dossier, ver. 1.4, February 2011. http://www.symantec.com/content/en/us/enterprise/media/security_response/whitepapers/w32_stuxnet_dossier.pdf

Fischhoff, B. (1982). "Debiasing," in Kahneman, D., P. Slovic, & A. Tversky, eds. (1982) Judgment under Uncertainty: Heuristics and Biases. Cambridge UK: Cambridge University Press, pp. 422–444.

Foltz, A. C. (2012). "Stuxnet, Schmitt Analysis, and the Cyber 'Use-of-Force' Debate," Joint Forces Quarterly, v. 67-4, 4th quarter, 2012. http://www.ndu.edu/press/lib/pdf/jfq-67/JFQ-67_40-48_Foltz.pdf

Forrester, E. C., Buteau, B. L., & Shrum, S. (2011). *CMMI for services : guidelines for superior service*. Upper Saddle River, NJ: Addison-Wesley.

Fredericks, Brian (1997). "Information Warfare: The Organizational Dimension," in Robert E. Neiison, ed. (1997). *Sun Tzu and Information Warfare*. Washington, DC: National Defense University Press.

Fursenko, A. A., & Naftali, T. J. (1997). *One hell of a gamble : Khrushchev, Castro, and Kennedy, 1958-1964*. New York: Norton.

Garg, N. & Grosu, D. (2007). "Deception in Honeynets: A Game-Theoretic Analysis," *Proceedings of the 2007 IEEE, Workshop on Information Assurance*, United States Military Academy, West Point NY, 20-22 June 2007.

Gates, G. (2012). "How a secret cyberwar program worked," New York Times. 1 June 2012. http://www.nytimes.com/interactive/2012/06/01/world/middleeast/how-a-secret-cyberwar-program-worked.html

Gerard, P. (2002). *Secret soldiers : the story of World War II's heroic army of deception*. New York: Penguin.

Gerwehr, Scott, & Russell W. Glenn (2002). *Unweaving the Web : deception and adaptation in future urban operations*. Santa Monica: RAND.

Gilman, R. (2013). "Better Tools Through Intelligence, Better Intelligence Through Tools," SANS Computer Forensics and Incident Response, What Word in Cyber Threat Intelligence Summit 2013, Washington, DC, March 22, 2013.

Gilovich, T., D. Griffin, & D. Kahneman (2002) Heuristics and Biases. Cambridge UK: Cambridge University Press.

Glenney, W. (2009). "Military Deception in the Information Age: Scale Matters," in Brooke Harrington ed. *Deception: From Ancient Empires to Internet Dating*. Stanford: Stanford University Press.

Goffman, E. (1997). "On Cooling the Mark Out: Some Aspects of Adaptation to Failure," in C. Lemert and A. Branaman eds. (1997) The Goffman Reader. Oxford UK: Blackwell Publishers.

Gribkov, A. I., Smith, W. Y., & Friendly, A. (1994). *Operation ANADYR : U.S. and Soviet generals recount the Cuban missile crisis*. Chicago: Edition q.

Gueye, A. (2011). *A Game Theoretical Approach to Communication Security*. Dissertation, Electrical Engineering and Computer Sciences, University of California, Berkeley, Spring 2011.

Hadnagy, C. (2011). *Social Engineering: The Art of Human Hacking*. Wiley Publishing: Indianapolis, IN.

Hagestad, W. (2012). *21st Century Chinese Cyberwarfare*. London: IT Governance Ltd.

Haig, Leigh (2002). "LaBrea–A New Approach To Securing Our Networks," SANS Security Essentials (GSEC) Practical Assignment, Version 1.3Completion Date: March 7, 2002. https://www.sans.org/reading-room/whitepapers/attacking/labrea-approach-securing-networks-36

Harmer, P.K., Williams P.D., Gunsch, G.H., Lamont, G.B. (2002). "An Artificial Immune System Architecture for Computer Security Applications." *IEEE Transactions on Evolutionary Computation*, v. 6, no. 3, June 2002.

Harris, W. R. (1968). "Intelligence and National Security: A Bibliography with Selected Annotations." Cambridge MA: Center for International Affairs, Harvard University. Cited by Epstein (1991).

Harris, W. R. (1972). "Counter-deception Planning," Cambridge MA: Harvard University, 1972. Cited by Epstein (1991).

Harris, W. R. (1985). "Soviet Maskirovka and Arms Control Verification," mimeo, Monterey CA: U.S. Navy Postgraduate School, September 1985. Cited by Epstein (1991).

He, F. Zhuang, J. S. Nageswara, & Rao, V. (2012). "Game-Theoretic Analysis of Attack and Defense in Cyber-Physical Network Infrastructures," *Proceedings of the 2012 Industrial and Systems Engineering Research Conference*, Orlando FL, 19 May 2012.

Heckman, K. E., Walsh, M. J., Stech, F. J., O'Boyle, T. A., Dicato, S. R., & Herber, A. F. (2013). Active cyber defense with denial and deception: A cyber-wargame experiment. *Computers and Security, 37*, 72-77. doi: 10.1016/j.cose.2013.03.015

Henderson, S. J. (2007). *The dark visitor : inside the world of Chinese hackers*. Morrisville, NC: Lulu Press.

Hespanha, J. & Doyle, F. III. (2010). "Bio-inspired Network Science," in Robert E. Armstrong, Mark D. Drapeau, Cheryl A. Loeb, and James J. Valdes (eds.). *Bio-inspired Innovation and National Security*. Center for Technology and National Security Policy, National Defense University Press: Washington DC.

Heuer, Jr., R. J. (1981). "Strategic Deception and Counterdeception: A Cognitive Process Approach," International Studies Quarterly, v. 25, n. 2, June 1981, pp. 294–327.

Heuer, Jr., R. J. (1999). Psychology of Intelligence Analysis, Washington DC: Central Intelligence Agency. https://www.cia.gov/library/center-for-thestudy-of-intelligence/csi-publications/books-and-monographs/psychology-of-intelligence-analysis/

Heuser, Stephen J. (1996). Operational Deception and Counter Deception. Newport RI: Naval War College, 14 June 1996. www.dtic.mil/cgibin/GetTRDoc?AD=ADA307594

Hobbs, C. L. (2010). *Methods for improving IAEA information analysis by reducing cognitive biases*. IAEA Paper Number: IAEA-CN-184/276. http://www.iaea.org/safeguards/Symposium/2010/Documents/PapersRepository/276.pdf

Holt, T. (2007). *The deceivers : Allied military deception in the Second World War*. New York: Scribner.

Hoglund, G., & Butler, J. (2006). *Rootkits : subverting the Windows kernel*. Upper Saddle River, NJ: Addison-Wesley.

Hsu, L-T. (2010). *A Game Theoretical Approach for Decision and Analysis of adopting Proactive Defense Strategy*. Thesis for Master of Science, Department of Computer Science and Engineering, Tatung University, July 2010.

Huber, T. (1988). *Pastel: Deception in the Invasion of Japan*. U.S. Army Command and General Staff College: Fort Leavenworth Ks.

Hutchins, E., Cloppert, M., & Amin, R. (2011). *Intelligence-Driven Computer Network Defense Informed by Analysis of Adversary Campaigns and Intrusion Kill Chains*. Paper presented at the 6th International Conference on Information Warfare and Security (ICIW 2011), 17-18 March 2011, Reading, UK.

Irvine, C.E., Thompson, M.F., Allen, T.K. (2005). "CyberCIEGE: gaming for information assurance," Security & Privacy, IEEE, vol.3, no.3, pp. 61–64, May-June 2005

Jajodia, S., Ghosh, A. K., Swarup, V., & Wang, C. (2011). *Moving target defense : creating asymmetric uncertainty for cyber threats*. New York: Springer.

Janczewski, L., & Colarik, A. M. (2008). *Cyber warfare and cyber terrorism*. London: Information Science Reference.

Johari, R. (2007). Future of the Internet, from http://itunes.apple.com/itunes-u/the-future-of-the-internet/id384229952?mt=10#ls=1

Joint Chiefs of Staff (2006) Joint Publication 3-13 Information Operations, Washington, DC: Department of Defense.

Jones, R. V. (2009). Most Secret War. London: Penguin.

Jowers, K. (2008). "Phishing scam turns out to be an inside job." Army Times, April 1, 2008.

Kott, Alexander & Gary Citrenbaum, eds. (2010). *Estimating Impact: A Handbook of Computational Methods and Models for Anticipating Economic, Social, Political and Security Effects in International Interventions.* New York: Springer, p. 8 ff.

Krekel, B. (2009) Capability of the People's Republic of China to Conduct Cyber Warfare and Computer Network Exploitation. McLean VA: Northrop Grumman Corporation.

Krekel, B., Adams, P., and Bakos, G.(2009). *Capability of the People's Republic of China to Conduct Cyber Warfare and Computer Network Exploitation.* Northrop Grumman Corp. for U.S.-China Economic and Security Review Commission: McLean, VA.

Krekel, B., P. Adams, and G. Bakos (2009). Capability of the People's Republic of China to Conduct Cyber Warfare and Computer Network Exploitation. Northrop Grumman Corp. for U.S.-China Economic and Security Review Commission: McLean VA.

Krekel, B., P. Adams, and G. Bakos (2012). *Occupying the Information HighGround: Chinese Capabilities for Computer Network Operations and Cyber Espionage.* Prepared for the U.S.-China Economic and Security Review Commission by Northrop Grumman Corp., March 7, 2012. http://www2.gwu.edu/~nsarchiv/NSAEBB/NSAEBB424/docs/Cyber-066.pdf

Kumar, S., Paar, C. (2006). Break DES for 8980 Euros. Retrieved from http://www.copacobana.org/paper/CHES2006_copacobana_slides.pdf

Lai, R. and S. Rahman (2012). "Analytic of China Cyberattack," *International Journal of Multimedia & Its Applications*, V.4, N.3, June 2012, p. 41. http://airccse.org/journal/jma/4312ijma04.pdf

Langner, R. (2013). To Kill a Centrifuge: A Technical Analysis of What Stuxnet's Creators Tried to Achieve. Hamburg: The Langner Group, November 2013. http://www.langner.com/en/wp-content/uploads/2013/11/To-kill-a-centrifuge.pdf

Lessig, L. (2006). Code: And Other Laws of Cyberspace. http://codev2.cc/

Lindsay, J. R. (2013a). "Stuxnet and the Limits of Cyber Warfare." University of California: Institute on Global Conflict and Cooperation, January 2013. http://www.scribd.com/doc/159991102/Stuxnet-and-the-Limits-of-Cyber-Warfare

Lindsay, J. R. (2013b). "Stuxnet and the Limits of Cyber Warfare." Security Studies, V. 22-3, 2013. https://sites.google.com/a/jonrlindsay.com/www/papers/StuxnetJRLSS.pdf

Macintyre, B. (2012). Double Cross: The true story of the D-Day spies. Great Britain: Bloomsbury Publishing.

Mandiant (2010). M-Trends: The advance of the persistent threat. https://www.mandiant.com/resources/mandiant-reports/

Mandiant (2013). APT1: Exposing One of China's Cyber Espionage Units. http://intelreport.mandiant.com/Mandiant_APT1_Report.pdf

Mark A. Stokes, M. A., J. Lin and L. C. R. Hsiao (2011). The Chinese People's Liberation Army Signals Intelligence and Cyber Reconnaissance Infrastructure. Project 2049, November 11, 2011. http://project2049.net/documents/pla_third_department_sigint_cyber_stokes_lin_hsiao.pdf

Martin, C.L. (2008). *Military Deception Reconsidered.* Thesis Naval Postgraduate School, Monterey, California.Macintyre, B. (2012) *Double Cross: The true story of the D-Day Spies.* Bloomsbury Publishing, London.

Masip, J. Garrido, E. & Herrero, C. (2004). "Defining Deception," *Annals of Psychology*, Vol. 20, No. 1, pp. 147-171,

Masterman, J.C. (2000). *The Double-Cross System.* Lyons Press: New York.

McAfee Labs. Signed Malware. Accessed 2012. http://blogs.mcafee.com/mcafee-labs/signed-malware-you-can-runbut-you-cant-hide

McNair, Philip A. (1991). *Counterdeception and the Operational Commander.* Newport, RI: Naval War College.

McPherson, Denver E. (2010). *Deception Recognition: Rethinking the Operational Commander's Approach.* Newport RI: Joint Military Operations Department. Naval, War College

Mengin,F. (2004) ed. *Cyber China: Reshaping National Identities in the Age of Information.* Palgrave Macmillan: New York.

MITRE Corporation (2012). Threat-Based Defense: A New Cyber Defense Playbook. http://www.mitre.org/work/cybersecurity/pdf/cyber_defense_playbook.pdf

MITRE Corporation (2012a) "Active Defense Strategy for Cyber." Technical Papers, July 2012. http://www.mitre.org/sites/default/files/publications/active_defense_strategy.pdf

Muñiz, J. Jr. (2009). *Declawing the Dragon: Why the U.S. Must Counter Chinese Cyber-Warriors.* Thesis Master of Military Art and Science, U.S. Army Command and General Staff College: Fort Leavenworth KS.

Object Management Group. (2008). *Business Process Maturity Model (BPMM).* OMG Document Number: formal/2008-06-01. Retrieved from http://www.omg.org/spec/BPMM/1.0/PDF, p. 72.

Office of the Director of National Intelligence (2007). "Iran: Nuclear Intentions and Capabilities," November 2007, http://www.dni.gov/press_releases/20071203_release.pdf

Ollmann, Gunter. (2010). Opt-In Botnets. Retrieved from https://www.damballa.com/downloads/r_pubs/WP_Opt-In_Botnet.pdf

Online Password Cracking . Accessed 2012. https://www.cloudcracker.com/

Parkour, M. (2010). An Overview of Exploit Packs Retrieved from http://contagiodump.blogspot.com/2010/06/overview-of-exploit-packs-update.html

Postel, J. (1980). User Datagram Protocol. Retrieved from https://tools.ietf.org/html/rfc768

Press, W.H. & Dyson, F.J. (2012). "Iterated Prisoner's Dilemma contains strategies that dominate any evolutionary opponent," *Proceedings of the National Academy of Science*, v. 109 no. 26, pp. 10409-10413.

Provos, Niels and Thorsten Holz (2007). Virtual Honeypots: From Botnet Tracking to Intrusion Detection. Boston MA: Pearson Education.

Rankin, N. (2009). *A genius for deception: how cunning helped the British win two world wars.* Oxford University Press, New York.

Rein, L. and Yoder, E. (2014). "Gone phishing: Army uses Thrift Savings Plan in fake e-mail to test cybersecurity awareness," The Washington Post, March 13, 2014.

Rid, T. (2013). "Cyberwar and Peace: Hacking Can Reduce Real-World Violence," Foreign Affairs, November/December 2013. http://www.foreignaffairs.com/articles/140160/thomas-rid/cyberwar-and-peace

Rowe, N. C. (2003). "Counterplanning Deceptions to Foil Cyber-Attack Plans," Proceedings of the 2003 IEEE Workshop on Information Assurance, West Point NY: United States Military Academy, June 2003.

Rowe, N., & Rothstein, H. (2004). Two taxonomies of deception for attacks on information systems. *Journal of Information Warfare, 3*(2), 27-39.

Rowe, N. C. (2004). "A model of deception during cyber-attacks on information systems," *2004 IEEE First Symposium on Multi-Agent Security and Survivability*, 30-31 Aug. 2004, pp. 21-30.

Rowe, N. C. (2006). "A taxonomy of deception in cyberspace," *International Conference on Information Warfare and Security,* Princess Anne, MD.

Rowe, N.C. (2007). "Deception in defense of computer systems from cyber-attack," in Andrew M. Colarik and Lech J. Janczewski, eds. *Cyber War and Cyber Terrorism.* The Idea Group: Hershey, PA.

Sanger, D.E. (2012). *Confront and Conceal: Obama's secret wars and surprising use of American power.* Crown: New York.

Sanger, D. E. (2012a). "Obama Order Sped Up Wave of Cyberattacks Against Iran," New York Times, June 1, 2012. http://www.nytimes.com/2012/06/01/world/middleeast/obama-ordered-wave-of-cyberattacks-against-iran.html

Sanger, D. E. (2012b). Confront and Conceal: Obama's secret wars and surprising use of American power. Crown: New York.

Spade, J.M. (2011). China's Cyber Power and America's National Security. Carlisle Barracks PA: U.S. Army War College.

Sawyer, R.D. (2007). *The Tao of Deception: A History of Unorthodox Warfare in China.* Basic Books: New York.

Schauer, F. & Zeckhauser, R. (2009). "Paltering" in Brooke Harrington, ed. *Deception: From Ancient Empires to Internet Dating.* Stanford, CA: Stanford University Press, 2009, pp. 38-54.

Shen,D., Chen, G., Cruz, J.B. Jr, Blasch, E & Kruger, M. (2007). "Game Theoretic Solutions to Cyber Attack and Network Defense," *Twelfth International Command and Control Research and Technology Symposium* (12th ICCRTS), Newport RI, 19-21 June 2007.

Shulsky, A. (2002). "Elements of Strategic Denial and Deception," in Roy Godson & James J. Wirtz *Strategic Denial and Deception: The Twenty-First Century Challenge.* New Brunswick NJ: Transaction Publishers.

Smith, D. L. (2004). *Why we lie : the evolutionary roots of deception and the unconscious mind.* New York: St. Martin's Press.

Software Engineering Institute. *People Capability Maturity Model (P-CMM), Version 2.0.* Carnegie Mellon University Technical Report CMU/SEI-2001-MM-01, July 2001.

Software Engineering Institute. *CMMI for Services, Version 1.3: Improving processes for providing better services.* Carnegie Mellon University Technical Report CMU/SEI-2010-TR-034, November 2010.

Somayaji, A., Hofmeyr, S., & and Forrest.S. (1997). "Principles of a Computer Immune System." *1997 ACM New Security Paradigms Workshop,* Langdale, Cumbria, UK.

Spade, J.M. (2011). China's Cyber Power and America's National Security. U.S. Army War College: Carlisle Barracks, PA.

Stech, F., and C. Elsäesser (2007). "Midway Revisited: Detecting Deception by Analysis of Competing Hypothesis," *Military Operations Research.* 11/2007; v. 12, n. 1, pp. 35-55.

Stech, F., Heckman, K. E., Hilliard, P., & Ballo, J. R. (2011). Scientometrics of deception, counter-deception, and deception detection in cyber-space. *PsychNology Journal, 9*(2), 79-112.

Stein, T., Chen, E., & Mangla, K. (2011). *Facebook immune system.* Paper presented at the 4th Workshop on Social Network Systems, SNS'11, April 10, 2011—April 13, 2011, Salzburg, Austria.

Sternberg, R. ed. (2002). *Why Smart People Can Be So Stupid.* Yale University Press: New Haven, CT.

Steven Marks, Thomas Meer, Matthew Nilson (2005). Manhunting: A Methodology for Finding Persons of National Interest, Monterey, CA: Naval Postgraduate School, p. 19.

Stokes, Mark. A., Jenny, Lin, and L.C. Russell. Hsiao (2011). "The Chinese People's Liberation Army Signals Intelligence and Cyber Reconnaissance Infrastructure," Project 2049 Institute. http://project2049.net/documents/pla_third_department_sigint_cyber_stokes_lin_hsiao.pdf

Stokes, M. A. and L.C. R. Hsiao (2012). *Countering Chinese Cyber Operations: Opportunities and Challenges for U.S. Interests.* Project 2049 Institute, October 29, 2012. http://project2049. net/documents/countering_chinese_cyber_operations_stokes_hsiao.pdf

Symantec. (2012). "The Elderwood Project." Retrieved from http://www.symantec.com/content/ en/us/enterprise/media/security_response/whitepapers/the-elderwood-project.pdf

Symantec. (2011). Internet Security Threat Report: 2011 Trends Retrieved from http://www. symantec.com/content/en/us/enterprise/other_resources/b-istr_main_report_2011_21239364. en-us.pdf

Symantec. (2011). "State of Spam and Phishing. A Monthly Report, June 2011. Retrieved from https://www.symantec.com/content/en/us/enterprise/other_resources/b-state_of_spam_and_ phishing_report_06-2011.en-us.pdf

Symantec (2012a). "The Elderwood Project." Retrieved from http://www.symantec.com/content/ en/us/enterprise/media/security_response/whitepapers/the-elderwood-project.pdf

Symantec (2012b). "Complex Cyber Espionage Malware Discovered: Meet W32.Gauss," Updated: 13 Aug 2012. http://www.symantec.com/connect/node/2416861

Symantec (2102c). "Complex Cyber Espionage Malware Discovered: Meet W32.Gauss," Updated: 13 Aug 2012. http://www.symantec.com/connect/node/2416861

TED (2011). "Ralph Langner: Cracking Stuxnet, a 21st-century cyber weapon." Mar 2011. http://www.ted.com/talks/ralph_langner_cracking_stuxnet_a_21st_century_cyberweapon.html

Temmingh, R. & Geers,K. (2009). "Virtual Plots, Real Revolution." In C. Czosseck and K. Geers (eds.) *The Virtual Battlefield: Perspectives on Cyber Warfare.* IOS Press: Amsterdam.

The Honeynet Project. (2004). Know Your Enemy: Learning about Security Threats. Retrieved from http://old.honeynet.org/papers/honeynet/

The MITRE Corporation. (2012). Cyber Information-Sharing Models: An Overview. http://www.mitre.org/sites/default/files/pdf/cyber_info_sharing.pdf

Thomas, T.L. (2004). *Dragon Bytes: Chinese Information-War Theory and Practice.* Foreign Military Studies Office: Fort Leavenworth KS, 2004.

Thomas, T.L. (2007). *Decoding the Virtual Dragon—Critical Evolutions in the Science and Philosophy of China's Information Operations and Military Strategy.* Foreign Military Studies Office: Fort Leavenworth KS, 2007.

Thomas, T.L (2009). *The Dragon's Quantum Leap: Transforming from a Mechanized to an Informatized Force.* Foreign Military Studies Office: Fort Leavenworth KS, 2009.

Torvalds, L. (2007). Tech Talk: Linus Torvalds on git, from https://www.youtube.com/watch?v=4XpnKHJAok8

United States Twelfth Air Force. Air Force Forces. (1996). Air Operations Center (AOC) Standard Operating Procedure (SOP), Combat Intelligence, Chap 5. Retrieved from http://www.fas.org/man/dod-101/usaf/docs/aoc12af/part05.htm

University of Southern California. Information Sciences Institute. (1981). Transmission Control Protocol, DARPA Internet Program, Protocol Specification. Retrieved from https://www.ietf.org/rfc/rfc793.txt

University of Southern California. Information Sciences Institute. (1981). Internet Protocol, DARPA Internet Program, Protocol Specification. Retrieved from https://www.ietf.org/rfc/rfc791.txt

Vakin, S.A., Shustov, L.N. & Dunwell, R.H. (2001). *Fundamentals of electronic warfare.* Norwood, MA: Artech House,

Wang, W., J. Bickford, I. Murynets, R. Subbaraman, A. G. Forte and G. Singaraju (2013) "Detecting Targeted Attacks by Multilayer Deception," Journal of Cyber Security and Mobility, v. 2, pp. 175–199. http://riverpublishers.com/journal/journal_articles/RP_Journal_2245-1439_224.pdf

Weaver, W. S. (2010). *Organizing for Operational Deception.* Fort Leavenworth, KS: Army Command and General Staff College, School of Advanced Military Studies Retrieved from http://oai.dtic.mil/oai/oai?&verb=getRecord&metadataPrefix=html&identifier=ADA523132.

Webb, M. D. (2006). *Creating a New Reality: Information Age Effects on the Deception Process.* Air University, Maxwell AFB, Alabama.

Whaley, B. (2006). *Detecting deception a bibliography of counterdeception across cultures and disciplines (2nd edition).* Washington, DC: Office of the Director of National Intelligence, National Intelligence Council, Foreign Denial and Deception Committee.

Whaley, B. (2007a). *Stratagem: Deception and Surprise in War.* Artech House: Norwood, MA.

Whaley, B. (2007b). The One Percent Solution: Costs and Benefits of Military Deception. In J. Arquilla & D. A. Borer (Eds.), *Information Strategy and Warfare: A Guide to Theory and Practice.* New York: Routledge.

Whaley, B. (2007c). Toward a General Theory of Deception. In J. Gooch & A. Perlmutter (Eds.), *Military Deception and Strategic Surprise* (pp. 188-190). New York: Routlege.

Whaley, B. (2007d). *Textbook of Political-Military Counterdeception: Basic Principles & Methods.* Washington, DC: Foreign Denial & Deception Committee, August 2007.

Whaley, B. (2010a). *Practise to Deceive: Learning Curves of Military Deception Planners.* Washington, DC: Office of the Director of National Security, National Intelligence Center, Foreign Denial & Deception Committee.

Whaley, B. (2010b). *When Deception Fails: The Theory of Outs.* Washington, DC: Office of the Director of National Security, National Intelligence Center, Foreign Denial & Deception Committee.

Whaley, B. (2012). *The Beginner's Guide to Detecting Deception: Essay Series #1. Foreign Denial & Deception Committee*, Office of the Director of National Intelligence, Washington, DC. Unpublished manuscript.

Whaley, B., & Aykroyd, S. S. (2007). *Textbook of political-military counterdeception : basic principles & methods*. Washington, D.C.: National Defense Intelligence College;.

Whaley, Barton, & Jeff Busby (2002). "Detecting Deception: Practice, Practitioners, and Theory," in Godson, R., and J. Wirtz, (eds.) (2002) *Strategic Denial and Deception: The Twenty-First Century Challenge,* New Brunswick, NJ: Transaction Publishers.

Whaley, B., & Webster, D. E. (1987). *When Deception Fails: The Application of Confidence Blow Off and Magical Out Techniques to Military Deception. (White Paper).* Mission Beach, California.

Whaley, B. (2007b) "The one percent solution: Costs and benefits of military deception," in Arquilla, J. & D. A. Borer, eds. (2007) Information Strategy and Warfare: A guide to theory and practice. New York: Routledge.

Whitham, B. (2011). "Defining Responsibilities for Tactical Military Cyber Deception Operations," *Journal of Battlefield Technology,* v. 14, no. 3, pp. 19–24.

Wick, Adam (2012). "Deceiving the Deceivers: Active Counterdeception for Software Protection," DOD SBIR Award O113-IA2-1059, Contract: FA8650-12-M-1396. http://www.sbir.gov/sbirsearch/detail/393779

Yetiv, S. (2013). National Security Through a Cockeyed Lens: How Cognitive Bias Impacts U.S. Foreign Policy. Baltimore: Johns Hopkins University Press.

Yuill, J. J. (2006). *Defensive computer-security deception operations processes, principles and techniques.* (Ph.D.), North Carolina State University. Retrieved from http://www.lib.ncsu.edu/theses/available/etd-10272006-055733/unrestricted/etd.pdf Available from http://worldcat.org/z-wcorg/ database

Zetter, K. (2011). "How Digital Detectives Deciphered Stuxnet, the Most Menacing Malware in History,"Wired,July11,2011.http://www.wired.com/threatlevel/2011/07/how-digital-detectives-deciphered-stuxnet/

Zhuang, J., Bier, V. M., & Alagoz, O. (2010). Modeling secrecy and deception in a multiple-period attacker-defender signaling game. *European Journal of Operational Research, 203*(2), 409-418.

Printed in the United States
By Bookmasters